GUERRILLAS OF DESIRE:
NOTES ON EVERYDAY RESISTANCE AND ORGANIZING TO MAKE A REVOLUTION POSSIBLE

Kevin Van Meter

IAS

AK PRESS

"Beautifully written, *Guerrillas of Desire* shows the power of the refusal of work of those capitalism has subjugated."
—**Silvia Federici, author of *Caliban and the Witch***

"Anyone interested in mutual translation between progressive political theory and social activism today must read this book."
—**Mark Blasius, Professor Emeritus of Political Science, The City University of New York Graduate Center and Center for LGBTQ Studies**

"Tracing Kevin Van Meter's political development from his first militant interventions as a young anarchist in the suburbs of Long Island to his encounter with autonomist Marxism, *Guerrillas of Desire* is an important exploration of the revolutionary possibilities of our time."
—**George Caffentzis, author of *In Letters of Blood and Fire***

"An ambitious work of theory and history that places autonomist Marxist ideas in direct conversation with contemporary anarchist practice, suggesting ways in which concepts such as class composition and everyday resistance, originally developed to analyze slave, peasant, and factory revolts, might aid modern day radicals operating within a bewildering political terrain marked by service work, toothless unions, insular affinity groups, and professional 'change agents.'"
—**Andrew Cornell, author of *Unruly Equality: U.S. Anarchism in the 20ᵗʰ Century***

"Kevin Van Meter gives us a fine, inspiring account of how generation upon generation of 'guerrillas of desire,' from peasant insurgents to slaves to housewives and industrial workers, have reproduced a culture of resistance and self-assertion in the face of power. But this eye-opening book does something more. It makes us see the problem of 'organizing' in a new and much more useful way, going beyond the tired discussion of how we're to achieve social revolution (insurrection? slow, patient 'education' of the working class?). We are already organized, Van Meter argues, we are already in revolt, and we always have been. The job of the organizer is to ask questions, to listen, and to cross-pollinate the wisdom of both open revolt and everyday resistance in communities everywhere. That's what makes revolutionary-becoming possible. Read this book, and put it into practice."
—**Eric Laursen, author of *The People's Pension: The Struggle to Defend Social Security Since Reagan***

"*Guerrillas of Desire* offers a powerful and bold thesis regarding the continuous and enormously potent social force embodied in the everyday resistance of working people. The refusal of work, mutual aid, and self-activity by everyday people are the kinds of rebellious, revolutionary, and creative expressions that Van Meter explores in these pages because they produce the possibilities and spaces for new social formations, new societies, and new worlds that can and must co-exist and thrive. Kevin Van Meter has written a truly remarkable book that I urge you to study, to sit with, to argue with, and to struggle with in the days to come. I know I will."

— **David Naguib Pellow, author of** *Total Liberation: The Power and Promise of Animal Rights and the Radical Earth Movement*

"With an activist heart and deep critical understanding of a life lived in radical politics, Kevin Van Meter's *Guerrillas of Desire* skillfully dissects stifling myths within US political movements and anarchism while chronicling the creative energy of self-activity. His liberatory beginnings and questions create open spaces for forging new paths or revisiting old ones in a quest for wider collective liberation."

— **scott crow, author of** *Black Flags and Windmills: Hope, Anarchy and the Common Ground Collective*

A very popular error: having the courage of one's convictions; rather it is a matter of having the courage for an *attack* on one's convictions!!!

—Friedrich Nietzsche, *Gesammelte Werke*

Guerrillas of Desire: Notes on Everyday Resistance and Organizing to Make a Revolution Possible

© 2017 Kevin Van Meter
This edition © 2017 AK Press (Chico, Oakland, Edinburgh, Baltimore)

ISBN: 978-1-84935-272-7
E-ISBN: 978-1-84935-273-4
Library of Congress Control Number: 2016954843

AK Press	AK Press
370 Ryan Ave. #100	33 Tower St.
Chico, CA 95973	Edinburgh EH6 7BN
USA	Scotland
www.akpress.org	www.akuk.com
akpress@akpress.org	ak@akedin.demon.co.uk

Institute for Anarchist Studies
PO Box 90454
Portland, OR 97290
www.anarchiststudies.org

The above addresses would be delighted to provide you with the latest AK Press distribution catalog, which features books, pamphlets, zines, and stylish apparel published and/or distributed by AK Press. Alternatively, visit our websites for the complete catalog, latest news, and secure ordering.

Cover design by Margaret Killjoy / birdsbeforethestorm.net
Cover illustrations by N.O. Bonzo / nobonzo.tumblr.com
Printed in the USA on acid-free, recycled paper

To all those who inhabit the small, nearly imperceptible moments. For it is their collectivized refusals, transgressions, everyday resistances, inquiries, creative expressions, and desires that will create a new world, one in which many worlds fit.

TABLE OF CONTENTS

PREFACE

lthough the reader encounters a preface first, it is often the last section to be written. I suspect this is for practical reasons rather than reflective or philosophical ones. Since the author must wait until the book is nearly finished to sum up the writing, provide an overview of intent, and recognize those who have helped produced it, such a document is written as deadlines approach. Or, as in this case, just after it has passed.

Nevertheless, I have always respected the beasts that haunt the writing process and the methods of the author. In moments when I need to be reminded why I write, I turn to George Orwell's essay by the same title. In "Why I Write" Orwell offered, "Writing a book is a horrible, exhausting struggle, like a long bout of some painful illness," a sentiment with which I concur. He continues, "One would never undertake such a thing if one were not driven on by some demon whom one can neither resist nor understand." This book is the result of a long process of exorcism, in which endless voices and demons have rattled my resolve and reverberated in my thoughts, and I feel a great responsibility to their words. It will be up to the reader to determine if I understood them at all.

Two illnesses have marked this work. The first, hypothyroidism, was diagnosed recently and hampered the completion of the book, which was written predominately during the 2015–16 school year, when I was on medical leave. The second, onset during my early days as a radical and organizer in the late 1990s, was a nagging cough that began every time I heard a fellow radical, organizer, or activist speak about "what is to be done"—a question almost always followed by suggestions as to what others should be doing. Instead I wanted to ask "How do people become what they are?" How do they become radicalized, become revolutionary, become other than what they were made by this society to be? It seemed to me then, as it does now, that we need to understand how revolutionaries emerge before we ask what is to be done with them. Or better still: what are we to do together?

These are not questions I have asked alone. Every piece of writing is a collective endeavor, and this book is certainly no exception. Conor Cash along with Craig Hughes and Stevie "Peace" Larson of the Team Colors Collective have been constant intellectual companions. Among the four of us, notions such as the refusal of work, contours of class struggle, methods of survival, and the role of everyday resistance have been debated feverishly. I have turned to Benjamin Holtzman periodically over the years to regain composure and focus, and he has always been considerate while setting me right, as have Andrew Cornell and Chris Dixon, new social movement historians who not only provided comradely challenges to my ideas but also suggested ways of improving upon them. Thomas Buechele, quoted in the introduction, provided me with the Stanley Aronowitz line from which I acquired the book's title. Charles Overbeck (of Eberhardt Press), Joseph Keady, Bryan Winston, scott crow, Alexander Reid Ross, Shane Burley, Brian Howard, Aaron Mallory, Vince Collura, Geoff Boyce, Sarah Launius, Alexandra Bradbury, Eric Laursen, Jack Bratich, and Spencer Sunshine provided feedback and recommended sources.

Additional recognition must go to Silvia Federici and George Caffentzis, as their mentorship and scholarship mark nearly every page of the text that follows. As well, Bruce Braun, Cesare Casarino, Vinay Gidwani, and George Henderson at the University of Minnesota, David N. Pellow at the University of California, Santa Barbara, Mark Blasius (who served as my official advisor for an earlier version of the text) and Forrest Colburn at the Graduate Center, City University of New York, and Conrad Herold of Hofstra University, served as guides and midwives to my intellectual development.

In April 2008, having just arrived in Portland, Oregon, I had a chance meeting with a fellow who was already known for clear writing and stoic positions, Kristian Williams. Nearly every week thereafter, Kristian and I have met to review our writing, read Orwell, rediscover the history of anarchism, and attempt to grapple with the current challenges facing revolutionary movements in the United States. Both in our friendship and in his official capacity with the Institute for Anarchist Studies, which has copublished this book with AK Press, Kristian has suffered as my editor of record. My tendency to be wordy or overemphasize secondary topics would have caused anyone difficulty, but he also had to coach me as I learned to write again after three years of academic writing in graduate school.

For the past twenty years, the Institute for Anarchist Studies has supported anarchist and radical scholarship across the planet. And the faith that Paul Messersmith-Glavin, Lara Messersmith-Glavin, Harjit Singh Gill, Sarah Coffey, and other board members had in me has been remarkable. Throughout the writing and publishing process Charles Weigl, Zach Blue, and the entire AK Press collective acted as publishers and understanding colleagues.

In February 2017, friends and colleagues met to discuss and critique the book during a dinner party. Individuals involved included Brandon Feld, Emily Tsing, Luis Brennan, Amelia Cates, Craig Florence (of Mother Foucault's Bookshop), Kira Smith, and others already mentioned. Furthermore, organizers in Portland, Oregon, with the Portland Solidarity Network, the Black Rose Federation, Industrial Workers of the World, Anarchist Black Cross, Incarcerated Workers Organizing Committee, Transformative Lenses Collective, and neighboring initiatives, were kind enough to share their thoughts with me shortly thereafter. In this regard, I want to thank Ayme Ueda, Casey Enns, Grace Covill-Grennan, Gibson Thorn, and Stephen Quirke for their comradeship.

Additionally, those with whom I have organized have afforded me the opportunity to field-test these ideas on making a revolution possible. Over the years, comrades in the Modern Times Collective, Long Island Freespace, Portland Solidarity Network, and other organizations have taught me in innumerable ways. I hope this book in some small way repays the cost of their lessons.

Before I knew that I was a revolutionary, a writer, or a scholar, Robert Lepley saw my potential as an organizer. It was only under his tutelage that any latent abilities emerged.

Thus far I have had the opportunity to live among friends in suburban Long Island, rural Vermont, Brooklyn, Tucson, Portland, and Minneapolis. Without the support of loved ones in these places I have called home—especially Abbey Friedman, Elizabeth Young, Stephen Colón, Phil Rutkowski, Sarah Hughes, and my family, but including many, many others—I would never would have overcome my illnesses and confronted the demons that drove me to produce *Guerrillas of Desire*.

PART I

1

INTRODUCTION: GUERRILLAS OF DESIRE

READING THE STRUGGLES. SUMMARY OF BOOK.

During an ill-fated job interview with the Association of Community Organizations for Reform Now (better known by its acronym ACORN) in 2000, I was able to observe the chasm between everyday practices of survival and the assumptions of Left organizers. As part of the interview process, I accompanied the local director on a day of door knocking in a predominately black, South- and Central-American immigrant neighborhood. The issue of the day: child care. Our task: sign up members and solicit donations. As we spoke with young mothers, grandparents, and a few fathers, the replies to our questions—"Are you willing to demand child care from your elected representatives?" "Are you willing to fight for your right to child care?"—should not have surprised us. "We already have child care," was the reply most often heard. Meaning that through collective efforts parents had cobbled together arrangements to ensure that their children were cared for while they worked without the costs associated with formal day care.

To the lead organizer such a thing was impossible. Day care was something the state provided following an organized demand. ACORN was unable to comprehend a fundamental difference articulated in 1975 by feminist scholar Silvia Federici as part of the international Wages for Housework campaign:

> It is one thing to set up a day care center the way we want it, and then demand that the State pay for it. It is quite another thing to deliver our children to the State and then ask the State to control them not for five but for fifteen hours a day…. In one case we regain some control over our lives, in the other we extend the State's control over us.[1]

It wasn't simply the visionless racial politics embodied by two white organizers knocking on the doors of poor people of color, to ask for money, or the inability to hear what those we spoke with were saying, but the gall of the whole endeavor. I turned down the job and instead began to look for answers in the historical record, in concepts of radical theorists, and in writings of militants from prior generations.

As the anti-globalization movement was waning in the early years of the new millennium, I began to think about how a set of concepts and metaphors, gleaned from a productive encounter between anarchism and Autonomist Marxism, could be used to examine mutual aid and the refusal of work.[2] Everyday resistance, practices of mutual aid and refusal of work, and overt forms of rebellion are mechanisms of a new society in formation. This is not to suggest that such actions prefigure or pre-determine a post-revolutionary society, but they point to the constant presence of a *possible* other world. There is a war going on in everyday life, and the role of this book is to perform a "culling [of] the historical wisdom," as scholar-activists Frances Fox Piven and Richard Cloward advocate, "that might inform mobilizations of the future."[3]

● ● ●

I grew up on suburban Long Island, frequently spending summers and other periods in rural Vermont. It should be noted that no one is *in* Long Island—there is no *in* to be. One is *on*, upon the highly segregated, sub-urban sandbar—not in, among the ecological, civic, or cultural lifecycles of the Island. The advantage afforded to me, to be part of these different environs, allowed the deadening boredom of Long Island to be countered by the fertility of rural Vermont.

There are two Vermonts. The hippie Vermont is the result of the back-to-the-land movement of the 1970s and the building of Interstate 91 (completed in 1978). Old Vermont, of small dairy farmers and town hall meetings, comprises the regions farthest from the freeway and far enough from ski areas as to not attract tourists. As a child I was terri-bly frightened by an annual game dinner there, where squirrel, venison, and even bear was served alongside roast chicken. Every firehouse and community hall in old Vermont had its own prized recipes. It wasn't so much the gamey meat, odd to my urban tastes and budding veganism, but the idea of the whole town eating in common and often in shifts. To sit, converse, share dishes, and pass bottles of wine at a table of neigh-bors was not a common experience for us flatlanders (as non-Vermonters were called). Mutual practices extended beyond the communal table into the operating principles of the community. The local state representative held office hours at the lunch counter of the local general store. Residents passing one another on a dirt road would wave. Municipal business was decided in monthly town hall meetings. There was no local police force.

Once my trepidation about eating in a communal setting passed, the cooperative ways of life buzzing amid the Green Mountains were preferable to suburbia. Urban radicals view the Green Mountains and the hill people of the United States, as populated by those who have succumb to the "idiocy of rural life" (a mistranslation of Marx).[4] Rather, I observed a beautiful sense of humility in cooperative ways of being, maintained in part by geographical seclusion. Suburban communities only *appear* to be less isolated, as they form invisible and armed borders in the landscape and in the minds of their inhabitants. New York City, just an hour away from my Long Island childhood home by train (if one could afford it), seemed to ooze the narcissistic, dominant US culture that was even then being exported around the planet.

In an attempt to locate cooperative ways of life in suburban Long Island, I began to ask older, more experienced radicals how one would go about locating the commons. Often the answers I heard were just impressions or the equivalent of whispers. Peter Linebaugh, who was on a speaking jaunt through the region, offered, "Keep digging until you find a commoner."[5] The Algonquian-speaking peoples of eastern Long Island, early potato farmers, and most recently the volunteer fire fighters who saved what was left of the Pine Barrens during the Sunrise Wildfire of 1995 are commoners. So too are long-term African American residents and recently arrived Salvadoran day laborers who have carved out spaces in between wealthier, whiter enclaves in what is referred to locally, and pejoratively, as "the black belt."[6]

In *The Magna Carta Manifesto* Linebaugh clarifies the relationship between the commons and commoners:

> First, common rights are embedded in a particular ecology with its local husbandry. For commoners, the expression "law of the land" from chapter 39 [of the Magna Carta] does not refer to the will of the sovereign. Commoners think first not of title deeds, but of human deeds: how will this land be tilled? Does it require manuring? What grows there? They begin to explore. You might call it a natural attitude. Second, commoning is embedded in a labor process; it inheres in a particular praxis of field, upland, forest, marsh, coast. Common rights are entered into by labor. Third, commoning is collective. Fourth, being independent of the state, commoning is independent also of the temporality of the law and state.[7]

Therefore, commoners and the commons are produced concomitantly. They do so by acting together in the contexts and environments within which they find themselves. Labor processes, such as those of the families I met on my dreadful excursion with ACORN, occur within particular contexts. Hence commons are created so that life cycles, growing cycles, and the earth on its rotational axis supplements and then replaces the time clock, business, television news, the election cycle, and the "tax season." These four attributes—local ecology, labor processes (but not work that is imposed), collective endeavors, and reordering of time toward ordinary life cycles—exist today. These common practices are not simply means of survival; they are factors in revolution. And they are not only shared by those who have inhabited Long Island, they can be found in the historical record among slaves, peasants, and workers.

●●●

Even in the inhospitable hinterlands of 1990s Long Island a few overt resistance movements thrived. Salvadoran day laborers, black churches, hip-hop crews (including Public Enemy), and the Do-It-Yourself (DIY) punk scene were a part of these collective endeavors. Drawing from the DIY punk scene, a group of activists instigated projects through the Modern Times Collective. In April 1998, a few individuals initiated a meeting that connected the punk scene, fledgling organizations such as Anti-Racist Action, Food Not Bombs, and a new General Membership Branch of the Industrial Workers of the World (IWW), and participants in international solidarity (East Timor Action Network), animal rights, feminist, and antiwar movements. With limited access to resources and members scattered across the island, these organizations initially became nodes in a network. Then as spring turned into summer these nodes were absorbed into a larger organizational body, the collective.

As the varying stages of the Modern Times progressed—initial network, formal activist collective, node in the counter-globalization movement, radical community-based organization—it became increasingly obvious to me that those who participated in our activities were drawn toward overt forms of organizing following personal experiences with informal and often covert forms of mutual aid and refusal. For instance, there was a young hardcore kid, just finishing high school and from working class Catholic stock, who worked nights sweeping floors at a chain supermarket. His general dissatisfaction with the cultural limitations of Long Island and the meaninglessness of his employment led him to slack off at work and school. As long as he did not fail or get fired, he would slide as close as possible to this precipice while using stolen time to listen to punk and read about revolutionary movements. That hardcore kid, Thomas Buechele, is now a doctoral candidate and instructor in sociology at one of the last truly public universities. He reflected to me during a recent shopping trip to the same chain supermarket, "Slacking on this job was one of many things that led me to get involved in Modern Times." During this time, he said, speaking about his late teens and early twenties, "I wanted to build a life worth living, [to carve it out] in a space that was deadening, where normalized depression surrounded me and when it was expressed it came across as arbitrary anger. Any ability I now have to think and process critically, to think through philosophical categories, I attribute to this overall experience."[8]

Labor historian and public intellectual Stanley Aronowitz serves as advisor to Buechele. Remarking on how working-class kids learn "how to refuse work, how to sabotage," Aronowitz reflects on his own upbringing. "Those like myself," he recalls, "who managed to play both sides of the street, never forgot that [the struggle against work] was better, despite the 'no money' economy, then the constant warfare with elders. We were *guerrillas of desire*, fighting for our autonomy against the entire apparatus of domination."[9]

●●●

As a formal activist collective, Modern Times modeled its organizing approaches on those of our anarchist elders and the anarcho-punk scene of the day. As with the collectives of rural Spain, we sought, as Sam Dolgoff suggested, "to introduce collectivist or cooperative ways of doing things into other aspects of [our] daily life."[10] However, as a self-identified anarchist collective, adopting an activist mentality prevented inexperienced organizers from being able to understand how their own needs connected to those of others in similar circumstances. Further, many of us believed that *we* were the agents of change, that we—"a small group of thoughtful, committed citizens"—were going to bring about a revolution.[11]

Hence, we followed the familiar pattern of using anarchist ideology as a lens through which to view the world while judging necessities and yearnings, experiences, and political activities accordingly. Summit protests and regional actions under the auspices of Critical Mass, Reclaim the Streets, and Direct Action Network followed. Modern Times was embedded in Philadelphia for the Republican National Convention for the better part of a month in 2000, hunkering down on couches and in community spaces. We returned to Long Island with our resources drained. Two dozen of our members spent time in jail. The impact on our local context was minimal; our lives were not improved. Over Labor Day weekend we held a mini-conference, what radicals during those years called a convergence, naming it "And Now for Something Completely Different."[12]

After this we used a modified Freirean pedagogy in the form of loosely organized long-term community dialogues, often involving upwards of sixty people.[13] In order to provide an opportunity for self-reflection, facilitators would periodically summarize the discussion and common themes raised by participants. The role of facilitator was limited to asking probing questions: "What hardships are you currently facing?" "What limitations are placed on your life?" "What kinds of collective projects could address your needs and desires?" As a result, those undercurrents of mutual aid and refusal embedded in life experiences, which had only periodically been noted prior, now reverberated throughout and beyond the collective. It was only when the anarchist ideology and activist mentality receded that the organizing project began to resonate with those outside our immediate sphere. By embedding the collective in our daily lives, we not only met Dolgoff's aphorism in word but also in deed.[14] In effect, dialogue participants and collective members wanted to build a life worth living on their own terms, according to collectively agreed upon principles.[15]

READING THE STRUGGLES

Two aspects of human life impressed me most during the journeys I made in my youth across suburban Long Island and in the Green Mountains of Vermont.[16] One was the ingenious methods of survival, authentic communication, daring acts of kindheartedness and mutuality, and an embodied, productive sense of commonality that confronted untold deficiencies in the material needs of existence. The other was that ongoing, seemingly endless struggle to improve the human condition; reorganization of ecological and spatial sensibilities and reordering of time toward an ordinary pace of life; and immense output of creativity and ideas even in the most inhospitable of locales with the most restrictive of conditions.

The first aspect articulates mutual aid, the second a degree of refusal. Being productive in common is where these excursions meet. As I began to investigate this nexus, other practices, methods of organizing, and forms of life popped out of the shadows like lightning bugs at dusk. Peter Kropotkin's *Mutual Aid* carries the subtitle *A Factor of Evolution*. Throughout *Mutual Aid* Kropotkin corrects the Social Darwinist misconception that competition defined human evolution. Then he humbly offers mutual aid as a factor in the unfolding of life on the planet, resulting in human societies. Everyday resistance is a factor in revolutionary struggle, not the sole factor. Answering how everyday resistance—refusals of work and practices of mutual aid—is a factor in revolution is the task of this book.

As a necessary aside, not all forms of everyday resistance should be celebrated and treated as a factor in revolutionary struggle. White male workers striking against the inclusion of black or female workers in the plant *might* be using a form of everyday resistance. But said strike is certainly something that revolutionaries and those committed to eliminating all forms of domination and oppression would, and should, oppose. As everyday resistance is a factor in revolutionary struggle, it is not the sole or only factor that requires due consideration.[17]

Guerrillas of Desire offers a contentious hypothesis: the fundamental assumption underlying Left and radical organizing, including many strains of anarchism, is wrong. I do not mean organizationally dishonest, ideologically inappropriate, or immoral. I mean empirically incorrect. Historical and current strategies on the Left and in radical movements are predicated on the assumption that working class and poor people are unorganized and not resisting. Hence the role of the activist, organizer, and insurrectionist is to activate, organize, and educate a disengaged population through various initiatives. Illustrating that everyday resistance is a factor in revolution and a form of politics, maintaining that its effects on overt rebellion and crises are measurable, requires the reversal of this assumption. Working class and poor people—as slaves, peasants, and workers in the industrial and social factory—are already organized and resisting.

Describing the myriad forms of everyday resistance under slavery, in peasant politics, and throughout the industrial and social factory is an immense undertaking. "Social factory" refers to the use of the factory model, beginning in the late 1960s and early 1970s, beyond the factory gates in other areas of capitalist production. On this concept, Silvia Federici and Mario Montano write, under the pen name Guido Baldi, "From the plant to the university, society becomes an immense assembly line, where the seeming variety of jobs disguises the actual generalization of the same abstract labor."[18] The transatlantic slave trade, peasant politics, and the industrial factory emerged during the era marked by the advent of capitalism and the modern nation-state—the period between the fourteenth century and the present. This book limits its focus to the refusal of work at it appears in everyday life and how this relates to and intersects with overt rebellions against work. Chapters 2 and 3 will address the revolt against work, examine self-activity and mutual aid, and consider how to apply a taxonomy of struggle to the historical record as "a sense-making machine" to understand these phenomena.[19]

Refusals by "guerrillas of desire" take place outside of the normal surveillance mechanisms of capitalism and the state, and relationships based in mutual aid are produced in this often temporary space. (Refusals of work and practices of mutual aid are two attributes of everyday resistance. I use the term "everyday resistance" to cover both.) These practices are intended to be illegible to the state, and so they should at all costs remain. *Guerrillas of Desire* is a historical work for this reason, as there is little concern that the guilty parties—slaves, peasants, and industrial workers long dead—would suffer state repression as a result of exposure here.[20] While I seek here to provide tools for contemporary struggle, mechanisms for uncovering and amplifying everyday resistance practices will need to be developed in situ.

Guerrilla attacks take place in valleys populated by tax collectors, managers, and bureaucrats. The guerrillas make incursions from the hills and liberated territories populated by commoners, whose ongoing acts of resistance produce the commons. Typically, an ambush is followed by a tactical retreat, and guerrillas use goods stolen in storehouse raids to meet the needs of the population. By addressing needs that the state and capital have not met and have refused to address, guerrillas develop a sense of solidarity and interdependence with the people. If the guerrillas can create a gravitational pull within a community, tugging the population further away from the state and capital, the general population will provide cover for guerrilla actions. The solidarity, communication networks, and mutual aid that already exist within the general population are given to guerrillas and used by them to carry out actions over a wider area. With increased support comes an increased chance of operational success and often the ability to avoid capture. Skirmishes erupt as guerrillas continue to enter and then flee the valleys for the relative safety of the hills. Raids on armories, sabotage of the machinery of production, arson of the slave masters' or bureaucrats' homes become part of assembled counter-narratives and counter-institutions. These are complementary practices, chosen contextually to address the immediate needs and desires of guerrilla forces. This is the model, anyway. However, models and theory should not be substituted for the complexities of concrete reality.

Search—dig, if necessary—until you find guerrillas of desire, historically and today: in concentration camps, prisons, kitchens, brothels, slave quarters, hillside peasant abodes, factory break rooms, and in rubble. "We are not in the least afraid of ruins," Spanish anarchist

Buenaventura Durruti is said to have uttered. "The pickaxe and the shovel are as important as the rifle."[21]

SUMMARY OF BOOK

The agents and acts I document, often by presenting existing scholarship, are remotely but substantively and genealogically connected to my own agency. As author, researcher, ethnographer, and organizer adopting a revolutionary position I am required to attempt three things: first, to write about encounters between ideas, texts, and practices; second, to discard assumptions of objectivity and ensure that theoretical abstractions describe concreteness; and third, to record the human qualities that acts of mutual aid and refusal express.[22] A book such as this one should reflect the complexities of human behaviors, identities, and diversity of the stories it retells.

Chapters 2 and 3, "Recognizing the New Society" and "From Concept to Metaphor," map the ideas offered by anarchism and Autonomist Marxism—with particular attention to mutual aid, working-class self-activity, and the refusal of work. The chapters 4, 5, and 6, "Under Slavery," "In Peasant Politics," and "Throughout the Industrial and Social Factory," apply the organizational and theoretical considerations of the prior chapters to complex phenomena taking place across vastly different spaces and times. In chapter 7, "On Organizing," I examine historical and current trends in Left and radical organizing in the US beginning with the ascent of neoliberal capitalism in the mid-1970s. Chapter 8, "To Make a Revolution Possible," summarizes the main points and indicates possibilities for future research.

There are two ways of reading this book. Understanding its structure will assist the reader in choosing a path. The first part (comprising the first three chapters) and the third part (chapters 7 and 8) form an arc that begins with theory and concludes by detailing historical and contemporary approaches to organizing. The arc moves through theoretical interrogations addressing the genealogies of anarchism and Autonomist Marxism, which influence the ideas throughout the book. Before concluding, our understanding of radical organizing is revisited, with any luck at a higher level of complexity and accuracy than at the outset. The central section of the book, part 2 (chapters 4–6) details everyday resistance under slavery, in peasant politics, and in the industrial and social factory. This section provides the historical evidence of everyday resistance under different regimes of capitalism with corresponding state forms.

Having read the introduction, one may choose to continue to chapters 2 and 3 to investigate the interpretation of everyday resistance, theory, and organizing that I provide. Another option is to jump from here to part 2 before returning to the earlier and concluding material. This second approach will allow the reader to view the evidence before considering my assessment of everyday resistance. Each approach addresses one of the aims of the book. The first approach seeks a productive encounter between anarchism and Autonomist Marxism; the second approach pursues an understanding of how everyday resistance is a factor in revolutionary struggle.[23]

Politics is about organization; it is also about choices. So too is reading.

2

RECOGNIZING THE NEW SOCIETY

RECORDING THE FACTS OF ITS EXISTENCE. THEORETICAL LINEAGES. AUTONOMIST IDEAS. WHAT IS THE WORKING CLASS?

The working class struggles against capitalism because its objective conditions of life force it to, not because it is educated to some "higher" consciousness by some outside force such as a political party. It would seem, also, that the struggle against capitalism includes all forms and levels of struggle, from individual to collective, from local to national (or international), from economic to political. In fact, it would be hard to conceive how the more general or radical forms of struggle, such as general strikes, factory occupations, or workers' councils, could occur without the preexistence of more limited forms of struggle: sabotage, local strikes, the organization of unions, and the like.[1]

—Martin Glaberman and Seymour Faber,
Working for Wages: The Roots of Insurgency

RECORDING THE FACTS OF ITS EXISTENCE

Recording resistance in everyday life is part of a larger task intended "to recognize the new society, align ourselves with it, and record the facts of its existence."[2] George Rawick's extensive oral histories of slave resistance, James Scott's writings about visits to the peasant village of Sedaka in Malaysia, C.L.R. James's studies of wildcat strikes in Detroit auto plants, and Silvia Federici's examination of skirmishes "against housework" are all attempts to reveal everyday forms of resistance and overt rebellion.[3] These four authors and others have believed that they were "closest to these events and [would thus] best serve them" since they had "trained themselves to recognize that the new society exists and to record the facts of its existence."[4] It is in these chronicles and the desire to align ourselves with "the new society," that we begin.

Herein "everyday" refers to forms of resistance that occur informally, while "overt" signifies the forms of rebellion that are formal in some fashion. Both clandestine and aboveground organizations are overt if they have or will declare themselves in opposition to the existing social order. While everyday resistance is an established concept, I have chosen the term "overt" to encompass that which is formal, public, planned, structured, and the like. The everyday and the overt, as well as resistance and rebellion, are points on a continuum. I wish to avoid the pitfalls of dichotomies such as spontaneous and organized, underground and aboveground, pre-political and political, and—worst of all—unconscious and conscious. Such dualism oversimplifies the phenomena they describe and is subject to ideological whims. As you read this book, the differences as well as the connections between everyday and overt should become increasingly clear.

Accounts of everyday resistance emanate from innumerable corners of the planet and are part of discourses with their own intellectual and revolutionary traditions. One of them began in 1964 in the London flat of seasoned revolutionary C.L.R. James, author of *The Black Jacobins*. James hosted a lecture there by American historian George Rawick on US history, and following the lecture James acted as inquisitor. Afterward Rawick realized that he had not fully grasped the self-activity of American slaves, and he went on to spend a good portion of the rest of his career collecting accounts to correct this. Forty-one volumes of *The American Slave: A Composite Autobiography*, for which Rawick served as general editor, were the result. Rawick published his most recognized piece in 1969—"Working Class Self-Activity," on the role of factory workers in 1930s industrial struggles—and by then he was already a few years into his research on the lives of American slaves. In 1972 the first volume of *The American Slave* was published, Rawick's own *From Sundown to Sunup*. Therein Rawick summarized his findings, focusing on the time that slaves had to themselves: the evening. Rawick's account is distinct from Scott's anthropology, James's history, and Federici's feminism. What unites these figures in a common project, however, is their contribution to chronicling practices of everyday resistance.[5]

Evidence shows that everyday resistance existed before the advent of capitalism, the rise of the nation-state, and development of the relations of power that flow through and animate these systems. However, it is one thing to document everyday resistance and another to argue that this resistance represents a "new society." What is detected in historical reports of everyday resistance is the possibility of other worlds, other ways of organizing the social order. Everyday resistance has been a way for people to survive under capitalism, obtain additional goods through theft, acquire a sense of autonomy by running away, forge counter-communities so that strikes and slowdowns have a base of support, maintain one's dignity, and attain a degree of freedom, even if only momentarily. Acts of resistance are performed under conditions of exploitation and oppression, domination and control. Historical reports of everyday resistance are glimpses of ways to organize life outside of capitalism and the state and experiments in (and examples of) new social relations. At the center of this resistance are complex human beings, the good, the bad, and the ugly.

There are various ways to interpret "the new society" in the present. One common version situates it amid disaster or stemming from exile; seeds of a new society can spring from the shell of the old.[6] One can also prefigure a possible other world by developing "countercultural lifestyles," "building and running counter institutions," "organizing ... with a horizontal orientation," and "creating and practicing more egalitarian modes of interacting."[7] And as part of a collective, an initiative in accordance with autonomist ideas could detect, inquire about, record, circulate, amplify, and intervene in the new society as it emerges.

"We are living in a nightmare," George Orwell offers in the spirit of this endeavor, "precisely *because* we have tried to set up an earthly paradise."[8] This book is just one possible interpretation based on particular theoretical lineages, a genealogical understanding of contemporary revolutionary movements in the United States, autonomist ideas, and the ability of working-class self-activity to confront state and capitalist discipline while forging new ways of being. In this chapter and the one that immediately follows, I will provide an approach for reading these struggles using ideas from anarchism and Autonomist Marxism.

THEORETICAL LINEAGES

In 1994 American autonomist Harry Cleaver published an article titled "Kropotkin, Self-valorization, and the Crisis of Marxism." The piece is an expression of Autonomist Marxism seeking a dialogue with anarchism. Thus far, it seems, there has yet to be a response. Cleaver's main argument is that there are similarities in anarchist-communist and autonomist thinking regarding the emergence of a post-capitalist society. Cleaver compares self-valorization—that is, "the diversity of autonomous efforts to craft new ways of being and new forms of social relations"—to mutual aid.[9] Peter Kropotkin, after studying animal societies, including human evolution, "affirm[ed] that in the ethical progress of [humans], mutual aid—not mutual struggle—has had the leading part."[10] Autonomists, on the other hand, base their conception of self-valorization on the tangible struggles of the working class under capitalism. Those familiar with Kropotkin's conception of mutual aid will already begin to see the similarities between the two concepts. In the conclusion to *Mutual Aid: A Factor of Evolution*, Kropotkin offers,

> It will probably be remarked that mutual aid, even though it may represent one of the factors of evolution, covers nevertheless one aspect only of human relations; that by the side of this current, powerful though it may be, there is, and always has been, the other current—the self-assertion of the individual, not only in its efforts to attain personal or caste superiority, economical, political, and spiritual, but also in its much more important although less evident function of breaking through the bonds, always prone to become crystallized, which the tribe, the village community, the city, and the State impose upon the individual. In other words, there is the self-assertion of the individual taken as a progressive element.[11]

Kropotkin views mutual aid as a factor in human and natural evolution, but a countervailing drive expressed as "self-assertion of the individual" is also at work against obligations imposed by society. It is important to note that Kropotkin is not referring to just hierarchical, authoritarian societies or just to democratic or anarchist ones. Mutual aid and self-assertion are common to *all* human societies. Moreover, this self-assertion entails both individuals' "efforts to attain ... superiority" and their efforts in "breaking through the bonds ... impose[d] upon the individual." To Kropotkin, the latter serves an important function since imposed bonds can prevent common, collective, reciprocal, and interdependent connections from emerging—and hence stifle ethical evolution. (Being aware of this, according to French anthropologist Pierre Clastres, so-called primitive societies create mechanisms, including the use of violence, to prevent the emergence of state relations— that is, "a separate organ of power, power separated from society.")[12] Arguably, the very question of how to balance self-assertion and mutual aid haunted Kropotkin until his death and has engrossed the anarchist movement ever since, although branches of it ignore one of these conflicting factors (social anarchists ignore self-assertion, insurrectionists ignore mutual aid).

To bring Cleaver back into these deliberations, self-valorization and mutual aid are not identical. In using mutual aid and self-valorization together, the first points to the cooperative ways of being that bolster all social life, while the second draws attention to "the autonomous elaboration of new ways of being, of new social relationships alternative to those of capitalism," as Cleaver puts it.[13] Theoretically, mutual aid has been a factor in all human societies, hence it exists in our current society as it will in a new one. Mutual aid is the cooperative and reciprocal activity that underpins all social life. The bonds that are formed as a result of this activity are as affective (emotional) as they are material, as conscious as they are unconscious. Self-valorization, on the other hand, only points to activity counter to capitalism, the state, and the relations of power that animate these systems. Self-valorization refers to new forms of life and values that are developed by an autonomous working class that did not exist previously. Thus, the concept does not describe preexisting or underlying activities the way mutual aid does. Mutual aid entails forms of cooperative activity that ground social life, refusal, and resistance before and after the development of new forms of life, while self-valorization only points to new forms. Hence these are both complementary and divergent, thus useful for delineating between different kinds of occurrences. Mutual aid and self-valorization can draw attention to phenomena that both anarchists and autonomists have identified through observations and included, as concepts, in their theoretical affairs.

Furthermore, there is the autonomist concept of working-class self-activity. "Self-activity" expresses the autonomous actions of the working class, encompassing both refusal and mutual aid in addition to overt struggle independent of unions or other official organizations of the Left (political parties, nonprofit organizations, progressive religious groups, foundations, etc.). "Self-activity" also indicates, more generally, activities that are directed and driven by their subjects, and it points to both continuous activities and relationships. Clearly, then, mutual aid is a type of self-activity.

In *Mutual Aid*, Cleaver noted, Kropotkin attempts to uncover prevailing events and sees mutual aid, self-assertion, and cooperation as vital for understanding resistance and rebellion. Encompassing Cleaver's observations on self-valorization, autonomists have identified individual and collective self-assertions that are outside of, and often against, the official organizations of the Left.

Cleaver inherited this idea from the prior generation of militants. Rawick, drawing from E. P. Thompson's monumental *The Making of the English Working Class*, argued that the wildcat strike illustrated an early stage of development that had two characteristics, "workers struggl[ing] simultaneously against the bosses, the State, and the union" and workers achieving "a much more direct form of class activity, by refusing to delegate aspects of their activity to an agency external to themselves."[14] Therefore autonomists, following Rawick, sought through observation and review of historical materials to record forms of resistance against bosses, the state, and self-appointed representatives of the working class.

Everyday resistance, mutual aid, and self-valorization taken together ("self-activity") are not, however, simply reactions to capitalism and the state. Working-class self-activity corroborates the class's autonomy. Cleaver summarizes this perspective:

> This insistence on the autonomy of working class self-activity, not only *vis-à-vis* capital but also *vis-à-vis* the "official" organizations of the class, e.g., the trade unions and the party, leads me to use the name autonomist Marxism to designate this general line of reasoning and the politics associated with it.... [T]he emphasis on workers' autonomy has led to the rejection of the orthodox Marxist argument that the only path to a post-capitalist society lies through a transitional socialist order managed by the party commanding the state in the name of the people. On the contrary, the process of building a new society, like the process of revolution itself, is seen as either being the work of the people themselves, or as being doomed from the start.[15]

To identify and document the new society is to align oneself with those building it: slaves, peasants, and workers. But just identifying this autonomous activity is insufficient, of course. Militants must recognize it and communicate its importance amongst themselves and circulate these stories between guerrillas who are resisting and rebelling. In so doing, the actions themselves are amplified and word of them circulates in fields, factories, workshops, offices, coffee shops, kitchens, bedrooms, and classrooms.

By discussing these concepts and complementary ideas that will be covered below, I intend to provide a method of defining and demarcating complex human behaviors. Thus far this discussion of theoretical lineages lacks a functional definition of "working class." After addressing autonomist ideas—which will aid in the overall understanding of class dynamics and struggle in everyday resistance and the relationship between the two—I will propose a definition of the "working class."

AUTONOMIST IDEAS

To conceptualize everyday resistance as part of a larger revolutionary tradition and go beyond the limitations of contemporary radical movements will require reconsideration of notions of capitalism, the state, and power. A turn toward Autonomist Marxism can aid in this undertaking, and it is useful to draw from the intersections of anarchist and autonomist traditions. In my assessment, Autonomist Marxism can assist contemporary revolutionaries in thinking through their ideas. Without an organized Autonomist Marxist presence in US radical movements (beyond periodic books and articles) it makes sense for autonomists to ally with these movements and provide conceptual and strategic aid. Analyzing how capitalism, the state, and power function, with the purpose of abolishing these systems, is vital for the revolutionary project. I begin with a reassessment of the notion of "workerism," since a reinvigorated class politics will be necessary for examining the other ideas that follow.

Beyond workerism

Workerism, as the belief that the working class is the central or only revolutionary subject, has been given a bad name, and rightly so. The word has come to mean a form of class reductionism. Arguably "workerism" in this sense has been used as a straw argument, parody, or insult to dismiss those who view class struggle as central to the revolutionary project. The term is related to the Italian *operaismo*, the precursor to the autonomist movements of the 1970s, a word that is often translated as "workerism."

In his history of the Operaisti, *Storming Heaven: Class Composition and Struggle in Italian Autonomist Marxism*, Steven Wright asks, "What then is workerism?" He answers,

> [*Operaismo's*] origins lie ... at the beginning of the 1960s, when young dissidents in the [Partito Comunista Italiano] and Socialist Party first attempted to apply Marx's critique of political economy to an Italy in the midst of a rapid passage to industrial maturity. In this they were motivated not by a philological concern to execute a more correct reading of Marx, but the political desire to unravel the fundamental power relationships of modern class society. In the process, they sought to confront *Capital* with "the *real* study of a *real* factory," in pursuit of a clearer understanding of the new instances of independent working-class action.[16]

Therefore the term "workerism" should be reconsidered, although there are elements of class reductionism in *operaismo*. Autonomist Marxists, since the Wages for Housework "Copernican revolution," as George Caffentzis once put it to me, at least in its American guises, has sought to define the working class broadly and take seriously the need to theorize the entirety of class struggle. Italian workerism provides clarity on the working class as autonomist subject as identified in Fiat factories in northern Italy during the massive strike wave of 1969, referred to as the Hot Autumn. These upheavals in Italy followed the global revolts of May 1968 (a month of unrest that peaked with student and worker protests in France and around the planet) and continued until 1970. The formation of workers' and students' councils provided the testing ground for the ideas of the movements of the period. Clearly, through our contemporary lens, the autonomous organizing of a working class in rebellion is far superior to its organizing by political party, union, nonprofit, cadre, or the like. But I do not bring up workerism to provide terminological clarity alone.

Workerism, in the crude economic sense, is not only a political position but the result of a battle that has taken place within Marxism and anarchism since the founding of the First International—the International Workingmen's Association (IWA)—in 1864. In advance of the IWA's founding, prominent organizer and French anarchist Joseph Déjacque, in the 1850s, advocated for equality between sexes and races.[17] Principled positions on racial and gender equality in the IWA were advanced periodically throughout the short life of the organization, hence some saw the importance of widening the scope of the class struggle. Robert Graham, historian of the anarchist role in the IWA, comments, "Women were to have equal status in the association, a position long championed by Déjacque and his associates."[18] Mikhail Bakunin stated in the "Principles and Organization of the International Brotherhood": "Woman, differing from man but not inferior to him, intelligent, industrious and free like him, is declared his equal both in rights and in all political and social functions and duties." Pierre-Joseph Proudhon's position on the "women question," on the other hand, reflected the worst attitudes of the day, being opposed to divorce.[19] The "American Sections" of the IWA, as historian Paul Buhle remarks in *Marxism in the United States: A History of the American Left*, "recognize[d] not only working class elements but also other citizens (in this case, women deprived of the opportunity of wage labor) as co-equals, including them as members by change of constitution (hitherto membership had been restricted to wage-earners)."[20] While the inclusion of women was at the behest of Republicans rather than anarchists, it illustrates the debate going on within the workers' movement of the time. As with their American counterparts, the "French Section" proposed that the 1867 Congress of the IWA consider "equality of men and women in social functions."[21] Lastly, while anticolonial sentiments were expressed by anarchists such as Elisée Reclus and others, the focus of much of the IWA's propaganda and organizational efforts were on male factory workers in countries undergoing the Industrial Revolution.

Returning to the US, early conflicts within the labor movement between the American Federation of Labor (AFL) and the Knights of Labor, then between trade unions and the IWW, focused on the inclusion of women and blacks in their ranks. The Knights ("however briefly") and IWW (determinedly) included "women reformers, seasoned eight-hour day advocates, supporters of impoverished immigrants, and Blacks," to which the AFL didn't have "claim."[22] The US anarchist movement, being heavily populated with recent immigrants in the late nineteenth and early twentieth century, was regularly involved in pro-immigrant and then antifascist activities. Its inclusion of African Americans, women, homosexuals, and other socially marginalized populations exemplifies anarchism's dedication to ideas such as free love and antiracism. There are innumerable other examples, but the issue at hand is how race, gender, and sexuality would be sidelined in favor of a class-struggle-only perspective. For instance, IWW militant Carlo Tresca's journal *Il Martello* helped shift the tenor of the anarchist movement. "While the focus on class struggle made the journal's politics clear," as Andrew Cornell reflected, "it left the contents narrowly focused: anything smacking of 'bohemianism,' such as consideration of modern art or the promotion of progressive gender roles, was out."[23] Such manifestations prevented anarchism and Marxism from taking more liberatory paths.

The question before us is how to reinvigorate workerism, in the post–Wages for Housework and autonomist sense, and place it in contact with the rich and substantive contributions offered by feminist, queer, indigenous, black liberation, immigrant, and other revolutionary traditions. Arguably what is missing from contemporary revolutionary movements is a class politics that holds other, complementary ideas closely with its own conceptions. Henceforth, everyday resistance, the refusal of the imposition of work, mutual aid and self-valorization, working-class self-activity, and an autonomous working class are conceptions that are part of this retheorized revolutionary endeavor.

Beyond capitalism

Capitalism was born in the violent process of enclosure—the enclosure of common lands and eviction of commoners—and concomitant primitive accumulation, which, as Marx noted, "precedes capitalist accumulation; an accumulation which is not the result of the capitalist mode of production but its point of departure."[24] In separating the population from the commons people lost access to the means of subsistence, and thereafter obtaining the means of survival meant working for someone else. Capitalism has undergone a continual process of restructuring since that time, the sixteenth century, in response to everyday covert and overt struggles against work. The working class is "dynamic, forcing, at times, capital to redefine itself and develop along new lines."[25] Resistance and rebellion of the working class as an active subject necessitates capitalism's reorganization of the production and reproduction process.

The central drive of capitalism is not simply the profit motive, the accumulation of capital (accrual of net wealth), or boundless growth ("need [for] a constantly expanding market").[26] Rather, as Cleaver remarked, capitalism as a social system is defined by the endless "imposition of work through the commodity-form."[27] Simply put, a commodity is a product or activity produced and sold in the capitalist marketplace. Without commodities, there can be no profit and markets. And since everything from food and clothes to housing and health care has been turned into commodities, which are only exchangeable for currency, workers need to obtain money to purchase what they need to survive. In effect, the working class must sell to capitalists their ability to work—what Marx refers to as *labor power*, which too is a commodity—to obtain a wage. Since capitalism requires human energy in the form of labor power to produce commodities, the working class maintains an important, central position in the production process. This position is the source of working-class agency. Without labor power, there can be no commodity production and no profit and markets. Hence workers are the source of profit and produce all wealth under capitalism, although this fact is concealed.

Bourgeois society might "appear as an 'immense collection of commodities,'" as Marx's first line of *Capital* argues.[28] But behind this facade, in its ideal, abstract form, capitalism is the ownership of the labor power manifest in commodities—private property defended by the artillery of the state. And the ability to impose the commodity form is the capacity to impose all other social relations.

Cleaver and Marx provide political definitions based on concern for the exploitation of labor power and the private acquisition of surplus value (value produced over the cost of labor and materials) produced by workers under the capitalist mode of production. And it should be noted that Bakunin and many in the anarchist tradition have accepted Marx's basic arguments about political economy. A simple, neutral definition of capitalism is this: an economic and political system with a "monetary system for producing bank-credit money; market exchange; and private enterprise production of commodities," which arises and functions under the shelter of the state.[29] A thorough review of varying and competing definitions of capitalism by the Left, orthodox Marxists, and anarchists would require volumes. But what many of these definitions have in common is that they criticize capitalism for exploiting workers within the wage system, as if we could just end exploitation and keep the work. By relying on Cleaver's definition of capitalism as the endless imposition of work, we are provided a broader understanding of how capitalism is a social system that "subordinates all of life to work and by so doing alienates those it forces to work and prevents them from developing their own paths of self-realization."[30] Yet no definition of capitalism is sufficient without discussing the working class. So, with prohibitions against class reductionism and rote workerism, the matter will be addressed below in an exhaustive description of the working class.

State: form and apparatus

In his rambling history *Demanding the Impossible: A History of Anarchism*, Peter Marshall offers that "all anarchists reject the legitimacy of external government and of the State, and condemn imposed political authority, hierarchy and domination."[31] The key phase here is "external government." Simple enough but not very instructive. While Kropotkin addressed the matter quite clearly in 1897's *The State: Its Historic Role*, misunderstanding remains. He proposed, "The *State* has also been confused with *Government*. Since there can be no State without government it has sometimes been said that what one must aim at is the absence of government and not the abolition of the State."[32] Clearly, contemporary anarchists view the absence of government and abolition of the state as an intertwined project, but they are without definitional clarity on the difference between these two concepts. Kropotkin elucidates:

> the State idea means something quite different from the idea of government. It not only includes the existence of a power situated above society, but also of a *territorial concentration* as well as the concentration *in the hands of a few of many functions in the life of societies*. It

implies some new relationships between members of society which did not exist before the formation of the State.[33]

Here Kropotkin incorporates a number of key themes: territory, authority, management of social life, internal relationships defined by hierarchy, and the state as a power over society (whereas government need not be a power over society). While the state always absorbs the governing body, is the opposite necessarily the case?

Reflecting on the role of the anarchists in the Spanish Civil War, Murray Bookchin adds to this debate:

> All states are governments, but not all governments are states. A government is a set of organized and responsible institutions that are minimally an active system of social and economic administration. They handle the problems of living in an orderly fashion. A government may be a dictatorship; it may be a monarchy or a republican state; but it may also be a libertarian formation of some kind. But without a rudimentary body of institutions to sort out the rights and duties of its members, hopefully in a democratic way, society would simply dissolve into a disorderly aggregation of individuals.... A state, by contrast, is a government that is organized to serve the interests of a privileged and often propertied class at the expense of the majority. This historic rise of the state transformed governance into a malignant force for social development. When a government becomes a state—that is, a coercive mechanism for perpetuating class rule for exploitative purposes—it invariably acquires different institutional characteristics.[34]

Bookchin begins to delineate the two and offers a perspective on the state that could be found equally among anarchists and many orthodox Marxists: that the state is the central committee of the bourgeoisie. This formulation relegates the state to a function supporting, administering, and policing at the behest of capitalism. Such an interpretation sets up the false idea that the central committee of the bourgeoisie can simply be swapped with the central committee of the working class (orthodox Marxists) or under-theorizes the vastness, power, and level of integration of the state in everyday life, believing that local institutions can simply replace centralized ones (as I suggest Bookchin does).

Whereas the definitions thus far provided are inadequate, there is another aspect of the anarchist conception of the state that is knotty. Nestor Makhno illustrates this problem when he says that the "modern State ... relies upon oppressive centralism, arising out of the direct violence of a minority deployed against the majority."[35] Makhno accurately describes the state of his day, but the notion that a state is "centralism" is insufficient today in a period marked by the decentralized relations of power—increasing power of local police and military forces, private foundations, and super political action committees; use of school boards to control curriculum and state legislatures to control federal voting redistricting; cuts to public housing and food subsidy programs; and an upsurge in militias and right-wing religious organizations. Yet this point compels further elaboration.

To reiterate: anarchists often see the state as form, as a personified, embodied authority that wields power over the population. Regularly "government" and "state" are equated by anarchists. Autonomist Marxists view the state as comprising apparatuses, as the machinery of government in addition to organizations that orbit the external authority. Both are animated by relations of power. The state as form hoards and employs power, while the state as apparatus (as both the government and its satellites) is animated by power. The former conception expresses the might and strength of the state (nationalist fervor, absolute authority, promise of renewal through elections, and salvation through obedience). The latter sees the imposition of order through coordinating bodies. Jim Crow, for instance, required the Ku Klux Klan, White Citizens' Councils, and Protestant Christianity in concert with elected officials, local police forces, and the Federal Bureau of Investigation, along with banks, landlords, and federal agencies that maintained segregated ghettos and redlined neighborhoods. Contemporary revolutionary movements require both formulations of the state.

To return to Kropotkin's definition of the state: the state as form is what he calls the "state idea." The idea of the state as the monopolizer of violence and concentrated relations of power, guarantor of relations of production, authority, and politico-military force both domestically and internationally requires a complementary conception of the functioning of the state as comprising apparatuses. In autonomist theory this means both the government itself—the machinery of government—and the numerous apparatuses that are technically external to the state but directly and indirectly coordinate with the official governing bodies. Such external apparatuses include private security firms, military contractors, religious and civil organizations, social service nonprofits, and para-state terrorist organizations such as militias and, historically, temperance unions. Adding state as apparatus to the anarchist conception of state as form allows revolutionaries to maintain the "state idea" while gaining a nuanced view of the operations of the state and its satellites.

The question of what "government" entails is thus far unanswered. The usefulness of Bookchin's notion of libertarian municipalism (of a governing social body directly controlled by its members) or Antonio Negri's constituent republic ("a government of the everyday") can only be resolved in revolutionary movements themselves.[36] Even such democratic manifestations of government can be tempered by the "self-assertion of the individual," and in a post-revolutionary society mechanisms will need to be identified, developed, and deployed to prevent the emergence of state relations. When French post-structuralist philosophers Gilles Deleuze and Felix Guattari call for the "war-machine" to "annihilate the forces of the State, destroy the State-form," they are referring both to the machinery of government, which requires attention toward its particularities in order to be annihilated, and to the very idea of a state authority, which must be politically, materially, and ideologically destroyed.[37] Their task is our own.

Power: potestas and potentia

So far my analysis has been hampered by the conception of power within contemporary radical movements and limited by the English language. If we were to map the etymology of the English word "power" back into its Latin roots, two terms would replace this singular concept: *potestas* ("able") and *potentia* ("to be able"). *Potestas* as authority, management, dominion, and the state. *Potentia* as potential, ability, influence, and productivity. To simplify, let me offer "power to direct" and "power to act" as inadequate English equivalents. Power is often seen in US Left traditions and movement contexts as an evil force beyond the control and will of the people, as a power of "authorities," power of the police and the carceral state, corporate power. Slogans such as "speak truth to power" (a nonsensical phrase) or "the powers that be" reflect how power is seen as something negative, as intangible. This is contradicted by notions such as Black Power, creating powerful movements, building power, "there is power in the union," and the like. Power always requires a qualifier. For many anarchists, power is evil, something to be attacked and undermined. But none of these conceptions improve our understanding of the relations of power that flow through and animate capitalism and the state with its apparatus.[38]

When capital captures cooperative laboring activity and directs it into the production process, imposing work, both conceptions of power are present. Furthermore, the state comprising apparatus uses the wills and desires of the populace to further its lust for territorial expansion as it Others and racializes those inside, those at its borders, and those beyond. There too *potestas* and *potentia* are present. It is baffling when radicals claim that they are in favor of power to act while rejecting power to direct, as both conceptions are intertwined. Anarchists who enact a system of transformative justice within a community are both acting and directing. When allies, supportive partners, and concerned community members generate an accountability process to address domestic violence, transform conditions that led to harm, heal affected parties, and prevent further harm, that is *potentia*. Exerting social pressure upon perpetrators of harm (though family, friends, partners, aware community members), and offering political and ethical inducements: these represent *potestas*. Simply put, the power relationships that construct transformative justice practices should be fundamentally different from relationships that produce and maintain the punitive, carceral state. Once we have put aside a simplistic or confused notion of power we can ask: What kinds of power relations exist, are being uncovered in recordings of everyday resistance, are we encountering at the limits of and within our collective endeavors? For instance, how are new forms of work being resisted and new social relationships emerging? Also: what kinds of power relations and configurations liberate us from those that define capitalism and the state as apparatus? Which kinds continue to snare us in these systems? How are punitive relations of power still present in accountability processes?

According to Foucault, "there are no relations of power without resistances." Such a claim extends the task of "reading the struggles" against domination, exploitation, and subjectification (the construction of the individual subject). Moreover, he proposes an "economy of power relations" that "consists of taking the forms of resistance against different forms of power as a starting point.... Rather than analyzing power from the point of view of its internal rationality, it consists of analyzing power relations through the antagonism of strategies."[39] Resistance uncovers relations of power, and it is our historic task not simply to lay bare these relations but to construct new relations between human beings.

WHAT IS THE WORKING CLASS?

Numerous concepts have now been introduced, and subsequent chapter will clarify each concept as a theoretical tool. Each of these—everyday resistance, commons and commoners, refusal of work, mutual aid, self-valorization, self-activity, and others—has its own histories, content, and contexts. When concepts make up a body of thought, a philosophy or revolutionary theory, they complement each other or conflict with one another. What everyday resistance does, when added to the concepts that make up Autonomist Marxism, is call attention to phenomena—to working-class self-activity—at the scale of everyday life and in the context of slavery, peasant societies, and the industrial and social factory.

Autonomists define the working class as such: autonomous from both capitalism and the official organization of the Left, broadly including all those who work under capitalism, based in relationships between workers rather than as a structural component of the economy or sociological category. Autonomists focus on the refusal of work and how the class is composed. Let us review each element in kind.

Workers' autonomy

"The working class," Glaberman and Faber suggest, "struggles against capitalism because its objective conditions of life force it to."[40] Since capitalism requires that individuals work for wages or access income through state or familial sources (partners and children access income indirectly through the wage earner), the working class *must* struggle against capitalism to obtain resources beyond its initial, meager wage. Class struggle emerges directly from the point of production of commodities, be it widgets or labor power, and in the battles around the length and intensity of the workday. But what does the working class confront?

Capitalists by definition control capital. Capital includes the means of production (tools, factories, raw materials, energy, etc.) and financial resources (money) that are part of the production cycle, which is set in motion in order to produce commodities. "The individual commodity," in Marx's assessment, "appears [as capitalism's] elementary form."[41] Cleaver's definition noted above relies on Marx's appraisal and on that basis Cleaver believes that "the generalized imposition of the commodity-form has meant that forced work has become the fundamental means of organizing society—of social control."[42] Since capitalists cannot create value with the means of production alone, even with automation and machinery, labor power must be employed in the production process. Labor power and means of production are brought together to act upon raw materials to produce commodities that contain both use-value (practical utility) and exchange-value (quantity of commodities that can be exchange for said commodity). Commodities are improved as labor power acts upon them, adding value to them in the process (which becomes surplus value). Then capitalists sell commodities in the sphere of circulation. The surplus value they obtain is the value produced by workers over and above the cost of production. And each commodity contains residue from deposited labor power, as if the commodity has captured bits of a worker's life force and energy in the production process.[43]

Marx's tenth chapter in *Capital*, volume 1, "The Working Day," provides the impetus for the focus on labor power: "Capital is dead labour which, vampire-like, lives only by sucking living labour, and lives the more, the more labour it sucks. The time during which the worker works is the time during which the capitalist consumes the labor-power he has bought from him. If the worker consumes his disposable time for himself, he robs the capitalist."[44] In effect, without the deployment of labor power as living labor in the production process capitalism cannot produce commodities. To cite biblical scripture, "the blood is the life."[45] Thus, living labor is the principal, necessary force in the production process; it is the host that capital, as dead labor, must have in order to live. The working class can rob capitalists, become Sabbatarians, or living labor can escape capitalist command and expend itself in cooperative, common endeavors. In this sense, at the point of production, at the very moment that the commodity is being produced through the expenditure of human labor power, the working class as living labor is an independent force, in operation autonomous from capitalism. And there are other moments during which it breaks free of capitalist discipline and the imposition of work entirely.

Capitalism attempts to maintain control over labor power at the same time as it efficiently exploits workers' ability to work.[46] To extract surplus value and hence profit, capitalism must organize the means of production and raw materials (what Marx called constant capital) and labor power (variable capital) in appropriate ratios. Since constant capital is used up at a relatively consistent rate, capitalists must pay workers less than the value they transfer to commodities in the course of the workday. It is in capitalists' interest to deploy labor power efficiently, periodically using labor-saving technologies such as automation to decrease the number of workers needed or replacing skilled workers with machines and unskilled ones.

Marx argued that the workday could only "vary within certain limits" and that hence the struggle around the workday was grounded in working hours, a "normal working day," and wages due for the rent of labor-power. Capital's interest "is purely and simply the maximum of labor-power that can be set in motion in a working day. It attains this objective by shortening the life of labour-power" as part of its "unmeasured drive" to accumulate capital.[47] A conflict emerges over the length and intensity of the workday, what Marx called absolute and relative strategies for creating surplus value. Relative surplus value strategy covers both the efficient exploitation of labor power and the use of machinery and ways of reorganizing production to increase the intensity of the exploitation of labor power. At times the working class has been successful in limiting capitalism's absolute surplus value strategy (winning the eight-hour day and weekend) and addressing relative surplus value (preventing automation and the replacing of skilled workers with machines and unskilled ones). Additional conflicts erupt between the amount of time needed for workers to gain enough wages to ready themselves to work another day, in addition to how that time is spent, and the time capitalism rents the worker to produce surplus value.[48] At these points of conflict the working class is struggling against capitalist authority. But Marx is only speaking about commodities as products here. He does not adequately address a particularly important commodity for capitalism: that of labor power itself.

"In Marx's account," Federici argues, "No other work intervenes to prepare the goods the workers consume or to restore physically or emotionally their capacity to work. No difference is made between commodity production and the production of the workforce. One assembly line produces both. Accordingly, the value of labor power is measured by the value of the commodities (food, clothing, housing) that have to be supplied to the worker, to 'the man, so that he can renew his life process.'"[49]

In orthodox Marxist (and adjacent workerist traditions) the emphasis on the production cycle ignores the cycle of reproduction of labor power, which arguably is the most important commodity in the capitalist system. Autonomists since Wages for Housework focus not just on the production of widgets but on the commodity of labor power. While the reproduction of labor power might appear to be a realm of relative freedom in the privacy of the home, especially with the feminist initiatives that have sought to reorganize social reproduction along more cooperative lines, capitalism and the state apparatus have launched countless counterattacks (wage freezes and reductions, welfare cuts, etc.) to exert control over this sector.

For capitalism the working class is simply labor power. Cleaver argues in *Reading* Capital *Politically* that the "working class as working class—defined politically—exists only when it asserts its autonomy as a class through its unity in struggle against its role as labour-power. Paradoxically, then, on the basis of this distinction, *the working class is truly working class only when it struggles against its existence as a class. The outcome … is not the creation of a pure working class after the revolutionary overthrow of capital but rather the dissolution of the working class as such.*"[50]

Broadly defined working class

Up until now I have revealed two ways that autonomists define the working class. First, the class can "craft new ways of being and new forms of social relations." In this it can force capitalism and the state to develop along new lines in addition to causing crises in these systems. Second, the working class is the primary antagonist in class struggle rather than simply being reactive to capitalism, and it is autonomous from capital, the state, and the official organizations of the Left. There is also a third general attribute that requires attention.

Autonomists define the working class broadly to include not only those working for wages (waged workers) but also those who obtain income through state benefits (welfare recipients) or are striving to obtain wages or income (the unemployed, disenrolled welfare beneficiaries), those whose work is unwaged (including students and housewives), and those who work to directly obtain basic needs for subsistence (such as slaves and peasants). It is important to acknowledge that while slaves are included in the expanded definition of the working class, African slaves in the Americas, as black proletarians, to use W.E.B. Du Bois's apt phrase, had a fundamentally different relationship with capitalism due to their bondage.[51] And in the same sense, peasants and landowners comprise classes, as "peasants are exploited by capital in the sphere of production."[52] While slaves and peasants are not generally understood to be part of formal, normal class relations, at least to Americans, they have been incorporated into contemporary strategies for accumulating capital.

In effect, as Glaberman and Faber contend, "workers work for others, who control the means of production," which is a social relation, and, as the Zerowork collective clarified, the working class is *"defined by its struggle against capitalism and not by its productive function."*[53] That is, "from capital's perspective" the working class is only a "factor of production" but from a working-class perspective it is a dynamic and complex agent, capable of its own liberation.

To summarize: in addition to what is considered the traditional manufacturing base, the industrial proletariat, this expanded notion of the working class includes students, housewives, slaves, peasants, the unemployed, welfare recipients, and workers in the technical and service industries. Hence the working class is defined in relation to *work*—be it waged or unwaged, productive or reproductive, material, immaterial, or affective—and to one another. But of course the owners of the means of production, as the owners of capital (i.e., capitalists), and their representatives—overseers, supervisors, bosses, managers—are directly defined by their relation to work, whereas bureaucrats, tax collectors, police, and security guards play key roles in disciplining the workforce and hence impose work indirectly upon the class as a whole. To differentiate between social classes, the specific relation to work needs to be identified. And a few issues need to be resolved: How is the working class composed? How and in what way is the working class "defined by its struggle against capitalism"?

Is the working class a structure or category?

What Autonomous Marxists and others are trying to accomplish with the concept of the working class is to explain the complexities of a set of human behaviors using a social classification. The time, energy, and very lives of the majority of the human species over the past five hundred years have been converted into labor power. Some individuals purchase this labor power, others manage and discipline it, and still more reproduce it. In a recent attempt at a definition of "class," Joanna Brenner offered, "Although the concept of class has not dropped from use, its contemporary meaning has become restricted to describing social stratification. Even in this sense, in which 'class' denoted a hierarchy of 'differences' (e.g., of income, education, culture), there is no agreed-upon meaning of class categories."[54] To delineate social stratification—working, middle, and upper class, with sub-demarcations such as lower-middle class—produces definitional and empirical problems. In this sense, class becomes an unchanging, fixed structural element in the economy or a sociological category applied universally to complex relations. Conceptions of class can be applied too rigidly or too vaguely as a form of individual prejudice.

Notions of class privilege and classism can make class seem just another item on the list of constraints imposed upon individuals. Class, Brenner writes, "risks being enveloped in a liberal discourse that focuses on individual transformation (e.g., 'recognizing one's privilege') while advancing moral imperatives (e.g., achieving more equal relations among people)."[55] Hence a contingent concept of class that considers the working class's level of integration into the production process must account for "historical specificity and try to account for the struggles over class."[56]

To address these problems anarchists and Marxists have argued that class is about power. In a similar fashion, Kathi Weeks postulates in *The Problem with Work* that class "is not a sociological category but a political one, and its boundaries depend on its particular composition at specific times and places."[57]

Refusal of work

The image of the working class comprising manual factory workers, usually white and male, disappears upon recognizing the refusals of slaves, peasants, prisoners, housewives, students, and office and service workers. The stereotype has always been a fiction, a narrow misrepresentation that has historically limited the potential of class struggle. According to autonomists, the dynamic, broadly defined working class becomes a class, a social actor, in relation to work only insofar as it is refused. The class makes itself through refusal and self-activity, against and beyond capitalism's attempt to make workers into commodities, nothing but labor power and potential labor power. Hence autonomists are interested in how the working class is composed vis-à-vis its struggles. That is, through the refusal of work, the working class becomes autonomous from capitalist command, the state apparatus, the party, and the union. At times these refusals force capitalism to develop new technologies and strategies to attack working-class power. Crises erupt within capitalism, or a "new era of social relations" is instituted as capitalism is restructured (as happened after the US Civil War, during the Green Revolution, and with the onslaught of "neoliberalism").[58]

Refusal specifically refers to acts of ignoring, disobeying, circumventing, countering, rejecting, or pilfering by employed and unemployed, waged and unwaged, and productive and reproductive workers, as well as those whose work is affective and immaterial. These workers neither control their work nor choose the what, when, where, and how of their work until they refuse it or decide to reorganize capitalist relations entirely.

However, questions arise: What about those who accept the regime of work or even relish it? Aren't there some workers who don't resist? What about structural unemployment? How can you refuse work when there isn't any? The concept of the refusal of work draws our attention to phenomena and is not a claim about all workers or all people everywhere. Within the social aggregate of the working class, as with any population, there is a diversity of opinions, experiences, and desires. The working class becomes more than labor power for capitalism when it refuses the imposition of work. Moreover, work is imposed on two scales: by the boss on the individual worker, as well as on the sector of the population that must access work to obtain income in a capitalist society. The individual worker must perform tasks in the course of the workday under the direction of the boss, but work is also imposed upon employed, unemployed, and those of piecemeal or precarious employment due to the need to obtain money to survive. The inability to access work and hence a wage is part of the imposition of a regime of work that requires an "unemployed reserve army of workers" or "relative surplus population."[59] To refuse work as an unemployed person is to refuse the imposition that requires one to receive a wage to obtain the necessities of life. Moreover, the refusal of work is not necessarily a conscious activity. Employees routinely work to rule (follow rules in minute detail) in order to slow down productivity, take longer than allowed lunch breaks, and ignore instructions from a supervisor in order to accomplish a work task. Each of these is an act of resistance.

If the working class is defined in part by its refusal of the imposition of work, then what can be said of those bosses and bureaucrats who impose work in one instance and refuse it in the next? Are these too part of the working class? The IWW adage that "the working class and employing class have nothing in common" is apropos here, and Wobblies exclude from membership those who have the power over wages and hiring or firing. In this definition an individual boss clearly imposes work upon individual workers, but bosses also impose work upon the general population as part of the aggregate capitalist class. Members of the working class, due to their position, have work imposed upon them that they cannot redistribute in the realm of production. (Historically, however, male workers were accustomed to redistributing work to wives, children, and unwaged workers performing the work of social reproduction. If working husbands' wages were cut, often wives were forced to do the same with less. Due to the struggles of women, gender-nonconforming people, and others against the patriarchal, nuclear family, this redistribution of household work has become less common.)

The working class becomes an active, possibly revolutionary subject, rather than simply an economic category or an inactive structural element in production, when it creates counter-communities and refuses work though everyday resistance, overt rebellions, and aboveground organizing. The working class as structure or category is made by capitalism, whereas the working class, in its own making, is a dynamic, active, and autonomous force.[60] But a worker's having relationships with other workers does not automatically include one in the class. If a worker is part of the structural imposition of work—not in the modest sense of setting schedules, taking breaks, or making minor production decisions but in the sense of imposing work and ensuring the effective exploitation of labor power—then they are not part of this autonomous class, regardless of relationships with other workers. Further, the relationships of the autonomous class are determined in situ: in relation to particular regimes of work, specific forms of resistance, and precise relationships between members of the class. The composition of the working class, where battle lines are drawn and positions are taken, is ascertained in the context of working-class struggle in particular times and spaces. Therefore, determining working class composition, its boundaries and limitations, in autonomist parlance begins with "reading the struggles" of the refusal of work and the kinds of relationships taking place therein, with due consideration to the divisions and forms of oppression. In these contexts, the new society is established and recorded with the possibility of other arrangements of productive, reproductive, cooperative, and creative activities, ones that address real human needs and desires, can be forged.

Class composition

One of the larger questions before us, and which encompasses this definition of class, is how to understand everyday resistance under different regimes of power (*potestas*). Periodically systems are replaced with new forms and capitalism is reorganized, partly in attempts to attack working-class power (*potentia*). It is important to understand the relations of power, production, and social reproduction as capitalism and the state apparatus seek to coordinate, capture, and impose. To produce and expand upon an analysis of workers' activities, an approach has been developed from the perspective of the working class in struggle, that of class composition. "By political recomposition," the Zerowork collective states, "we mean the level of unity and homogeneity that the working class reaches during a cycle of struggle in the process of going from one political composition to another. Essentially, it involves the overthrow of capitalist divisions, the creation of new unities between different sectors of the class, and an expansion of the boundaries of what the 'working class' comes to include."[61]

In an article titled "Marxian Categories, the Crisis of Capital and the Constitution of Social Subjectivity Today," Cleaver grounds the concept of class in concrete social relations, and brings us closer to the contemporary period. Class composition, he writes, is "explicitly designed [by autonomists] to grasp, without reduction, the divisions and power relationships within and amongst the diverse populations on which capital seeks to maintain its domination of work throughout the social factory—understood as including not only the traditional factory but also life outside of it which capital has sought to shape for the reproduction of labor power."[62]

Autonomists begin with a workers' inquiry by "reading the struggles," recording everyday resistance and overt rebellions, as the working class creates new relationships and new subjectivities, escapes capitalist command (even temporarily), and is recomposed (and often decomposed) vis-à-vis its struggle with capitalism and the state apparatus. The working class politically recomposes itself through the refusal of work and the "craft[ing of] new ways of being and new forms of social relations." As the working class acts in its own interests it goes through a process of political recomposition. Then, as capitalism and the state attack working-class power, they seek to decompose the class through cutting wages, undermining union organizing efforts and worker legal protections, instituting technological developments, imposing "austerity," raising the costs of reproduction, and fomenting divisions along lines of race, gender, sexuality, national origin, age, and ability, among others.

As Nick Dyer-Witheford notes, "The process of composition / decomposition / recomposition constitutes a *cycle of struggle*."[63] These cycles of struggle accumulate, furthering the contradictions and crises of capitalism. In this sense, according to Negri, the working class is a "dynamic subject, an antagonistic force, tending toward its own independent identity."[64] In this way, the working class is "defined by its struggle against capitalism." While it has thus far been implied, autonomists do not view the working class as a structure or category of social stratification. In the the *The Making of the English Working Class* E. P. Thompson argued,

> By class I understand a historical phenomena, unifying a number of disparate and seemingly unconnected events, both in the raw material of experience and in consciousness. I do not see class as a "structure," nor even as a "category," but as something which in fact happens (and can be shown to have happened) in human relationships. More than this, the notion of class entails the notion of historical relationship. Like any other relationship, it is a fluency which evades analysis if we attempt to stop it dead at any given moment and anatomize its structure.... A relationship must always be embodied in real people and in a real context.... If we stop history at a given point, then there are no classes but simply a multitude of individuals with a multitude of experiences. But if we watch these men [sic] over an adequate period of social change, we observe patterns in their relationships, their ideas, and their institutions. Class is defined by men as they live their own history, and, in the end, this is its only definition.[65]

Accordingly, class is neither a structural component of the economy nor a sociological category. Seeing class as structure limits the working class to a mere position within the economy rather than a dynamic force.

Class as a category relegates it to income or education level, waged industrial work, or sector of the population defined by party apparatchiks, union bureaucrats, wonky academics, or nonprofit do-gooders. Perennially someone will yell out at a radical meeting or gathering, "We have to get workers involved!" While ignoring the simple fact that all those assembled *are* workers, this is using class as an a priori sociological category. To define the working class relationally requires a rigorous inquiry and analysis of the contingency, subjectivity, and internal dynamics of a social aggregate of individuals ("sectors of the class") that must obtain wages, income, or subsistence directly (waged work, welfare, payment in goods and services) or indirectly (children, partner's wage). Hence the working class can be seen as the sector of the population that experiences the imposition of conditions that make work necessary. Through the refusal of this imposition, internal class relations are furthered, the class politically recomposes itself, and the possibility of a new society beyond capitalism is fostered. Then, of course, the working class comes into conflict with forces that control the means of production (capitalists), manage these means (overseers, landowners, supervisors, bosses, and managers), and maintain larger social relations that enforce the mode of production in the society in which capitalism and the state are functioning (relations with the likes of bureaucrats, tax collectors, police, and security guards). All must work, even capitalists. As Henry Ford boldly declared, "I don't expect to retire. Every man must work, that's his natural destiny."[66] For the bourgeoisie, what was once referred to as the "professional-managerial class," escaping the worst violence of these relations is possible through the coordination and imposition of work on others, even as it is imposed upon their own bodies.[67] In order to better control the working class, police and security guards are drawn from among the working class. As police and rental cops, members of the working class gain authority and a small degree of escape from their own powerlessness. Through their management and control of the working class outside of the factory, work is imposed upon the population in addition to the on-the-job impositions. Each social class has a complex set of internal and external relations such as these.

To suggest that the working class is defined by its relationships requires three things: "reading the struggles," determining the divisions that exist within the class, and ensuring that sectors of the working class aren't omitted from our conceptions and organizing. Agricultural and domestic workers were excluded from the Wagner Act, which passed in 1935 and serves as the foundation for labor law in the US. The exclusion of agricultural workers was tacitly accepted by sectors of the union movement until the rise of the United Farm Workers, which eventually led to the passage of the Migrant and Seasonal Agricultural Worker Protection Act in 1983. Domestic workers would have to wait until the development of a workers' center campaign that pushed for the 2010 Domestic Workers' Bill of Rights in New York State, with a few other states following. Housewives who did not earn a wage were also not considered working class. Autonomists sought to overcome these exclusions conceptually since the working class itself had endeavored to overcome these organizationally and politically. In this way, the concept of the working class can be carefully extended further to address other forms of exploitation and oppression, domination and control as it pairs with other conceptions in revolutionary theory.

An autonomist theory of class requires broad definitions of workers' autonomy and work refusal *and* an inquiry into the composition of the working class vis-à-vis capitalism. By beginning with a wide-ranging description and striving to understand class dynamics and struggles in particular contexts, revolutionaries can approach the working class as it is rather than as they imagine it or wish it to be.

Autonomists view the working class as all those who are refusing the imposition of work—employed and unemployed, waged and unwaged, productive and reproductive, material, immaterial, and affective. Not just those toiling in fields, factories, and workshops but those working in offices and coffee shops, kitchens, bedrooms, and classrooms. To review, work is simultaneously imposed on the population and upon individual workers. These workers face specific hours, wages or lack of wages, and pace on the job, and if they quit or are fired the need to work to obtain income is ever present. The guerrillas of desire, as I see them, are those refusing the imposition of work on the terrain of everyday life both as individual workers and members of the working class. Theft of time and materials, feigned illness, sabotage, arson, murder, exodus, and the myriad of other forms this refusal takes—as well as the process of creating counter-communities—can be found in everyday life. In his classic *Workers' Councils*, Dutch Marxist Anton Pannekoek states that "every shop, every enterprise, even outside of times of sharp conflict, of strikes and wage reductions, is the scene of a constant silent war, of a perpetual struggle, of pressure and counter-pressure."[68] It is through Pannekoek's lens that we begin to see the guerrillas of desire not only as a historical subset of slaves, peasants, and workers in the industrial and social factory but as a subset of the working class today struggling against the general imposition of work. By subset I mean that these guerrillas do not represent all of the struggles of the working class or the entirety of the struggle against the imposition of work but resist outside the gaze or comprehension of capitalism and the state apparatus. It is from the concepts of the working class and everyday resistance that the metaphor of the guerrillas of desire is derived.

3

FROM CONCEPT TO METAPHOR

THREE ILLUSTRATIONS OF THE PROBLEM. TOWARD RECONCEPTUALIZATION.
METAPHOR AS DREAM WORK OF LANGUAGE.

In early January 2006, a friend and I traveled to Austin, Texas, from New Orleans just months after Hurricane Katrina, enduring delays, engine troubles, and missed connections. By the time we reached Austin we were exhausted, not only from riding the Dirty Dog (Greyhound bus lines) but also from six weeks in New Orleans's Algiers neighborhood volunteering at the Common Ground Health Center.

While in Austin we met with Harry Cleaver to discuss Autonomist Marxism, class composition, radical movements, and other pressing matters. We had not slept well or eaten a decent meal in at least a fortnight. Cleaver invited us into his home and served us an exceptionally strong pot of coffee, and we chatted for the better part of two hours. I noticed that a framed poster of the cover from the second and final print issue of *Zerowork* hung on his wall.

Our intent was to produce an interview for *Clamor*, *Left Turn*, or some similar movement publication that would popularize a concept that could allow revolutionaries to move beyond the "stuckness" of the period after the counter-globalization movement ended. In our view we were trying to escape the whirlpool of ideology, cheap sloganeering, and seemingly endless attempts at resurrecting the counter-globalization movement. A composition-based approach to class and social movements, in our minds, offered a necessary corrective to the overemphasis on political consciousness. Different questions would be asked once movements adopted the concept of class composition. By substituting queries such as "what are the emerging struggles?" and "how is the working class composed?" (which would bring us to "how are revolutionary movements organized?") for "what do people believe?" and "do I agree with them?" radicals could begin to ground themselves in the everyday struggles of the working class and thus initiate a new cycle of struggle.

Speaking on this matter during conversation Cleaver offered,

Throughout the history of Marxism, questions have arisen. What is to be done? Where do you organize? Resources are limited, so Marxists have always looked for those sectors of the working class that seem to have the most leverage or seem to be the most dynamic and are those who are most likely to be on the foreground of the class struggle.

It is easy to understand why they have done it; I just don't think we can afford to have that attitude anymore. We need to recognize that capital is global. Struggles are happening all over the place, and our problem is connecting them up in such a way that makes them all stronger.... Our problem, our *big* problem, is to understand concrete struggles taking place all over, but on the other hand we need to understand the connections.[1]

Avoiding or actually rejecting the search for a singular revolutionary subject, he continued, "What we see by looking historically are these cycles of struggle. What hasn't been studied enough is the formation of movements and how they gel and come together. You have these molecular struggles going on all the time and all over the place, but under what circumstances do they begin to link up? How does that linkage catalyze? It is like a formation of crystal from a liquid. Something happens, and even in the literature that deals with class composition and cycles of struggle, it has not received much in the way of analysis."[2] Focusing on the specificity of struggles jointly with the connections between them requires a relational approach to class and a broad definition of the working class. By returning to a grounded, open, and comprehensive theoretical project, contemporary revolutionaries begin with a reassessment of their ideas in relation to their contexts. If, as Cleaver told us, "we cannot afford to privilege particular sectors," then we must locate the points of conflict in everyday life and examine how overt rebellions emerge.

We cannot align ourselves with ideas alone. Adherents of radical views often rely heavily on ideological positions—that is, sets of ideas and ideals that are both analytical and prescriptive in relation to how society does and should function. When one establishes ideological positions before intervening in a situation, one will find one's understanding colored by the original outlook alone. A radical, Cleaver announced, can "come into a community and bring an ideological perspective, a politics, a set of ideas which are completely disassociated from what is going on in that community. This doesn't work." Autonomists, he suggested, "are saying that you need to start from where you are materially. This means the relationships that exist, if you want to forge stronger relationships."[3] Cleaver's words reflect an old maxim of union and religious-based organizing: meet people where they are, not where you want them to be.

Throughout our dialogue we weaved back and forth between discussions of organizing and clarifying questions on autonomist concepts and ideas. "In [Autonomist Marxism]," Cleaver said forcefully, "we begin with the struggles and are trying to understand the dynamics of these struggles."[4] By beginning with the cycle of struggles we start to see how everyday resistance (proto-insurgencies) develop into overt rebellions and movements (small-scale insurgencies) and how these insurgencies, if successful, are generalized across the population (major insurgency).[5] And the knowledge of these struggles is not limited to the militant. "Most people just get a sense of the struggles and whether or not they had an impact," Cleaver continued, "They don't go in, doing analysis and trying to understand the composition of struggle. But local people, of course, do. Local people overwhelmingly never write it up. They are too busy making history to write about history."[6] One of the many tasks for militants—for organizers and organic, working-class intellectuals—is to extend this local knowledge by recording these histories, aligning with and circulating them.[7]

As our conversation progressed, we inquired into the history of *Zerowork* and *Midnight Notes* and Cleaver's relationships with Italian Operaisti and earlier generations of Marxists (C.L.R. James, Martin Glaberman, George Rawick, Grace Lee Boggs, and others).[8] I returned again and again to the question: "What is class composition?" Cleaver would ask in turn about the setting: Class composition in what context? Where? Which movement are you referring to? He became frustrated, even irritable, which in hindsight seems completely understandable. In my exhaustion and narrow-mindedness, a different approach eluded me.

Since the interview did not go as planned, it has never been published. Why it failed has clear implications for revolutionary movements in the United States and how theoretical concepts are deployed.

What I did not yet fully understand was that I wanted Cleaver to provide a definition of class composition, and hence the working class, that was universal, that could be applied similarly and steadfastly across the US. Of course, to separate the concept of class composition from the concrete and complex human behaviors it describes, from the actually existing struggles of the working class, is to render it useless. Our ideas, conceptions, and theories about how the world is arranged and how it could be are not cooked up in academic cauldrons as things to be exhibited or added to curriculum vitae. Nor are they torches to lead the working class out of darkness. Nor are they cobblestones to throw through bank windows or Kalashnikovs to shoot the bourgeoisie (as much as these might be needed). Our ideas, and the concepts and metaphors that express and arrange them, directly affect our efficacy as revolutionaries and the success of class struggle. The revolutionary project entails the constant reconsideration of ideas, which in turn requires a series of open-ended questions. It demands that militants conduct inquiries and experiment with new as well as time-tested approaches to organizing.

All told, the interview was a flop. I obstinately failed to take in Cleaver's message. But the reason why it flopped is interesting, and it is related to the reasons why revolutionary theory in the US has failed. The distorted view of social reality and the limited understanding of the world that impedes contemporary revolutionary movements is the result of attempting to apply abstract, fixed concepts as "things" in a context in which they do not pertain.

THREE ILLUSTRATIONS OF THE PROBLEM

Three illustrations will demonstrate the failure of revolutionary theory in the US. The first addresses the problem of deploying stale concepts in different contexts. The second will speak to the similar drawback of hastily adopting concepts into anarchist or radical theory from other traditions. The third will survey the arrangement of ideas as fixed structures (anarchism, orthodox Marxism) or open assemblages (Autonomist Marxism). Although the first discusses insurrectionary anarchism, the second covers white privilege, and the third addresses anarcho-primitivism and social ecology, the problems I identify are not limited to any variant of anarchism or other tradition.

First illustration

On the evening of February 22, 2010, the editors of *We Are an Image from the Future: The Greek Revolt of 2008* spoke at the Internationalist Bookstore in Chapel Hill, North Carolina.[9] This was the first of a fifty-date tour of the US, which would bring them to the Iron Rail in New Orleans, Monkeywrench in Austin, Boxcar in Bloomington, Red Emma's in Baltimore, and Wooden Shoe in Philadelphia, among other bookstores. In addition to these anarchist haunts, there was an obligatory anarchist book fair and a few stops at collective spaces that would close shortly thereafter. The tour marked a sudden shift in US anarchist politics—or, per its proponents, "post-politics"—toward an insurrectionist and later nihilist turn. No longer was *The Coming Insurrection* simply a catchy title for a book, it was moving from a proposition to a certainty.[10]

Seeing themselves reflected in the declassed insurrectionists of Greece, US anarchists applied the "lessons" of the 2008 rebellion to their own contexts. The upheavals in Greece occurred following the police murder of a young student. The lessons included these: street battles are the pinnacle of revolutionary action; insurrections are in themselves strategies, not just tactics—anything else is just liberalism (although that term is rarely defined); once one stops being obedient, then "life is magical."[11] If a popular insurrection had been launched in Greek streets, why not American ones? Well, the histories, conditions, class composition and networks of social relations, and worker protections and social safety nets troubled by austerity measures differed greatly between the two countries. To replicate the Greek conditions, Americans would have to go back to the 1940s and resurrect the Greek National Liberation Front, nearly fifty thousand strong, in the war against fascism and then squat buildings in the 1970s and then work for decades building infrastructure.[12] When American insurrectionists launched "attacks" in Oakland, Portland, Seattle, and elsewhere between 2010 and 2016, they lacked the informal relationships and formal institutional arrangements of their Greek counterparts. Thus, they had limited resources to continue their struggle and to resist repression.

Insurrection as a concept, like class composition as a concept, requires that one consider content, context, and its histories and its relationship to other notions. I suggest that the insurrectionist turn in the US has neither fulfilled its promise or potential nor made a serious and lasting contribution to the strength of revolutionary movements. The error lies in applying successful (or spectacular but disastrous) tactics to situations and contexts without subsequent and necessary consideration of the complexities involved.

Similar misappropriations and misapplications took place in the counter-globalization movement, when Situationist and Zapatista slogans adorned banners and flyers. More recently a South American variant of platformism (the need for tightly structured anarchist political organizations) called *especifismo* (anarchist insertion into mass movements) has influenced anarchist organizers in North America. The groundwork for this development was laid by the "mass anarchist" perspective of *Black Flame: The Revolutionary Class Politics of Anarchism and Syndicalism*, written by two South Africans from an "internationalist" perspective.[13] In part, the success of organized anarchism and other revolutionary traditions in the US will be the result of militants' ability to inquire into their own circumstances without being encumbered by ideas developed in different contexts.

Second illustration

French philosopher Michel Foucault argued, "We have to be there at the birth of ideas, the bursting outward of their force: not in books expressing them, but in events manifesting this force, in struggles carried on around ideas, for or against them."[14] This bursting forth and "bursting outward" of ideas correspondingly requires that philosophers, scholars, and militants who are attuned to these ideas give them a designation, describe them, and circulate them within and between radical currents.

Contemporary anarchism and other radical traditions have created concepts, inherited some, and adopted others. Accompanying inherited and adopted concepts are often underlying, unacknowledged attributes. For instance, the current understanding of white privilege in US Left and radical movements derives from the precursors provided predominantly by the Weather Underground (WUO).[15] The WUO in focusing its attention on the pervasive nature of white supremacy in the US called for whites to follow the "progressive demands of people of color," says Dan Berger in *Outlaws of America*, "and mandated that white people challenge themselves and other whites, at personal and institutional levels, in the struggle for racial justice."[16] It is quite possible that the popularity of this notion of white privilege illustrates that white radicals see addressing racism in the US as needed for revolutionary transformation. Nevertheless, many of the attributes that accompany this notion are incompatible with anarchist and autonomist principles.

WUO members believed in "the primacy of confronting national chauvinism and racism among the working-class whites."[17] This sector of the population had an "invested interest" in imperialism, as stated in the WUO's "You Don't Need a Weatherman to Know Which Way the Wind Blows" statement.[18] The WUO's view of the white working class, which they had little contact with, is troubling. Especially when considering their "fight the people" catchphrase, directed at the class they believed was hopelessly racist and duped by capitalism. In their minds, the WUO vanguard would inform white working people how to act against white supremacy, although their mechanism for divestment in white privilege is unclear and at times contradictory. The WUO's own practice of desperate and often brutal self-criticism helped shape the commandment "Check your privilege," although that phrase came later. The dismissal of white workers along with self-flagellation and guilt are present in the litany of "I" statements in Peggy McIntosh's popular "White Privilege: Unpacking the Invisible Knapsack" and other bridges between the WUO's time and our own.[19]

Alternatively, US movements could look to the Sojourner Truth Organization's earlier conception of "white skin privilege," which the Weather Underground vulgarized, wherein racism and whiteness was an impediment to organizing on shop floors and in communities. The Sojourner Truth Organization (STO) sought to move the white working class toward abolishing whiteness and capitalism. STO's conception developed during the early 1970s when white revolutionaries in the US were grappling with their role in dismantling white supremacy. STO members viewed white privilege as a social dynamic that needed to be addressed by white organizations as part of a larger revolutionary strategy. As historian Michael Staudenmaier summarized: "The whole purpose of developing the analysis of white skin privilege was to pave the way for collective action."[20] The STO's Noel Ignatiev viewed the WUO position as misguided since "the short-term interests of white workers are harmed by the embrace of white skin privilege"; hence whites are capable of dismantling whiteness—and should do that—without first aligning with the WUO's anti-imperialist analysis.[21]

The Weather view of white privilege has overshadowed that of the STO. The former shifts easily from seeing the white working class as invested in white supremacy to seeing the class being essentially and unchangeably complicit in the racial order, while the latter requires an engagement with the class and as such has built-in prohibitions against judgment and damnation. While both conceptions rely on the understanding that there is a role for white working-class people in the fight against white supremacy, these roles are viewed differently. With the subcultural nature of contemporary movements, the WUO's "fight the people" notion has been amplified. Currently, since class struggle and the economic terrain have been given secondary status when appearing at all, movements have adopted the WUO view that "privilege" is primary. Hence members of the white working class, in this formulation, must address their perceived racism *before* addressing their own interests, *before* organizing or working alongside movements of color. WUO vanguardism, inherent in this notion of white privilege, becomes a prohibition against acting and engaging in the messiness of organizing among and between sectors of the working class.

As these ideas influence movements we can test their accuracy and usefulness by looking at the outcomes. With the rise of the radical right in the US we can deduce that our conception of white privilege has neither inoculated the working class against fascism (or the white middle class that was partly responsible for bringing Donald Trump to power) nor enrolled the class in the project of abolishing white supremacy. To rethink the role of the white working class in a multiracial struggle to abolish capitalism will require a return to the STO's vision, with due consideration given to our core principles as revolutionaries. As things stand, however, many conceptions in the anarchist or autonomist lexicon conflict with the anti-authoritarian tendencies of these traditions.

Third illustration

It would be nearly impossible to locate a political theory that did not begin with a claim about the world. John Zerzan and Murray Bookchin, proponents of anarcho-primitivism and social ecology respectively, both rely on notions of the natural world and human beings' role in it in order to produce an ethics and, in turn, a politics. Zerzan claims that human beings began their downfall when they left the state of nature. As he puts it, "civilization is also separation from an original wholeness and grace."[22] It is not surprising then that his ethical commitments to live "unmediated" by civilization suggest "future primitive" politics. If one were to examine these theories closely one would discover that part of Zerzan's argument is similar to Marx's conception of alienation, which Zerzan applied to all of human history rather than just to capitalism, and one would also detect a residue of the Judeo-Christian myth of the fall from grace and original sin. Bookchin quite differently observes "a deep-seated continuity between nature and society."[23] His "organic societies" reveal a mutualistic ethics that require participation in community politics, which he dubs "libertarian municipalism." Bookchin's dialectical naturalism—as the unfolding of nature into organic, human societies—resembles a long-abandoned orthodox Marxist notion of dialectical materialism applied to the natural world. The ethical and political commandments that emerge from these claims only allow their adherents to view their own positions as good and others as evil. Even when Zerzan's and Bookchin's theories intertwine or resonate they are defined by their own independent structures.

Gilles Deleuze and Felix Guattari refer to these types of structures as "arborescent"—tree-like. They are defined by hierarchal, dependent relationships (objective claims are the roots, morals or ethics are the trunk, and politics are the branches and leaves) that reinforce false dichotomies (good and evil), narrow thinking (only thinking within one's own tree system), and totalizing principles (unwavering universal claims).

But there is another way of looking at philosophy and revolutionary theory, another image of thought. This alternative assemblage of interconnected concepts (rhizomes) and connections between concepts (shoots), which I will refer to as a conceptual apparatus, will provide the revolutionary project with a new approach.[24]

TOWARD RECONCEPTUALIZATION

"Concepts by their definition," Cleaver suggested during our interview, "are abstract—they are abstracting from concreteness. So the way you convince someone the concept is useful is to demonstrate how it draws your attention and focuses you on phenomena that turn out to be important [but] that might, in many cases, not be apparent."[25]

Phenomena create problems for thinking beings and our "sense-making machines." In attempting to address this, Martin Glaberman and Seymour Faber offer:

> It should be understood that definitions or concepts in the social sciences are not absolutes, and they are not "things" that are true or false. Definitions are tools that help us understand reality, and help us clarify the categories with which we examine the nature of human society. They can be more or less useful. They can clarify and make more perceptible our view of those elements of society that we are examining. Definitions are not universals and should change with changes in society. In the worst case, definitions poorly framed can distort our view of social reality and limit our understanding of the world.[26]

As the conditions and contexts in which we operate change, so should our concepts, and we can craft new concepts and discard inoperable ones. But one cannot haphazardly play with the definition of a word because its usefulness as a means to communicate will erode. Rather, improving the precision of our ideas must be done using organized and consistent methods, especially when refining concepts we have inherited.

There are four steps needed in examining our ideas: inquiry and examination of contexts, review of inherited concepts, creation of new concepts, and construction of an apparatus of concepts. Perhaps a fifth step should be stated: repeat the process over and over. But how do we find a productive way forward?

To address this question Friedrich Nietzsche suggests triumphantly,

What dawns on philosophers last of all: they must no longer accept concepts as a gift, nor merely purify and polish them, but first *make* and *create* them, present them and make them convincing. Hitherto one has generally trusted one's concepts as if they were a wonderful dowry from some sort of wonderland: but they are, after all, the inheritance from our most remote, most foolish as well as most intelligent ancestors.... What is needed above all is an absolute skepticism toward all inherited concepts.[27]

All that said, what is the autonomist conceptual apparatus suitable for investigating everyday resistance?

From Everyday Resistance to Guerrillas of Desire

Up until now I have argued that theoretical concepts are part of "a sense-making machine," that they allow us to understand complex and often previously unobserved human activities. Since I am examining the historical record, the purpose here is to develop a conceptual apparatus to examine the evidence. Then the conceptual apparatus can be used to determine if forms of the refusal of work, mutual aid, and self-activity extend or do not extend into the contemporary period.

In order to deploy the concept of everyday resistance in revolutionary struggle we must determine its content (what it describes) in addition to its form and function (how it fits within a larger theoretical apparatus). A taxonomy of struggle, a type of conceptual apparatus, will function to assist in identifying, cataloging, and comparing forms of everyday resistance across time and space.[28] Mutual aid, solidarity, and communication networks serve as the basis for counter-communities of guerrillas and overt rebels (one category of analysis), while the refusal of work is a testament to the multiplicity of expressions and the myriad of forms everyday resistance can take (another category). Self-activity is where these two categories meet.

Moreover, in addition to concepts, metaphors often propagate our ideas, provide an emotional outlet for desires, and allow one's mind to wander toward various political horizons. Metaphors stand in for what they describe. They are not the thing itself.

An analogous concern is that there is a fundamental difference between creating a metaphor from an observation and creating one from observation relayed through a concept. The former moves from imagination, prejudice, and superstition to intuition without the requisite stage for reason, reflection, and developing common notions (as suggested by Baruch Spinoza's theory of knowledge).[29] While metaphors should be intuitive, if they are not based upon accurate observations and coherent, clear abstractions, they will not communicate our ideas and stories well. As previously stated, concepts and metaphors are different rhetorical and theoretical devices that in turn produce different results.

"Guerrillas of desire," as a "newly invented metaphor," does not describe slaves, peasants, and workers engaging in everyday resistance per se but rather encapsulates their complexity while producing ideal and striking images in the mind of the reader, it is hoped. The guerrillas of desire seek to elope with the reader's imagination, fleeing the dead and worn-out metaphors of contemporary radical politics.[30]

METAPHOR AS DREAM WORK OF LANGUAGE

A metaphor, properly formulated, can extend a concept. The shift from concept to metaphor is done to move an idea from an analytical and productive tool within revolutionary theory toward a mechanism for collective, collaborative dreaming and animation of desire. If we were to first produce a metaphor, draw out a concept, and then attempt to apply it to concrete struggles it would lose its ability to function. It would be too abstract as to be useful. Moreover, when revolutionaries take metaphors for concrete reality, they confuse their dream worlds and desires with actually existing phenomena, immanent options, and grounded, strategic possibilities. The conceptual apparatus, as a rational and well-defined application of theory, does not serve all the needs of the revolutionary project. In effect, I am proposing that there are two theoretical structures that result from abstraction and that each have their role to play. Metaphors can clarify meaning. Metaphors speak to the emotions and animate desires for liberation, creation and destruction, sensuality, and collective action—for *potentia*. Metaphors can also animate desires to dominate, to control—for *potestas*.

Thus far I have avoided defining the "desire" in "guerrillas of desire" since I wanted to ensure that we did not begin and end in abstraction. By "desire" I simply mean the force that animates human and social bodies. Desire is striving, will to action, toward self-assertion of the individual and crafting new ways of being (what Spinoza refers to as *conatus*). Desire, as with *potestas* and *potentia*, combines in novel and interesting ways to drive human beings to act. Desire does not act alone. Rather, it requires a vehicle for its expression: a partner in sexual relations, others to organize collective actions with, artistic mediums and instruments with which to work creatively. Desire is immensely productive, as it produces social relations, forms of life, and relations of power.[31]

To be a guerrilla would be to connect desire to the possibilities of guerrilla action and the results these could have in the world: theft of time and materials, feigned illness, acts of sabotage, arson, murder, exodus, and the myriad forms this resistance can take, along with the counter-communities needed for these acts to occur.

Guerrillas invest relations of *potentia*—liberating corn from a grain silo, burning down a storehouse, carving out a community in the least likely places (as did maroons—communities of escaped slaves—in swamplands)—and intertwine these with *potestas*—the likes of slitting the throat of an overseer, farm manager, foreman, or abusive husband passed out on the couch. The desire for power is held by the police officer and prime minster but also by every guerrilla of desire. For it is often that these guerrillas only possess desire with nothing else to their name. It is by acting that they access power.

The metaphor "guerrillas of desire" is part of "the dream work of language," and to understand a metaphor "is as much a creative endeavor as making [one]."[32] The expression "guerrillas of desire" is an attempt to create a set of stories—using guerrilla war as its framework—that sets fire to the imaginations of those who encounter these words. It is here that the stories of resistant, rebellious slaves, peasants, and workers will combine and be amplified. In this way, conceptualization and in turn metaphor creation are directly connected to the project of "recording the existence of the new society," of producing the future in the present and the dreams that come from "the next step we are going to take." In this way, as a form of guerrilla war, the guerrillas of desire are more like the Zapatistas than previous guerrillas. In a poetic communiqué, Subcomandante Marcos speaks to this sentiment perfectly:

> In our dreams we have seen another world, an honest world, a world decidedly fairer than the one in which we now live.... This world was not a dream from the past, it is not something that comes to us from our ancestors. It came from ahead, from the next step we were going to take. And so we started to move forward to attain this dream, make it come and sit down at our tables, light our homes, grow in our cornfields, fill the hearts of our children, wipe our sweat, heal our history. And it was for all. This is what we want. Nothing more, nothing less.[33]

It is exactly this dream world that our metaphorical structure allows us to access as resistance and rebellions are dreams that arise out of everyday life. While the concept of everyday resistance will re-situate and initiate reconsideration of anarchist and autonomist theory, strategy, and organizing, it is complemented and extended by the metaphor of the guerrillas of desire. Revolutionary politics, especially in their anarchist guise, have always included rich and substantive metaphors. The dream world of guerrillas of desire should fuel not only the possibilities afforded by seemingly endless guerrilla war in everyday life but may also stoke the engine at the center of the revolutionary project. It is in these conceptions and metaphors that a revolution is made possible.[34]

PART II

4

UNDER SLAVERY

FROM PLANETARY ENCLOSURES TO THE MIDDLE PASSAGE.
SLAVE GUERRILLAS AND THE US CIVIL WAR. CREATING COUNTER-COMMUNITIES.
A MULTIPLICITY OF EXPRESSIONS, A MYRIAD OF FORMS. GENERALIZED REVOLT AGAINST WORK.

> **Under slavery, as under any other social system, those at the
> bottom were not totally dominated by the master class. They
> found ways of subverting the worst of the system and even at
> times of dominating the masters.**[1]
>
> —George Rawick, *From Sundown to Sunup*

Historically, the guerrillas of desire can be found constantly circulating
in the Americas under the system of chattel slavery as it existed from
the sixteenth to the nineteenth century. Slaves undertook a whole set of
resistant practices, such as the "deliberate slowing up of work, destruction of property, feigning illness and pregnancy, injuring oneself, [and]
suicide."[2] "Slaves pulled down fences, sabotaged farm equipment, broke
implements, damaged boats, vandalized wagons, ruined clothing, [and]
set fire to outbuildings, barns, and stables; mistreated horses, mules,
cattle and other livestock, [and] stole with impunity."[3] And slave women
resisted sexual assault while fighting for the autonomy of the black home.[4]

In addition to these forms of everyday resistance, slaves throughout
the Americas fled plantations, formed maroon communities, and waged
ongoing battles against the slavocracy from these encampments. Herbert
Aptheker observed in an article titled "Slave Guerrilla Warfare": "The
mountainous, forested, or swampy regions of South Carolina, North
Carolina, Virginia, Louisiana, Florida, Georgia, Mississippi, and Alabama (in order of importance) appear to have been the favorite haunts for
these black Robin Hoods. At times a settled life, rather than a belligerent
and migratory one, was aimed at, as is evidenced by the fact that these
maroons built homes, maintained families, raised cattle, and pursued
agriculture, but this type of life appears to have been exceptional."[5]

Extraordinary or not, forms of everyday resistance point to the resilient and organized behavior of maroons, which in turn challenges the narrative of slave docility. This guerrilla war, both "exceptional" and ordinary, prevented those in slavery from being completely "dominated by the master class" and was a vital component in the building of counter-communities and in the "creation of their humanity."[6] In this spirit George Rawick fittingly titled his book *The American Slave: From Sundown to Sunup* as night was the time that slaves had for themselves, a time when they were able to construct their own lives.

In his encyclopedic history of slave resistance Aptheker observed that of the 250 actual or attempted slave rebellions in the United States, each developed directly out of the resistance practices of slaves. Aptheker sees these revolts grouped in cycles of struggle lasting an average of eight years. Occurring in clusters from 1790 to 1802, 1810 to 1816, 1820 to 1832, 1835 to 1842, and with major rebellions in 1856 and 1860, the struggle of slaves in general intensified until the onset of the Civil War in 1861.[7] Capitalism and the state apparatus were forced, in innumerable ways, to respond to the struggles of slave guerrillas, eventually leading to the numerous crises that brought about the war. To respond to the crisis of command and control, the state responded with slave patrols, legislation to aid in the return of runaway slaves, and violent disruption of "conspiracies" between slaves and poor whites. Importantly, slave patrols were a departure from the paternalism and racism that underpinned the slave system. Kristian Williams offers: "Beginning in 1661, the slave codes shifted the responsibilities of enforcement from the overseers to the entire White populace." In 1721, a South Carolina statue "enabling any White person to apprehend and punish runaway slaves" was revised "to shift its focus from runaways to revolts."[8] Although slave revolts were responses to specific conditions on a plantation or in a region, they were part of a larger historical configuration. As Eugene Genovese remarked in *From Rebellion to Revolution: Afro-American Slave Revolts in the Making of the Modern World*, "The revolts of black slaves in the modern world had a special character and historical significance, for they occurred within a worldwide capitalist mode of production. Accordingly, they contributed toward the radical though still bourgeois movement for freedom, equality, and democracy, while they foreshadowed the movement against capitalism itself."[9]

In many ways slaves liberated themselves.[10] It is not that slaves discovered the "contradictions of capital" or developed the correct revolutionary consciousness. Rather, chattel slavery (as a form of capitalism) required the endless imposition of work in order to extract surplus value and accumulate capital, resources, and power (*potestas*). When slaves disrupted work at the point of production by "being lazy" or "carelessly" breaking tools they also refused capitalist command as expressed by the overseer and slave master. Everyday resistance of slaves thus had political and wide-ranging consequences.[11]

FROM PLANETARY ENCLOSURES TO THE MIDDLE PASSAGE

From its very beginning, the transatlantic slave trade was part of a global process of large-scale primitive accumulation, of which the enclosure of common lands across Europe was a preliminary thrust. Twelve million, five hundred twenty-one thousand, three hundred and thirty-seven captives, or thereabouts, were enslaved between 1501 and 1875, comprising the bulk of the human cargo transported on Portuguese and British ships disembarking in Brazil, the British colonies, and the US.[12] Thus began capital's march across the globe. Nation-states extended beyond their initial borders. Capitalism and the nation-state would henceforward be intertwined. The merchant class and then the bourgeoisie, in their incessant, unquenchable desire to acquire wealth, expressed imperialist and colonialist tendencies as they sought to dominate resources and lands beyond Europe. Since the monopoly of violence within a territory was codified through international agreements between nation-states— such as the Treaty of Westphalia and the Treaty of Tordesillas—these treaties became the basis for carving up the planet's lands inhabited by brown and black peoples and divvying them up for the white and European ones.[13] For instance, the Berlin Conference of 1884–85 served not so much as a peace agreement between European nations (and formation of a bloc against US, Russian, and Japanese interests) as it did dividing up the conquest of Africa. Therein the continent was divided by European powers that maintained sovereign control over the territories under their jurisdiction.

In response to European peasant struggles and in the endless search for raw materials and cheap labor, capitalists, supported by the bourgeoning state apparatus, began an attempt to enslave the indigenous peoples of Brazil and then the entirety of the Americas. Through its colonies in Brazil, European capitalism (specifically Portuguese in this case) confronted an auto-consumptive, reciprocal, and communally based economy. That is, indigenous societies in Brazil cooperatively produced goods that were readily distributed to members of the community through traditional and ceremonial practices. This was a form of life historian Stuart B. Schwartz refers to as "based on production for use rather than for exchange, a system which provided a comfortable livelihood without concern for profit in the Western sense."[14] Capitalism could not extract surplus value from these communal systems. Hence, the *encomienda* system (wherein the Crown granted the right of colonists to demand labor and tribute from the local population) and the enslavement of the native peoples together comprised the strategy for capturing work and disciplining the population. Indigenous Tupinamba communities in what would later become Brazil began trading their minute surpluses with Europeans. These initial exchanges soon expanded to a point at which trees were being harvested for Europeans. In the 1530s, as more Portuguese settlers came to Brazil, increased agricultural production was needed to sustain this growing population and the colonists sought African workers to replace indigenous ones.[15]

Within thirty years the indigenous peoples' massive exodus from the plantations and their refusal of the regime and pace of work, to which they were unaccustomed, began to reach crisis levels characterized by low output, products of poor quality, and massive waste of time and materials. This destabilization created opportunities for further resistance, through which both guerrilla wars and overt rebellions broke out. As Schwartz describes it,

> In 1567 a general slave insurrection swept the region of the Bahia Reconcavo [around Salvador, Brazil]. Masters were killed and slaves fled the cane fields in large numbers. [Additionally there] was a large-scale Millenarian resistance movement called *Santidade*, which flourished among escaped Indian slaves and formed *aldeia* [autonomous villages] ... in the region of southern Bahia. Combining Roman Catholic and native beliefs, the *Santidade* followers began burning sugar mills and plantations in the 1560s, and despite Portuguese military reprisals their activities continued into the seventeenth century. In 1610 their numbers were reported at twenty thousand and included escaped blacks as well. As late as 1627 their raids continued in the southern Reconcavo and served as a beacon to those still in captivity.[16]

Schwartz continues, "By far, the most common form of slave resistance in colonial Brazil was flight, and a characteristic problem of the Brazilian slave regime was the continual and widespread existence of fugitive communities called variously *mocambos*, *ladeiras*, *magotes*, or *quilombos.*[17] Consequently, in the 1570s the Portuguese turned to the African slave trade to fulfill their labor requirements.[18] This massive undertaking, unparalleled in human history, attempted in part to directly counteract the effectiveness of the greatest weapon indigenous guerrillas had at their disposal: exodus.[19] As the Portuguese and other European powers, often in the form of chartered companies, shifted from using indigenous slaves to African ones, the ability of guerrillas to resist by simply running away decreased considerably. While African slaves often fled plantations, without the knowledge of the local terrain they lacked the main advantage indigenous peoples had over their European captors. While the enslavement of Africans provided the necessary labor power for early capitalism in the Americas, resistance dogged every aspect of this endeavor. European slavers faced similar challenges in Africa as they did in the Americas, and they often employed African warlords to capture slaves.[20]

During the Middle Passage, slaves used what leverage they had to resist, including noncooperation, mutinies, and, in extreme cases, starving themselves to death. Once on the ship, slaves were largely at the mercy of the ship's crew. Seen as cargo, their underlying value was equivalent to other commodities and to sums of money. One particularly egregious incident illustrates this point. In 1781, the captain of the *Zong* discovered that his sickly slaves were consuming too much food and water, hence threatening the profitability of the voyage. He threw 132 of them overboard and then filed an insurance claim.[21] The ensuing court cases were found in favor of the insurance company and not the slave ship, but no criminal charges were filed. As a result, the *Zong* massacre became a cause célèbre for abolition.

The history of slave resistance and rebellion, as the history of transatlantic slave trade itself, is varied and marked in blood. Enslaved Africans took guerrilla form, and their desire to be free forced the state to provide massive resources to slavers. Within the depths of the slave ship, in their diseased and rat-infested holds, packed tightly to maximize profits, the men were separated from their wives, children from their mothers. But, as C.L.R. James reflects, such estrangement could not prevent the slaves from undoing the chains that bound their hands and feet "and hurl[ing] themselves on the crew in futile attempts at insurrection."[22] Every so often, although the exact number of cases is unknown, these attempts were not futile. Sixty years after the *Zong*, in November 1841, mutinous passengers on the slave ship *Creole* "overpowered the crew [and] sailed for the British West Indies," where slavery had been abolished."[23]

Slave guerrillas, as one would expect, continued to resist enslavement after their arrival in the Americas. As I will explore in more detail shortly, one of the most successful forms of slave resistance was feigning illness or mental or physical defect. Strategically deployed in the slave market, this form of everyday resistance would drive down the price of the slave and could cost a former owner dearly. This was just part of a web of practices used by the guerrillas, practices that define the counter-communities that emerged during the era of slavery and would continue afterward. Such everyday resistance, as well as the overt rebellions and mutinies as noted above, contributed to the political and economic crises that led to the US Civil War and the end of slavery in America.[24]

SLAVE GUERRILLAS AND THE CIVIL WAR

The historical record illustrates that slaves resisted bondage at every turn and that organized slave revolts, which often included poor whites, occurred with some frequency.[25] Responding to the "problem" of fugitive slaves and the fear of rebellion among certain sectors of the white southern populace, the slavocracy pressured the federal Government into adopting the Fugitive Slave Act in 1850. But this prevented neither escape nor disorder. Historian Cedric J. Robinson offers: "It was not ... some sort of mathematical mean between the political sentiments, economic interests, and moral consciousness that inspired ... two mutually contradictory but historically complementary public acts [the Fugitive Slave Act and John Brown's raid at Harpers Ferry] (each in its own way, of course, proved to be a necessary condition for the civil war that followed)."[26] The Fugitive Slave Act could not hold back slaves in exodus. And while slaves did not join John Brown's incursion as he expected, his action did reverberate throughout the country, with secondary and tertiary effects that would amplify white southern dread and black longing for freedom. Cyclical upheavals caused great alarm south of the Mason-Dixon Line and were used by the slavocracy to consolidate political power. "The linkage in southern minds between slave insurrection and civil war," Civil War historian Brian Holden Reid contends, "may explain why so many sceptics who were not persuaded by secessionist arguments, hurriedly supported the Confederacy once the die was cast."[27] He goes on to describe two cases that caused widespread terror among the slavocracy: John Brown's 1859 raid (and the lasting memory of it) and an aborted rebellion in October 1861 that sought to unite slaves with Union forces. In the first instance, the raid on Harpers Ferry was contagious among southern slaves and free blacks in the North. The same had been true with news of the Haitian Revolution seventy years prior and with Nat Turner's revolt in 1831. In the second case, the 1861 rebellion, a mere six months following the battle at Fort Sumter that opened the war, the slavocracy feared that rebellious slaves would undermine the Confederacy by uniting with the Union army. Robinson points to the period of struggle between the Fugitive Slave Act and Harpers Ferry, while Reid draws our attention to the period between Brown's raid and the onset of the war.

Even though slaves had been fleeing plantations since the onset of slavery, an uptick in such acts, often with the organized assistance of free blacks, sympathetic whites, and the Underground Railroad, occurred in the late 1840s. Thus the political class of the southern states lobbied strongly and successfully for passage of the Fugitive Slave Act as the 1850s began. Concern over slaves in exodus was particularly prevalent along the Mason-Dixon Line, intensifying the fear among members of the slavocracy. "The sight of slaves fleeing en masse," historian Max Grivno observes, "taught masters and mistresses that slaves were becoming dangerous investments. The border skirmishes that erupted from the 1830s through the 1850s would teach slave owners just how dangerous their human chattels were."[28] Skirmishes took place in the South, along the border, and in the North as well. "The Fugitive Slave Act galvanized northern blacks," David Williams argues in *I Freed Myself: African American Self-Emancipation in the Civil War Era*.[29] Williams writes, "Across the North, blacks stepped up efforts to form unofficial militias, neighborhood patrols, and other self-protection societies ... [b]ut it was in the South that rising resistance stoked slaveholder fears and pressed the slavery issue to a breaking point.... Reports of rising resistance, up to and including murder, became more and more common throughout the 1850s."[30] Exodus and insurrection clearly led to fear among whites invested in the slave system, forcing political crises that federal and state governments would not resolve, and in some instances could not resolve, without going to war.

While Turner's and Brown's rebellions reverberated throughout the country, these upheavals began to have serious economic and political consequences for the survival of the slave system. "Revolts made a substantial contribution to the amelioration of the material conditions of slave life," Genovese surmises, "for they provided one of the major spurs to the abolition of the African slave trade. In the US, especially, the closing of the trade, with its attendant rise in the price of labor, compelled slaveholders to adopt measures designed to guarantee the productivity and reproduction of their labor force."[31] These innovative measures to ensure production of cotton, hemp, rice, tobacco, and sugarcane were concomitant with increased exploitation, surveillance, and ruthlessness and violence of overseers. In addition to the resistance and rebellion thus far addressed, practices such as theft, sabotage, and arson were used against the slave system. But even with these forms of resistance and rebellion, the slave system continued to be incredibly profitable. Slavery continued to be economically viable while the ability to impose work on slaves as individuals and as a class eroded. This erosion of labor discipline, as we will see below, threatened the long-term feasibility of the system.

For the duration of the Civil War, slaves launched insurrections, sabotaged farm implements, set storehouses ablaze, and fled to join the Union Army. Escaped slaves based in maroon communities waged guerrilla warfare. Genovese notes, "The peak of nineteenth century maroon activity came during the war, when long hidden groups appeared in full view and many others arose among slaves deserting the plantations."[32] Two hundred thousand slaves abandoned the plantations to work for the Union Army during this period, "destroying the South's ability to supply its army."[33] As the war progressed, slaves deserted for the North.

Slaves' resistance and rebellion mattered. Historian John Ashworth writes, "We are ... driven to conclude that black resistance to slavery was a key factor in the Civil War."[34] Scholar Bernard Mandel underscores this: "Unquestionably the most persistent, thorough and effective anti-slavery force in the nation was the slaves themselves. For three hundred years they resisted bondage and exploitation by every means that ingenuity and courage could devise.... In the 1850's the resistance of the slaves mounted, and during the Civil War many seized the opportunity to overthrow their oppressors as soldiers in the Union armies of liberation."[35]

It is important to note, as scholars remind us, that slave self-activity was not the only factor in the liberation of slaves—war was necessary to unravel the slavocracy and reweave the American economy.[36]

As the Civil War ended and Reconstruction commenced, struggles continued. In the section titled "The Working Day" in the first volume of *Capital*, Karl Marx recorded his observation of the battles that were to follow the war: "In the United States of America, every independent workers' movement was paralyzed as long as slavery disfigured a part of the republic. Labour in a white skin cannot emancipate itself where it is branded in a black skin. However, a new life immediately arose from the death of slavery. The first fruit of the American Civil War was the eight hours' agitation, which ran from the Atlantic to the Pacific, from New England to California, with the seven-league boots of the locomotive."[37]

From crisis new opportunities for working-class organizing directly confronted the forces of capitalism and the nation-state. Black militants and politicians of Reconstruction forged new relations between the races, while union members, predominantly white and European, launched the planetary struggle for the eight-hour day. African Americans went from branded slaves to black workers, but labor emancipation efforts were often hobbled by white supremacy.[38] Within a year of the end of the Civil War the International Workingmen's Association picked up the charge to limit the working day. This struggle and those that followed, including our own, are possible because of those who came before: indigenous and black guerrillas. The black community was made in these struggles, and it was made when women fought to maintain their families and bodies from the predilections of slave masters, in the evenings after the sun had set, and it was made in the fields when slaves broke tools against trees and rocks. The kinds of counter-communities and myriad forms of everyday resistance used by these guerrillas require further elucidation.

CREATING COUNTER-COMMUNITIES

Enslaved guerrillas used a network of social relationships and unique modes of communication that defined slave communities. In effect, guerrillas seek to be indistinguishable from the community while drawing upon its resources, and slave populations did this, existing within and against the system of slavery. Often community activities took place below the surface and beyond the perception of the overseers, and normal everyday interactions were used as cover for resistance operations. For these reasons, I refer to these relations as those of a counter-community: counter to the logic of the slave system, counter to the imposition of work, counter to the material and spiritual deprivations that slaves experienced day to day. Resistance and rebellion occurred regularly under slavery and afterward. As Rawick reflects: "The slave revolts came out of the natural development of the black community and were a stage in the development of that community."[39]

To employ the aforementioned taxonomy, there were three intersecting attributes within these counter-communities that furthered everyday resistance: solidarity, communication, and mutual aid.

Solidarity

A sense of solidarity seems to have permeated social relations within slave communities, and trust among the slaves was necessary for communications networks to function and for mutual aid to function. Without a sense of common experience, common purpose, confidence in one another, and belief that what they did "from sundown to sunup" was sacred and secret, a counter-community could not have maneuvered around and against the slavocracy. To construct their culture of survival, slaves purposely modified Bible verses and maintained or reconstituted traditional African practices. To subvert the slave order and develop cohesion among themselves, they shared meager resources, sang together in the fields, and held their own religious services. Thus, there were discursive as well as material and spiritual elements to slave solidarity. These practices and the resultant cohesion evolved concomitantly.

In the following example from Alice and Raymond Bauer, slaves had positions traditionally held by whites, replacing sadistic overseers who traditionally administered punishments: "In some cases, it was noted that the slave resisting punishment took pains not to treat his fellows with any more than the absolute minimum of violence. With such demonstrations of solidarity among the slaves it is not surprising to find a slave telling of how he and his fellows 'captured' the institution of the driver."[40] Since punishment for everyday acts of resistance or modest indiscretions were inevitable, if a slave could capture the "driver" or overseer role, penalties for insubordination could be mitigated. Moreover, this camaraderie among slaves often took place publicly, observed by the entire plantation or citizens from the surrounding region. Then, of course, solidarity was extended as one slave boasted to another how he had captured a position usually reserved for the overseer or master. The act of even a single guerrilla telling others of such resistance is quite profound and reflects the sense of solidarity that was necessary for more complex communications networks to function.

Communication

Slave communication took place via informal networks throughout the plantation and indeed connected plantations with one another. Rumors spread through these networks, along with news about loved ones and information helpful for those seeking to flee or rebel. Freed slaves developed their own communities and often continued to communicate with those who were still enslaved. Rumors surrounding the Haitian Revolution of 1789 circulated among slaves in the US, which was of much concern to the slave-owning class.[41] Since it was claimed that Africans could not govern themselves, a successful slave rebellion seven hundred miles off the coast of Florida directly threatened the slavocracy. In addition, word of local rebellions or even individual acts of resistance spread far. Rawick supposes, "There must be ways whereby individual acts of repression become known throughout the community, ways whereby individuals learn from each other that resistance is legitimate, and ways whereby individuals learn from each other of particular ways to resist."[42] Communication moved not only between slaves within one plantation but also, in a fragmented way, between slaves and maroons elsewhere. Shipments of slaves from one region to another, contact between slaves from neighboring plantations, "grog shops" (unlicensed liquor stores) where slaves came into contact with poor whites, and chance meetings in towns and cities, are only the most general contact points. Of course, parents would teach children, and knowledgeable slaves would teach the newly arrived. Slaves who worked in their masters' homes or were rented out to others would pass along useful information throughout the community. As slaves, moved so did news of resistance, rebellion, and possible freedom.

By extension, the church and religious services became spaces outside of the daily routine for communication and the formation of bonds among the slave populace. Further, slaves used religious teachings to justify their actions and used its arguments against slavery as a whole.[43] The relatively free zones of slave religious observances developed to such a point that the slaveholding class had to respond, which is why they began to surveil and limit church activities.[44] A degree of surveillance is hinted at in Alabama's 1833 slave codes requiring black preachers to "be licensed thereto, by some regular body of professing Christians immediately in the neighborhood, and to whose society or church such negro shall properly belong."[45] Originally planned by the slave-owning class as a method for *preventing* uprisings, black churches became spaces in which rebellions were fomented.[46] Moving through and extending beyond these spaces—referred to as "hush-harbor meetings" by slaves themselves—myths and songs spread the stories of the slaves' resistance and rebellion.[47] In song and eventually in their lives, slaves became free.

The mythic tales of Br'er Rabbit were among many stories that would allow slaves to imagine their freedom and share notions of everyday resistance. Rawick expands on this: "There are a variety of myths and folktales from black populations in Africa and the New World in which a relatively weak creature succeeds in at least surviving in his competition with greater beasts, usually by trickery.... He is often absurd, but he is also filled with life and keeps struggling against his situation."[48] Alex Lichtenstein writes, "Trickery is used by 'Br'er Rabbit' in numerous instances not only to steal livestock from men, but to lay the blame on others or cheat his accomplices, so he can distribute the food to his own family or sweetheart."[49] Within the "trick" there is a counter-narrative that presents stealing, lying, and cheating as legitimate under slavery. Slaves were able to momentarily escape the cruel conditions of their enslavement in telling these folk tales. The craving for freedom was momentarily satisfied, while the possibility of achieving it was furthered. From these components—sense of commonality, communications networks, folktales—mutual aid and resistance emerged.

Mutual Aid

Slaves assisted one another, brought food to those who were hungry or had run away, and created a vibrant Underground Railroad to assist escaped slaves. These acts of solidarity and mutual aid allowed slave communities to improve their immediate, material conditions while serving as a base of operations for further action by guerrillas and rebels. Reciprocal relationships were based in specific regions—"a particular praxis of field, upland, forest, marsh, coast," as Peter Linebaugh suggested speaking about commoners. Slaves escaping through the Underground Railroad would use local resources and hiding places. They could run away with the expectation of receiving food and other supplies. As John Hope Franklin and Loren Schweninger outlined in *Runaway Slaves: Rebels on the Plantation*:

> Many runaways sustained themselves while on the run by tapping into the clandestine slave economy. Those who remained in the vicinity of their old plantation often kept in close contact with fellow slaves, who provided them with supplies from the master's storehouse. Those who moved into towns and cities brought what they had stolen to trade, barter, and sell. And those who sought to move greater distances were in regular contact with slaves who were willing to buy or sell various items or to trade stolen goods for food and clothing. Runaways took cattle, hogs, sheep, livestock, rice, cotton, corn, whiskey, poultry, grains, meats, even baskets, brooms, and farm tools.[50]

Runaway slaves and those who stayed behind to manage the underground economy dealt in pilfered goods—that their own labor had indirectly paid for.

A MULTIPLICITY OF EXPRESSIONS, A MYRIAD OF FORMS

Enslaved guerrillas used many tactics in their struggle against what has been called the peculiar institution. These tactics included theft, sabotage, feigned illness, suicide, slowdowns and wildcat strikes, exodus, arson, and assassination. Exploring the particulars of these forms will lead us toward an understanding of the generalized guerrilla war against the regime of power that defined slavery, which are part of the echoes of refusal that haunted early capitalism.

Theft

Theft was likely the most common form of everyday resistance under slavery, and the act entailed the reclamation of one's own work, the basis of plantation wealth. To combat this widespread activity, slaveholders adopted two strategies, one aversive (violent punishment) and the other coercive (giving slaves plots where they could grow their own crops, in the hope that this would reduce their need to steal). The latter was an attempt to destroy the underground economy and bring all of slaves' economic activity under the control of the state. South Carolina in 1740 passed the "Act for the Better Ordering and Governing Negroes and Other Slaves in this Province," which prohibited slaves from engaging in the sale of any item without the explicit permission of the master. This aspect of the law was ineffectual, and theft continued. In 1796 a law was passed to prevent grog shopkeepers from selling goods purchased from slaves without the master's permission. State regulations continued with subsequent acts that increased fines on those who had traded illegally with slaves (1817) and then prohibited any purchase of goods from a slave (1834). The slaveholding class was desperate to keep this clandestine economic activity under control and limit contact between slaves and poor whites, whom had begun to explore their common interests.

At its core, the struggle against theft was a struggle for power. As guerrillas pilfered the property of their masters, they developed ethical positions to justify this activity. In this, Alex Lichtenstein, whose scholarship directs this section, believes that "slaves made a clear distinction between the legitimate 'taking' of property from whites and the reprehensible 'stealing' from their fellow slaves. Such mixed feelings were the result of the contradiction between slaves' Christian sense of morality ... and their desire or need to steal."[51] The goods that slaves took were not exclusively used for their own consumption but were often bartered and found their way into underground networks. Grog shops were spaces where slaves could sell goods, alcohol could be purchased, and blacks and poor whites came into contact and formed relationships. These establishments were usually owned by non-slaveholding, poor whites, and when the slave masters or the state sent vigilante patrols to suppress them, class antagonisms arose.

The distinction between taking and stealing created a problem for the slave system. Additionally, it illustrated solidarity between slaves and an awareness of who benefited directly from slaves' work. Furthermore, theft was an instrument of economic resistance against a set of legal frameworks and relations of power. In this regard, theft can be read as a battle over the products of one's work. Theft threatened the entire social order, as "the constant pilfering of goods disrupted the plantation production system and eroded the social control of slave labor that made such a system possible and profitable."[52]

Sabotage

Slaves made a habit of destroying tools on the plantation, included breaking farm implements and working livestock to death. Capitalism, the state, and the disciplinary order had to respond to these tactics. Capitalism would react by creating heavier and sturdier tools (technological improvements), the state generated new legislation, and then the cycle would begin again. Given the subtleties and the low risk of getting caught, it is unsurprising that sabotage was one of the most common forms of slave resistance. Masters thought that the slaves were simply being mischievous since they believed it was their nature to do so. Aptheker notes that "the carelessness and deliberate destructiveness of the slaves, resulting in broken fences, spoiled tools, and neglected animals, were common phenomena."[53] Since this made it quite difficult for the master to implement new farming techniques, this lowered both the productivity and the profitability of the plantation. Essentially the slaves hindered progress and development of the plantation system by these actions. The point came when "mules were substituted for horses because horses could not stand up under the treatment of the slaves."[54] Slaves attacked the master's property as it was the most immediate representation of his authority.

The development of the "nigger hoe" (as it was then called), following the failure of the "Yankee hoe," is a vivid example of the power (*potentia*) of everyday resistance as it forced capitalism to adapt to the actions of the enslaved. As described at the time: "The 'nigger hoe' was first introduced into Virginia as a substitute for the plow, in breaking up the soil. The law fixes its weight at four pounds—as heavy as a woodman's axe.... The planters tell us, as the reason for its use, that the negroes would break a Yankee hoe in pieces on the first root, or stone that might be in their way."[55] Maintenance of the slave system, as with the tools themselves, was a constant battle between the disciplinary order and the everyday struggles of these guerrillas.

From Feigning Illness to Suicide

Faking illness was a common tactic. The masters, not wanting their slaves to die, often allowed a day off for a sick slave. Choosing the opportune moment, a slave would often feign illness on the auction block to lower their price, thereby reaping revenge upon a cruel master or, in some cases, preventing the sale altogether.[56] A slave who feigned illness at the auction block did so when the master was vulnerable. While being "shipped from Jamaica in 1709," Darold D. Wax writes: "Jenny was lame and in poor health, which, coupled with her attitude, made it almost impossible to find a buyer for her."[57] Jenny, by combining illness with insolence regained some semblance of control over her fate. Illnesses would also arise in interesting patterns with "everybody sick on Saturday, and scarcely anybody sick on Sunday" (the slaves' day off).[58] In a similar fashion, women would feign illness or pregnancy and, for the short time before they were inevitably discovered, be granted both time off from the most strenuous work and additional food. These "pregnant" women must have understood that their lie would be discovered and that they would be punished, but the short-term relief from work and increase in rations must have been just too tempting.

As a permanent escape, there are examples of slaves who committed suicide, performed acts of self-mutilation, and even killed their own children. While these are not common forms of resistance, they do arise throughout the history of slavery. Suicide was an act of refusal, ultimately removing oneself from enslavement.[59] It is a testament to the brutality of slavery that numerous slaves killed themselves, often in groups, rather than remain the property of another. At times, the Bauers write, "new slaves commit[ed] suicide in great numbers. Ebo landing in the Sea Islands was the site of the mass suicide of Ebo slaves who simply walked in a body into the ocean and drowned themselves."[60] Aptheker notes, "On at least one occasion, in 1807 in Charleston, mass suicides occurred; in this case two boatloads of newly-arrived Negroes starved themselves to death."[61] And not just suicide: there are accounts of slaves cutting off a hand, arm, or leg to make themselves less useful to their masters. From illness to infanticide, suicide to self-mutilation, slaves sought to flee their bondage.

Slowdowns and wildcat strikes

Many southern doctors found that slaves often exhibited signs of mental illness, and some believed this to be widespread. Symptoms of "Dysaethesia Aethiopica" were said to include mischief, destruction of property, theft, and working and performing tasks too slowly. In recognizing that their labor only benefited the master, slaves expressed their indignation by refusing work, working slowly, and being generally uninterested in their tasks. Bauer and Bauer commented, "It is thus not surprising that one finds many recurring comments that a slave did not do half a good day's work in a day."[62] Numerous slaveholders commented that the slaves had to be constantly monitored to get them to work, that they would do all they could to resist up to the point of being punished.

For the system to operate, overseers and slave owners believed that they needed to be constantly present and consistently willing to use the whip to get slaves to work. But were slaves simply indifferent to their tasks or were they deliberately working slowly? On one plantation it was recorded that slaves neglected to guard the cattle and "were fully aware that the cattle were ruining the sugar cane, but kept right on singing and dancing."[63] I suggest that they were at times indifferent, at times deliberate, and at times both of these. What is key is that their actions were an expression of the need to control their own destiny.

By refusing work slaves gained leverage over their role in the production process. By striking they threatened the increasingly fragile nature of the slave system, particularly as the Civil War approached. Slave strikes were a logical next step in the refusal of work, and these were often combined with other forms of everyday resistance, such as theft, sabotage, arson, and running away. We can say with some confidence that wildcat strikes could not have been undertaken without the everyday actions of the slaves, as "individual acts of truancy became slave strikes."[64] To expand upon this, the Bauers write, "The slaves were well aware of their economic value and used it to good advantage. The skilled laborers among the slaves knew their worth and frequently rebelled against unsatisfactory work situations. Slaves who were hired out would run away from the masters who had hired them and then either return home or remain in hiding until they felt like returning to work."[65]

At times these instances of everyday resistance and slave strikes became especially effective. During the profound crisis of the Civil War period, "in the absence of many slaveholders, overseers, and patrollers, hundreds of thousands of slaves worked sporadically or not at all other than for their own immediate needs.... In the South, the slaves systematically sabotaged the war effort by refusing to produce."[66] Resistance and rebellion in times of crisis, when the disciplinary order has broken down, compounds the situation and leads to further crisis and hence opportunity for revolution, as nearly occurred during the Civil War.

Exodus

As described earlier, the simple act of running away was quite an effective tool that the slave possessed. The Underground Railroad, through which runaway slaves fled to the North, sometimes all the way to freedom in Canada, "was no regularly organized institution. Rather, the runaway slaves naturally utilized the resources of the black community—the slave quarters and the homes of freedmen."[67] The slave counter-community served everyday resistance directly. In Brazil, Mexico, the Caribbean, and everywhere slavery existed, the slaveholding class responded to the constant flight of slaves in the form of legislation, slave patrols, punishment of slaves who assisted runaways, and attacks on maroon communities. Preventing an exodus of slaves was necessary to maintain the slave system and disciplinary order. When slaves ran away they challenged the very fabric of the slavocracy and created the possibility of another society. The state and slaveholding class responded with legislation. The national Fugitive Slave Act, passed in 1850, "mobilized some Northern whites into a movement to abolish slavery and protect fugitives, [but] it was the fugitive slaves who created the need for the Fugitive Slave Act," Rawick deduced.[68] Rather than being granted freedom, slave guerrillas, through their resistance, at times in concert with poor whites, made freedom possible.

"Departure out of ... Egypt," as Frederick Douglass referred to his own case, can be seen in two general categories: taking temporary leave of the plantation and running away to form maroon communities.[69] There is a difference, of course, between truant slaves and escaped ones, and women were more likely to be the former, as historian Stephanie M. H. Camp reveals in works such as *Closer to Freedom: Enslaved Women and Everyday Resistance in the Plantation South.*[70] Exodus was combined with other forms of everyday resistance, and "solidarity was often extended to runaway slaves who stole food from plantations as their sole means of survival."[71] These small acts grew into communities that existed outside of slavery, against, and beyond it.

Communities such as this existed in Haiti when the Haitian Revolution thunderously announced itself in 1789. In *The Black Jacobins*, a marvelous text on the subject, C.L.R. James states that in Haiti, those "whose boldness of spirit found slavery intolerable and refused to evade it by committing suicide, would fly to the woods and mountains and form bands of free men—maroons. They fortified their fastnesses with palisades and ditches. Women followed them. They reproduced themselves. And for a hundred years before 1789 the maroons were a source of danger to the colony. In 1720, 1,000 slaves fled to the mountains. In 1751 there were at least 3,000 of them." James continues, "Many of these rebel leaders struck terror into the hearts of the colonists by their raids on the plantations and the strength and determination of the resistance they organized against attempts to exterminate them."[72]

In Brazil, *cimarrones* (escaped African slaves) became *vagabundos*; they formed *mocambos, ladeiras, magotes,* and *quilombos*—communities of resistance.[73] Many of these communities were quite large. As Schwartz declares, "One *mocambo* was reported in 1723 to have over four hundred inhabitants, but size alone was not the sole determinant of *mocambo* danger ... as word of these events reached the slave quarters of the *engenhos* and planters feared a similar outbreak."[74] Maroon communities became a beacon for runaway slaves as well as those still living on the plantation. While armed revolt was a concern and "rumors of planned slave revolts [in Brazil] circulated in 1719, 1725, and 1756, the main problem continued to be *mocambos*."[75] Armed revolts and conspiracies could be put down, but preventing the individual slave from leaving the plantation was a much greater challenge. The Quilombo dos Palmares, which existed for nearly a century, was one of the longest-running communities of slave guerrillas in Brazil. It had its own form of government and its own agricultural system, neither of which were common among maroon communities.[76] Palmares, like other such enclaves, was more than simply a community of runaway slaves—it was a threat to the existence of the entire regime of power that defined slavery.

Arson and assassination

For slaves who chose not to flee or were unable to do so, different tactics were sometimes used: arson, poison, and assassination. A lit match placed in a barn would threaten an individual plantation, but a series of such fires could level a region and destabilize the slave state. The fear that arson struck among members of the slaveholding class was enormous. Aptheker clearly sees the threat this activity posed: "Arson was more frequent and appears, indeed, to have been one of the greatest dangers to antebellum Southern society.... Members of the hated patrols were at times especially selected by the slaves to suffer the destruction by a slave-created fire." He says that "fires deliberately created by individual slaves in protest against their oppression and as a means of revenge against their exploiters" spoke to fellow slaves and sent clear messages to the slave-owning class: we will not passively accept our enslavement.[77]

Arson was a danger to the pre–Civil War American South since slaves were the vast majority of the population. The flames of a burning "big house" was reflected in the faces of the entire slave community. Arson was common because it was easy and at times struck not only the master's immediate property but surrounding lands as well.

When a master's family was poisoned, more often than not the culprit was a woman. It was women who most often had access to the master's house and kitchen. Female slave guerrillas would poison a particularly brutal master and his family; occasionally they would poison themselves and their own kin to escape enslavement. Seemingly the only method of preventing this was the trust a master held in his house slaves. However, "in 1751 South Carolina enacted a law providing the death penalty, without the benefit of clergy, for slaves found guilty of attempting to poison white people."[78] But legislation would not prevent slaves from killing those who enslaved them.

GENERALIZED REVOLT AGAINST WORK

Understanding slave revolts is key to grasping the revolt against work. Slavery, which contributed greatly to the early processes of industrialized capitalism, can be considered a testing ground for capitalism, the state apparatus, and methods of worker resistance that would develop later. The slaves keenly understood that they were not benefiting from their work. As mentioned above, slaves viewed the "taking" of goods from the master as morally acceptable and often necessary for their survival, but pilfering from a fellow slave or a poor white's crops was "theft." In this gray area between necessity and solidarity, slaves as agents of their own liberation become clearer. As a class, slaves destabilized the regime of power that defined slavery. As Michael Hardt and Antonio Negri explore in their book *Empire*: "European capital would not relinquish slave production until the organized slaves posed a threat to their power and made that system of production untenable.... Political unrest did of course undercut the economic profitability of the system, but more important, the slaves in revolt came to constitute a real counter-power."[79]

Only when we see slaves as part of the working class, functioning autonomously from capital and the state apparatus, does the effect of their resistance on the regime of power that defined slavery come into focus. "Only when the slaves, through their own struggles," Rawick argued, "saw the necessity and possibility of freedom, could they struggle to overcome, to transcend that bondage."[80] These are themes that will be explored in the following chapters on the peasantry and the class of industrial and social workers. It is the resistance against capitalism, against the imposition of work, that defines the working class.

5

IN PEASANT POLITICS

FROM PLANETARY ENCLOSURE TO THE WITCH HUNTS.
PEASANT GUERRILLAS AND THE GREEN REVOLUTION. CREATING COUNTER-COMMUNITIES.
A MULTIPLICITY OF EXPRESSIONS, A MYRIAD OF FORMS. GENERALIZED REVOLT AGAINST WORK.

> **Formal, organized political activity, even if clandestine and revolutionary, is typically the preserve of the middle class and the intelligentsia. To look for peasant politics in this realm is to look largely in vain.**[1]
>
> —James C. Scott, *Weapons of the Weak: Everyday Forms of Peasant Resistance*

James Scott, who has been at the forefront of recording everyday peasant resistance for the past four decades, believes that one needs to look beyond the official organizations of the Left to find the fire burning in the belly of the peasant, the agricultural worker worldwide. Peasant politics, he asserts, "is less a pitched battle than a low-grade, hit-and-run, guerrilla action."[2] To carry out insurgence, peasant guerrillas use a myriad of symbolic and concrete forms of resistance that stem from the communal relations and active solidarities that weave their communities together. Scott writes in one of his taxonomical essays on the subject, "There is no organization to be banned, no conspiratorial leaders to round up or buy off, no rioters to haul before the courts—only the generalized noncompliance by thousands of peasants."[3] Such noncompliance is rooted in the material conditions and relations of power that define peasant life. The power (*potentia*) of guerrillas vis-à-vis capitalism, the level of integration into capitalism, the strength of the agricultural sector in the economic life of the country, and the power (*potestas*) of the state apparatus are all factors that define the limits upon this activity. It is within these contexts and against these limits that peasants struggle. These circumstances, in all their variety, and constraints, with varying degrees and relations of power, are the result of primitive accumulation, colonization, slavery, witch hunts, sovereign power wedded to the nation-state, and the march of capitalism across the globe.

The enclosure process, an ongoing factor in capitalist development, has always sought to unravel and subsume noncapitalist relations of agricultural production. These forms, as Pierre Clastres asserts, "wouldn't do, and ... didn't last: the Indians were soon put to work, and they died of it." Thus, the transatlantic slave trade and the further subjugation of black and brown bodies was necessary to impose the regime of work in early capitalism. Clastres continues, "Two axioms seem to have guided the advance of Western civilization from the outset: the first maintains that true societies unfold in the protected shadow of the State; the second states a categorical imperative: man must work."[4] It is this imposition of work that demonstrates how "peasants are exploited by capital[ism] in the sphere of production."[5] Peasant guerrillas attack this imposition and in the process create oppositional cultures. Forms of everyday resistance, such as sabotage and the theft of grain, are similar to those found under slavery. But while both peasants and slaves are agricultural workers, the former have a fundamentally different relationship with capitalism than one of bondage. Simply put, peasants are agricultural workers who are not slaves. The category "peasant" includes itinerant and tenant farmers, sharecroppers, migrant farmworkers, indentured servants, and, importantly, subsistence farmers outside of capitalism. Peasants may rent, own a small amount of land, or simply work the land of others. They may pay a fee, tax, or portion of their crop to landlords, banks, and state bureaucrats. The distinction between peasants and farmers is a political one, and agricultural workers may be referred to as serfs, landless, migrants, subaltern, *campesinos, paysan, krest'ianin, raiyat, nongfu,* and *fellah* depending on the narrator.[6] In a social movement context, Via Campesina defines "a peasant" as

> a man or woman of the land, who has a direct and special relationship with the land and nature through the production of food and/or other agricultural products. Peasants work the land themselves, rely above all on family labour and other small-scale forms of organizing labour. Peasants are traditionally embedded in their local communities and they take care of local landscapes and of agro-ecological systems.
>
> The term peasant can apply to any person engaged in agriculture, cattle-raising, pastoralism, handicrafts-related to agriculture or a related occupation in a rural area. This includes Indigenous people working on the land.[7]

Hence the term "peasant," as reflected in the expansive definition, is a heterogeneous and fluctuating one.[8] Historically, peasants predated enclosure, but they took on new characteristics, new positions in the overall economy, with the onset of capitalism and its march across the planet. The purpose here is to examine peasants as part of the rural working class and political subjects equivalent to their urban and sub-urban counterparts.[9] When exploring the forms of peasant resistance, symbolic action, the criminalization of communal behaviors, and the revolt against work, the metaphor of the guerrillas of desire will allow us to explore this activity over a broad set of time periods and geo-graphical spaces.

FROM PLANETARY ENCLOSURE TO THE WITCH HUNTS

Between October 25 and November 3, 1842, Karl Marx contributed to the *Rheinische Zeitung* five articles on the theft of wood. In these im-passioned pieces, Marx decries the legal apparatus enclosing Europe's communal lands. This juridical attack on customary rights was a way of decomposing the relationships and means of subsistence that up to that point had defined peasant life. This process of primitive accumula-tion, of enclosure, was a violent one. Laws were developed to punish, by fines or prison, the gathering of berries, dead leaves, and fallen branch-es. Henceforward collecting fallen timber and the natural abundance of the woods would be criminalized. Commenting on Marx's articles, Peter Linebaugh writes:

> Under this progressive erosion of their material power, a life and death struggle took place for the re-appropriation of wealth, a struggle that was endemic, highly price sensitive, and by no means restricted to timber and fuel rights.... In the spring women and children ranged through the fields along the Rhine and its tributaries, the Mosel, the Ahr, and the Lahn, cutting young thistles and nettles, digging up the roots of couch-grass, and collecting weeds and leaves of all kinds to turn them to account as winter fodder.[10]

Without access to gleaning the woods for subsistence the very exis-tence of the Rhenish peasant population was considerably undermined. In the developing lexicon, "woods" and "forest" become opposing terms. Woods were common, forests were enclosed. On November 3, 1842, Marx, in his final article from this series, admonished the forest owners and legislators for criminalizing customary access to the woods,

What is the basis of your claim to make the wood thief into a serf? The fine. We have shown that you have no right to the fine money. Leaving this out of account, what is your basic principle? It is that the interests of the forest owner shall be safeguarded even if this results in destroying the world of law and freedom. You are unshakably determined that in some way or other the wood thief must compensate you for the loss of your wood. This firm wooden foundation of your argument is so rotten that a single breath of sound common sense is sufficient to shatter it into a thousand fragments.[11]

As an expression of the conflicts occurring in European peasant societies, this "theft" took place within the enclosing commons. The larger context of enclosure included the shift of manufacture in home or workshop to factory.[12] Alongside the control and capture of common life, peasants detached from the land began to flow into the cities and therefore into the factories as cheap labor. But for those who stayed behind, and for agricultural workers thereafter, their relationship with the land they lived upon shifted from one of subsistence and communal rights to one of dependency on landlords. The displaced French peasants would become famous for throwing their sabots—the wooden shoes that were adapted for muddy fields—into the gears of the machines. It is from this activity that the word "sabotage" comes. As peasants were removed from the commons and arrived in cities, they discovered that a set of laws overseeing public space had been constructed there as well. Begging, emigration, and certain types of public behavior considered disorderly (loitering, intoxication, etc.) were criminalized.[13] Further, gleaning at the edges of the city was banned to erode subsistence practices peasants carried into urban environs.

An entire state-apparatus was constructed across Europe to produce, through decree, a class of workers that would accept the horrid conditions in the industrial factories. Once separated from their means of subsistence, these new city dwellers had to survive by finding wage labor or obtaining "public relief" so that, in this regard, they found themselves dependent upon either capitalism or the state apparatus. The flow of peasants was now dictated by legalized violence and the requirements of the growing labor market.

Capitalism also required an apparatus for *enforcing* decrees and sought to prevent wayward peasants from escaping urban areas for rural or wild ones where they could subsist off the land. Many did escape, though, and thereafter participated in land expropriations and the theft of goods. As Scott offers, "the pace of 'forest crime' rose as wages declined, as provisions became more expensive, and where emigration was more difficult; in 1836 there were 207,000 prosecutions in Prussia, 150,000 of which were for forest offenses."[14] Proto-police forces—beadles, constables, or bailiffs—were created to punish theft from the forests and fields and to enforce these new laws.

As peasants were flowing into the cities two key commodities were being forged: workers and the forest. That is, labor power and resources, both needing to be extracted. Privatization of forest rights required a discourse and knowledge so that the forest could be managed within capitalism. These discourses justified the exclusion of those who did not have the correct intellectual tools and harvesting practices to maintain the integrity of the forest.[15] The woods, as a part of the commons, came under the direction of scientific forestry. Schools were created to teach new techniques, while traditional knowledge was undermined and suppressed. Enclosures of the common woods was part of a larger discourse on private property rights swirling around Europe at the time, which would shortly come to infect all social life.

As peasants' lives were restricted under these new regulations and state apparatuses, other processes attacked the relationships at the core of the peasants' way of life. Witch hunts in Europe during the sixteenth and seventeenth centuries separated women from sources of power, communal activities, and each other. Unmarried women who had once survived by gleaning in the woods and fields were forced into wage labor or dependent relationships with husbands, fathers, and the patriarchal state. Transgressions of new moral legislation would be met with violence and the threat of being burned at the stake. The witch hunts were part of a larger war on crime.[16] Men and women were not just targeted as peasants or thieves but because of their standing in the social order. Silvia Federici, in her epic volume on the subject, *Caliban and the Witch: Women, the Body and Primitive Accumulation*, describes the effect of this process on women: "The witch-hunt destroyed a whole world of female practices, collective relations, and systems of knowledge that had been the foundation of women's power in pre-capitalist Europe and the condition for their resistance in the struggle against feudalism."[17] Patriarchal systems of domination were vocalized as male members of the community asserted increasing power over women in the home and in public. As "ale wives," women had previously controlled male access to alcohol, gained a source of additional income through sales, and collected nettles as a bittering agent for the beer they produced. When beer laws came into effect and hops replaced nettles, a key women's role in public and private spaces shifted to men, official breweries, and the church.[18]

The period being described by Marx, Linebaugh, and Federici, is when many of our modern institutions originated, though the earliest enclosures can be traced to the twelfth century. While much attention has been given to how the enclosures forged a new class of proletarians, of industrial workers, insufficient consideration has been given to the peasants, to agricultural workers whose lives were forever altered by enclosure. Such a process did not take place only during the birth pangs of capitalism. Rather, ongoing mechanisms of enclosure continue today and increasingly bring areas of life under capitalist control, as access to the dwindling means of subsistence are eroded further by the imposition of wage labor and legal frameworks of exclusion.[19] Two contemporary examples of struggles against enclosure include the indigenous peasant Ejército Zapatista de Liberación Nacional in the jungles of Southwest Mexico and demands for increasing local control over agricultural land taking place across India. Peasants, broadly defined to include indigenous populations, continue to challenge capitalism and state apparatuses as they struggle to maintain their communal and ancestral lands. Migrant agricultural workers, family farmers, and those producing for subsistence outside of the market are social actors that the state is still attempting to manage. While peasant populations used tactics of everyday resistance prior to the advent of capitalism, our exploration of the peasant guerrillas of desire might commence with the enclosure process but it must address resistance both to agricultural production under capitalism and to the violence of enclosure.

PEASANT GUERRILLAS AND THE GREEN REVOLUTION

In order to examine the myriad forms and expressions of everyday resistance since the onset of capitalism, a brief case study of a particular instance of capitalist crisis will ground our project. The Green Revolution, beginning in the 1930s and ending in the late 1960s, used military technology (e.g., pesticides—chemical formulations created for battlefield use and then appropriated for domestic use) to increase agricultural yields and food production.[20] The stated purpose was to increase food security on a planetary scale. In fact, the political motives are clear: decompose peasant power, prevent the spread of communism and left-wing governments, further the enclosure process, reestablish imperialism, and globalize capitalist control of agriculture, and with it a key aspect of social reproduction and survival—agriculture—is further subsumed into capitalism. Food production, once in the hands of peasants and small farmers, was captured by multinational corporations, international bodies, and First World governments. The Green Revolution was an attack on the peasantry: a period of capitalist attack on working-class power globally and taking place simultaneously in the separate Soviet and Western blocs. Vandana Shiva, addressing this matter in *The Violence of the Green Revolution: Third World Agriculture, Ecology and Politics*, argues,

> The Green Revolution was necessarily paradoxical. On the one hand it offered technology as a substitute to both nature and politics, in the creation of abundance and peace. On the other hand, the technology itself demanded more intensive natural resource use along with intensive external inputs and involved a restructuring of the way power was distributed in society. While treating nature and politics as dispensable elements in agriculture transformation, the Green Revolution created major changes in the natural ecosystems and agrarian structures. New relationships between science and agriculture defined new links between the states and cultivators, between international interests and local communities, and within the agrarian society.[21]

Although technology serves "as a substitute for both nature and politics," its deployment increased commodity production within the limits of the workday. Since less labor power was needed, there was less need for peasant workers, and consequentially a large portion of the population was thrown out of the agricultural sector, adding to the reserve army of workers in urban areas. During the Green Revolution the relative strength of the peasantry vis-à-vis capitalism and the state apparatuses declined. Decomposition of peasant power was accomplished in three ways: applying the factory model to agriculture, Taylorizing agricultural production, and using labor-saving technologies to decrease reliance on labor power.

Shiva continues, "The Green Revolution was not the only strategy available. There was another strategy for agrarian peace based on reestablishing justice through land reform."[22] But of course this strategy was not the one chosen. Western governments, led by the United States, had their own approach to increase agricultural production after World War II. The Green Revolution used pesticides to increase yields, and it had the effect of taking an area of life that had a certain element of autonomy and placing it under capitalist command. The Green Revolution was an extensive undertaking that was directed, at least initially, at the developing world, and agricultural production under capitalism was reorganized. Agricultural yields were increased by controlling irrigation, instituting mono-cropping, developing high-yield varieties (new strains that produced more salable commodities per plant), and using pesticides. The result was the increasing and continuous consolidation of food production and the loss of political power by peasants and small farmers. Harry Cleaver states,

> The story of the Green Revolution is far more than one of plant breeding and genetics. It is woven into the fabric of American foreign policy and is an integral part of the postwar effort to contain social revolution and make the world safe for profits. When understood in this broader perspective, the Green Revolution appears as the latest chapter in the long history of increasing penetration of Third-World agriculture by the economic institutions of Western capitalism. Thus the term Green Revolution encompasses not only the increased output associated with a new technology but also the political, economic, and social changes which have produced and accompanied it.[23]

The thrust behind the Green Revolution was not simply to create an insecure food system that simultaneously increased yields and decreased access to subsistence and low-cost foodstuffs but also to create a timid peasantry. The peasant population, sufficiently decomposed, would not refuse, rebel, or attempt to reorganize agricultural production along more communal and self-sufficient lines. The introduction of new technologies often followed peasant uprisings and rebellions, and, when these technologies were not sufficient, war was declared. Bombs were dropped on Southeast Asia. Low-intensity warfare was instituted against peasants and indigenous peoples in Central America.[24]

The effects of the Green Revolution have been disastrous, albeit in a way far more diffuse than China's famine-causing "Great Leap Forward" or low-intensity warfare against peasants in the Global South. Thus, large swaths of the peasant population were (and continue to be) removed from their communal lands. Without access to land for subsistence, insecurity in local and regional food systems develops. With food insecurity comes an increase in famine and malnutrition. Dependency on international corporations for seeds and food distribution follows. The Green Revolution is part of the attempt by capitalism to reorganize planetary agricultural systems, of which biotechnology, structural adjustment programs (which include conditions requiring agricultural production for export rather than subsistence), and "neoliberalism" are related initiatives.

Against these plans, peasants across the planet have participated in a series of resistance activities, from carving out plots from larger farms and reclaiming public lands to overt rebellions. Counter-plans are used by peasants in two ways: first, as they maintain their communal structures in the face of enclosures, and, second, as they refuse work as agricultural workers under capitalism. Intertwined with these activities is a set of symbolic and material resistance practices that can be found in everyday life. Occasionally these practices form the base from which overt rebellions are launched. Most commonly, peasants have found alternative approaches to reshape their lives and the agrarian societies of which they are part.

CREATING COUNTER-COMMUNITIES

Solidarity, communication, and mutual aid are vital to the formation of a counter-community that in turn serves as a base for acts of resistance and survival. Peasant counter-communities are opposed to the logic of the agricultural systems that are imposed upon them and extract the products of their labor. Further, in times of drought or famine, networks of support are extended beyond attending to the material shortages that peasants experience day to day. In effect, counter-communities are the product of solidarity, communication, and mutual aid, and in turn they reproduce these for the fortitude and maintenance of agrarian society. Untangling the complexity of the relationships between peasants and relations of power in agricultural production requires concepts that allow precise attributes and characteristics to be examined and highlighted. Our examination of counter-communities under slavery occurred within bounded geographical and chronological limits: the transatlantic slave trade in the Americas between the fifteenth and nineteenth centuries. In this chapter our geographical boundaries are broader and time periods less distinct, outside of examining the Green Revolution. As such, these, as with the forms of everyday resistance described below, should be considered categories of common practices found in peasant politics.

Solidarity
In a situation where "open declarations of defiance are replaced by euphemisms and metaphors; clear speech by muttering and grumbling; open confrontation by concealed noncompliance or defiance" (in the words of James Scott), a general sense of commonality and solidarity is important.[25] A sense of trust is required for those involved in resistance and often criminalized activities. Solidarity was a necessary component of all the historical forms of everyday resistance described here. A "conspiracy of silence" can be found historically among peasant populations,

and it "consisted of three elements: the refusal to report crime, the refusal to identify criminals, and the refusal to tell the truth about crime."[26] While noncompliance with authorities reflects one general form of solidarity, it implies a second: peasant reliance on traditional methods of addressing social transgressions, methods that maintained the integrity of the community. Peasants distinguish between gleaning and theft just as slaves separated "taking" from a slave master and "stealing" from one another.[27] As forest laws and other tools of the state criminalized activity previously thought of as necessary for peasant sustenance, a split between the state's laws and peasants' self-regulation necessarily developed. The witch hunts, with "ordinary" prosecutions for "witchcraft," sought to control the behavior and morality of the masses, and this was part of the new forms of crime control and social regulation developing in the fifteenth and sixteenth centuries.[28] "Witches" and peasants had their codes, while the state had its own. Within this rift peasants have fostered what we might call a bifurcated ethics, with one set for public transcripts and another for hidden ones. So-called conspiracies of silence are only possible when a considerable sense of solidarity has permeated the peasant counter-community. And, to communicate, peasants often use "euphemisms and metaphors," "muttering and grumbling," and other means to ensure that the landlord, supervisor, or boss is unable to understand them.

Communication

Taxes, development practices, market transactions, laws, and the imposition of mono-cropping or specific farming methods (e.g., use of tractors or pesticides) are often not directly confronted but rather are nibbled away at through "gossip, slander, the rejection of demeaning labels, the withdrawal of deference."[29] The collection of taxes, to take one such example, is undermined somewhat through "slander" and constant complaining about where tax monies go. Within peasant communities such a counter-narrative is part of the overall justification for everyday resistance and, when it occurs, overt rebellion. In reference to peasant resistance, Scott describes these activities as "requir[ing] little or no coordination or planning; they make use of implicit understandings and informal networks; they often represent a form of individual self-help; they typically avoid any direct, symbolic confrontation with authority."[30] A popular culture of resistance emerges from the same set of activities, and they reinforce one another. What in effect these counter-narratives provide is the capacity to carry out raids and theft without formal organization.

Scott sees many forms of communication and everyday resistance as substitutes for direct confrontation, offering, "In place of open insult, the use of gossip, nicknames, and character assassination; in place of direct physical assault, the use of sabotage, arson, and nocturnal threats by [a] masked man; ... in place of labor defiance, shirking, slowdowns, and spoilage; in place of the tax riot or rebellion, evasion and conceal-ment."[31] What, in part, is illustrated here is that there is a spectrum from "insult" to "sabotage" and "evasion." Communication networks enable everyday resistance and are part of the actions themselves. Communi-cating with fellow peasant guerrillas can be as simple as complaining about the boss, and this "amount[s] to an exchange of small arms fire, a small skirmish, in a cold war of symbols between rich and poor."[32] Thus, communication is not a separate category of activity that takes place prior to everyday resistance. Rather it is part of a set of activities that circulate throughout peasant communities. And, as messages and metaphors move among guerrillas and potential guerrillas, the symbolic and material base for further everyday resistance and overt rebellion is produced. Such activity has been common among slave guerrillas and will be found throughout the industrial and social factory.

Mutual aid

In the course of peasant life, counter-communities and black markets often develop and overlap. As Michael Jiménez describes, in Colombia in the early twentieth century, "In order to avoid the reve-nue collection agents, the peasantry developed extensive networks to protect a contraband economy based primarily on the production and sale of untaxed liquors." He continues, "Some women manufactured and distributed cigarettes in nearby towns in violation of revenue laws, but, most importantly, they were key players in the production and marketing of local fermented and distilled liquors."[33] Other goods have also travelled outside the view of the tax collector, and at times items such as armaments and medicine are exchanged in this fashion. These illegal activities require informal community institutions, cohesion, and communication.

The Mexican peasantry, for example, has historically had a high level of civic and social participation due to a series of communal practices. The *ejido, comunidad indigena,* and *pueblo* have all led to an increased level of direct participation in the community. These institutions, and at times the municipality as well, have been used to express demands and solve the needs of the community. Ann Lucas de Rouffignac, in her study of the Mexican peasantry in the early 1980s, describes this activity: "Peasants organize themselves in a myriad of ways (from the total parcelization of the land [as parcelization can be a response to the efforts of larger landowners to create undifferentiated plots]—through the formation of *grupos solidarios* of various sizes and characteristics who work together for specific productive or commercial tasks—to complete collectivization)."[34] These forms of organized response, mutual aid, and community initiatives do not simply reorganize life; they create spaces for other activities. De Rouffignac continues, "For peasants in the Mexican countryside, the integrity of the peasant community, the *pueblo*, is where they can begin to create space for their own self-valorization activities, not capital[ism's]."[35]

Peasants did not just seek control over land, they sought to govern their own corporal existence. Poor women and gender-nonconforming people throughout the history of capitalism have had their bodies and sexuality subjugated to the interests of men and to capitalism in general. Thus, in peasant societies, sexual violence has been used interpersonally as a weapon against women and, by proxy, against the autonomy of the peasant household. In Colombia during the 1920s, this concern became a point of struggle: "The deep anxiety aroused by planters' sexual predations was certainly as responsible for fueling the organized opposition of the rural poor ... as demands for the alteration of work obligations or efforts to guarantee the autonomy of the peasant household."[36] Sexual violence is just another way that plantation holders maintain control over the peasantry. Peasant women create safe harbors to protect the peasant household, and this is done in two ways: by emphasizing communal ways of organizing and by creating networks and relationships with other women. By forging spaces outside of the disciplinary order and gaze of landowners, women agree to provide a sense of physical or affective safety for one another, and hence they produce relations with men on their own terms. The power of peasant women is part of the larger network of relations that construct peasant counter-communities.

An entire area of life is created in these counter-communities and institutions, and these are made possible through solidarity, communication networks, and acts of mutual aid. As with cooperative labor, forms of everyday resistance require these elements.

A MULTIPLICITY OF EXPRESSIONS, A MYRIAD OF FORMS

Peasant guerrillas have used several tactics to gain an advantage over a landlord, tax collector, or state bureaucrat. Similar to the tactics of resistant slaves, these include theft, sabotage, work slowdowns, wildcat strikes, squatting, exodus, and finally arson and murder. Further, as general taxonomical groupings, the kind of counter-communities and forms of everyday resistance are specific to the contexts, histories and traditions, and relations of power—strength vis-à-vis capitalism and the state—that the particular peasants find themselves in. As with slave guerrillas, and for that matter worker guerrillas, these general categories are abstractions from concrete phenomena, and to really understand the particular expressions and forms operating in a specific context one must inquire into everyday resistance in situ.

Theft

As we saw above with the enclosure of woods in Europe, in northern India during the latter part of the nineteenth century "the inception of commercial forestry ... signaled a dramatic change in the level of state interference with the everyday life of the peasantry," as Romachandra Guha notes.[37] Scholars have recorded similar cases among peasants in Egypt and elsewhere.[38] In the attempt by nascent capitalism to prevent the peasantry from having access to the means of subsistence, an entire legal apparatus emerged. With a monopoly on the legitimate use of violence the state has the ability to define crime and hence constitute public order. The struggle over the definition of crime is as important to our understanding of peasant resistance as the criminal acts themselves.

Thefts of small quantities of grain or similar commodity go almost unnoticed yet can comprise considerable additions to the peasant diet. Speaking particularly of peasants in eighteenth-century Poland, Jacek Kochanowicz writes that "any manorial property that could be stolen was. Grain was taken from barns, fish were taken from ponds. Fruit trees were cut down."[39] Grain contained residue of peasants' own labor, and stealing grain was one way that peasants reclaimed the product of their work. As peasants stole commodities they would often tell stories about their daring feats. Describing highland Peru in the mid-twentieth century, Gavin Smith explains, "The villagers are known as 'the foxes' and, in the talking of their tactics, they endlessly contrast the cunning of the fox with the strutting by empty courage of the rooster."[40] In these stories peasants themselves are able to play with the idea of committing "cunning" acts as they attempt to gain an advantage over the landowning class or the intermediaries who purchase their agricultural products. Theft is not always simply the taking of goods or the cheating of a landowner: the struggle over land itself often used this tactic as well. In Poland, "small pieces of land were added to peasants' strips little by little."[41] With added pieces of the landowner's property, they were able to produce additional crops, thus contributing to greater yields for the market and for themselves.

Sabotage

Destroying the machines of production, exhausting livestock, and breaking farm equipment are the most instantaneous forms of resistance because these means of production are the most immediate representation of the landlords and landowning class. As we saw with guerrillas under slavery, farm implements are easy broken, and such damage could appear as normal wear and tear.

During his fieldwork in Malaysia, James Scott observed how peasants responded to capitalism's attempt to decrease the importance of their labor and the power of the peasant community: "Batteries were removed from the machines and thrown in irrigation ditches; carburetors and other vital parts such as distributors and air filters were smashed; sand and mud were put into the gas tank; and various objects (stones, wire, nails) were thrown into the augers.... Starting in 1976, when combine-harvesting began with a vengeance, peasant acts of vengeance likewise spread throughout the paddy-growing region."[42] In this specific instance, these methods were used to protest the use of the combine-harvester in the fields, which deskilled peasant work and decreased the need for peasant workers. Hence it was a direct attack on their level of composition. When anonymous individuals committed these acts in the night, word of the actions spread through existing communications networks, while anonymity was maintained by a diffuse culture of resistance.

Slowdowns and wildcat strikes

As a strategic suspension of work, a strike is usually associated with unions and industrial workers. But under certain conditions wildcat strikes have been launched in peasant communities. While in Malaysia in the 1970s, Scott discovered that "if the farmer has a reputation for stinginess, the women will strike, as they do once or twice a year. The 'strike' is not announced, but everyone understands what is happening."[43] This sort of community work stoppage in Malaysia is frequently combined with a boycott of a particular intermediary acquiring their goods. For where work is imposed on peasants, they periodically strike until better conditions are granted. At these times, we see an antagonism over the conditions of work—for instance, how often a paddy must be thrashed—and these smaller work stoppages and avoidances habitually circulate and become strike actions. In a similar respect, strikes take place at strategic moments—at harvest time or during a land sale or collection of taxes or tribute—to maximize effect on landowners and bureaucrats. For tenant farmers or migrant farmworkers, harvest might well be the only time when their power is such that they can force a price or wage increase respectively. Harvest is when peasants have some semblance of control over the product to be turned over to the landowner—fruit and vegetables will lose their value if they spoil.

Squatting

Squatting is one way in which our peasant guerrillas can gain control over the land that they cultivate. Consequently, squatting has been employed throughout the history of peasant struggle, and the battle over land has been a central antagonism during every capitalist epoch. It emerged during the enclosures as peasants struggled to maintain their ancestral lands, and it continues to be a common tactic of peasants across the planet. Currently in Brazil the 1.5 million members of the Movimento dos Trabalhadores Rurais Sem Terra (Landless Workers Movement) are squatting land under the slogan "Occupy, Resist, Produce!" Land occupations are often combined with other tactics. Nicaraguan peasants during the 1970s operated similarly. Forrest Colburn observes: "Throughout rural areas, peasants seized land and farms they claim were idle or abandoned. Strikes were a continuing problem. Although many of the workers' demands were undoubtedly justified, continued labor indiscipline was crippling the economy. Many owners of private farms and government officials administering state farms claimed that labor indiscipline was their most serious problem. Labor productivity was widely held to be down at least 25 percent."[44] As revolution broke out in Nicaragua in July 1979, this process was expanded and furthered. Colburn again: "Peasants and rural laborers acting on their own seized many farms, particularly those of absentee landlords."[45] Here we see peasants taking advantage of a situation by occupying the lands that were left fallow by landlords and going on strike when it was most advantageous. It was these instances of resistance and the support of the peasant population for the Sandinistas that led to the revolution.

During the same period peasants were struggling to maintain their hold on squatted lands in the highlands of Peru. Since the late 1940s villagers had occupied their ancestral lands and defended themselves against eviction and the repression that had followed. From 1963 until 1973 there was a declared war, which included arson, sabotage, and deception. This resulted in a series of treaties, but each time the government looked for the signatories they had disappeared.[46]

Exodus

Throughout the history of capitalism, the peasantry has sought to control the land that it cultivated or its own labor power by fleeing. Toward these ends they have often defended themselves or seized goods and land by means of arson and murder. As was the case for guerrillas of desire under slavery, these tactics have often resulted in direct relief from a particularly brutal landowner. Beyond the theft of goods, lands, and time, destroying the machinery of production, and striking, the peasant's "ultimate form of 'passive' resistance was to run away."[47]

Capitalism's need for peasant labor fluctuates, and for that reason the state often restricts migration in the attempt to retain peasants in a country or regions. Jiménez found that in Colombia, "Taking flight was an extreme, though not unusual, response to the pressures from departmental officials, but certainly disturbing to the planters desiring stable work forces."[48] A number of factors determine if exodus will become a successful strategy. These include the option of returning to communal or ancestral lands, the possibility of obtaining other forms of work, the level of participation by peasants fleeing, and the extent of internal cohesion. Supplementary to this is the ability of peasant guerrillas to obtain support in the form of goods and resources from the counter-communities in which they participate. Here mobility depends on the agency of the peasant population as defined by their political power and the strategic use of this power during crises and labor shortages. At moments when the state is attempting to restrict peasant and migrant movement, exodus becomes a revolutionary strategy. When forced migration, enclosure of land and resources, and involuntary urbanization is the state's strategy, land seizures open revolutionary possibilities for peasants. I am not suggesting that peasant guerrillas are readily reactive to state dictates. Rather, the choice of exodus or land occupation as a strategy is dependent upon the conditions peasants find themselves in, their needs and desires, and the limits capitalism and the state impose upon peasant life.

Arson and assassination

Arson and assassination, while perhaps not as common in peasant politics as under slavery, have been used by peasant guerrillas toward several ends. These final two tactics are the most direct and carry the most risk. Arson and murder should be considered part of guerrilla warfare as they are often committed by individuals or groups in secret, outside of the context of an overt struggle. Arson against a grain silo or a landowner's home can be a single act of revenge or but one such act of many in a protracted struggle.

In the early twentieth century, India experienced a series of extended peasant struggles, and arson was used at times in the battle over the forests. As Guha describes this, "In 1916 a number of 'malicious' fires were set in the newly constituted reserved forests.... The 'deliberate and organized incendiarism' of the summer of 1916 brought home to the state the unpopularity of the forest settlement and the virtual impossibility of tracing those who were responsible for the fires."[49] During a similar period of struggle in Egypt, scholar Nathan Brown sees that murder became a suitable tactic. He explains, "A primary weapon used by peasants was direct physical—often murderous—attack. Assassinations of local officials and notables unsettled many landowners and other members of the elite."[50] Clearly the most dangerous of the tactics discussed here, assassination is a direct strike against the representatives—landowners or state bureaucrats—of the power structure. And it should be noted that suicide is currently common among peasants in the Global South as a reaction to the immiseration caused by neoliberal capitalism.[51] All of the tactics described here are an attack on the power of the elite classes, capitalism, and the state, and together represent a generalized revolt against work.

GENERALIZED REVOLT AGAINST WORK

Refusal of work by peasants situates them within the working class. It is clear from our descriptions of the struggle taking place in peasant politics that the peasantry is resisting the imposition of work on a daily basis.

Writing about Polish peasant resistance in the eighteenth century, Kochanowicz summarizes how peasants refused work discipline, stating that they "resist[ed] labor obligations, ... perform[ed] them carelessly [and] showed up late for work, worked carelessly, and took prolonged lunch breaks."[52] The slowdown is part of the generalized revolt against work, and the attempt to thwart capitalist command can be described as "counter-planning in the fields." Kochanowicz continues about Poland, with words that could have been used to describe peasant resistance elsewhere: "They brought the worst tools and weakest animals to work. They resisted, often successfully, the introduction of more efficient, but more labor-intensive tools [at least in regard to the energy expended by individual peasants], for example scythes instead of sickles for harvest."[53]

Everyday peasant resistance became an increasing problem for the Chinese state during Mao Zedong's Great Leap Forward (1958–61). The forced collectivization and farming practices of the Great Leap Forward led to the largest human-caused famine in modern history (1959–61).[54]

Peasant guerrillas created cracks in the state system, leading to reforms, and attacked the collective and ideological controls that defined this state-capitalist regime. Peasants chose four main areas of resistance: manipulation of official policy, creation of their own policy, aggressively overproducing commodities, and inflating costs.[55] Resistance continued into the subsequent period of reform. "In the years 1979–89," Daniel Kelliher explains, "state and peasant fought, cooperated, cheated, stumbled, lied, and compromised their way toward reform of everything fundamental in rural life."[56] He notes: "Peasants do not merely resist state policy (a passive act); they reshape policy into something new, something the state never intended (a creative act)."[57] Here, as with earlier resistance to Mao's policies, Chinese peasants resisted the reorganization of their lives in accordance with state command and the imposition of work as they sought to create new forms of life.

In a similar fashion, Colburn describes the resistance of Nicaraguan peasants as they attacked the amount of time spent working: "Rural laborers throughout Nicaragua spontaneously took advantage of the near anarchy in rural areas to reduce dramatically their labor obligations. Those employed for daily wages simply cut back on the length of the workday."[58] David Zweig also contributes an example of peasants attacking the intensity of their work, writing about China of 1966–86: "In one team, peasants spent more time during the busy summer season planting potatoes in their own fields than working on [compulsory] collective land."[59] By decreasing the length of the workday, peasants can force capitalism to develop new strategies to contain this resistance and decompose its organizational power. When these forms of daily revolt against work combine, they increase peasant pressure on a regime of work. There is a point at which "individual grievances become collective grievances," Scott maintains in *Weapons of the Weak*, and whole new sets of potentialities arise.[60]

As these individual acts accumulate and become collective, aspects of the social order and capitalist command begin to break down. Brown describes this development in Egypt with an example that illustrates the power of collective action among peasant guerrillas: "They could ignore or evade unfavorable policies; they could slack off if they received too little for their crops or labor. Such passive resistance has been held responsible for completely disrupting economic policies over much of the continent of Africa in recent years."[61] Peasants often find themselves resisting the imposition of work that is coordinated by a state-capitalist regime, and the cost of resistance is often brutal suppression of their activities. Resistance takes place in direct ways, such as negotiating over wages, and in indirect ways, including haggling over the price of crops.

Peasant guerrillas fit into a larger continuum of war in everyday life under capitalism. While these activities were certainly extant before the enclosure of the commons worldwide, capitalism's attempt to impose work discipline and, by extension, the state's role in fixing the population in once place, preventing access to the woods and forms of subsistence, and breaking up allegiances developed following the enclosure. Peasant resistance in everyday life can come together and form overt rebellions. These merge into cycles of struggle that connect with other sectors of the working class. Finally, these connections intersect historically with the resistance of guerrillas struggling under slavery until the late nineteenth century and with those struggling throughout the industrial and social factory.

In the following chapter, as I describe work in both the industrial and social factories—both productive and reproductive work—we will begin to see similarities with slave and peasant guerrillas of desire on an allegorical level, as well as the struggles of both productive workers inside the factory and reproductive workers outside of the factory on a conceptual level.

6

THROUGHOUT THE INDUSTRIAL AND SOCIAL FACTORY

FROM PLANETARY ENCLOSURES TO THE FACTORY SYSTEM.
WORKER GUERRILLAS AND NEOLIBERALISM. CREATING COUNTER-COMMUNITIES.
A MULTIPLICITY OF EXPRESSIONS, A MYRIAD OF FORMS. GENERALIZED REVOLT AGAINST WORK.

> Against this monster, people all over the world, and particularly ordinary working people in factories, mines, fields, and offices, are rebelling every day in ways of their own invention.[1]
>
> —C.L.R. James, Grace C. Lee (Grace Lee Boggs), and Pierre Chaulieu (Cornelius Castoriadis), *Facing Reality*

The period that E. P. Thompson describes in his astounding 1963 book *The Making of the English Working Class* was not simply the end of the original enclosure movement and the onset of the Industrial Revolution but also correspondingly a period of intense class struggle. Between 1790 and 1830 initial rumblings of workers in England's industrial districts developed into organizations, such as the London Corresponding Society. Organizations emerged from a set of activities in the lives of the workers and from the everyday resistance and overt rebellions that the factory system sought to contain. Following the enclosures in Europe landless peasants migrated en masse to the urban regions, and they brought forms of association and communal practices from the village, including production of alcohol, theft of wood, and the practice of women sharing their dwellings with other women, thus providing some relative freedom from the increasingly patriarchal household.[2] Hence, urbanized peasants, in effect proletarians, were not simply forged in capitalist fire, they were active in fashioning their own subjectivities. Thompson writes,

> The making of the working class is a fact of political and cultural, as much as economic, history. It was not the spontaneous generation of

the factory-system. Nor should we think of an external force—the "industrial revolution"—working upon some nondescript undifferentiated raw material of humanity, and turning it out at the other end as a "fresh race of beings." The changing productive relations and working conditions of the Industrial Revolution were imposed, not upon raw material, but upon the free-born Englishman.... The factory hand or stockinger [weaver] was also the inheritor ... of remembered village rights, of notions of equality before the law, of craft traditions. He was the object of massive religious indoctrination and the creator of new political traditions. The working class made itself as much as it was made.[3]

As early proletarians made themselves they were creating distinctive working-class cultures and ways of life while struggling against new forms of power (*potestas*) that were emerging. "Free-born Englishmen" were regulated by the state in the political sphere and by the incipient bourgeoisie in the economic sphere. Entire regimes of production and reproduction were set in motion and discourses developed to justify the imposition of work and the accumulation of capital. Class struggle then, as now, involved a complex interplay between the making of the working class by capital and the state and the resistance, rebellion, and ways of life made by working people. The Levelers (in the early 1640s), Diggers (late 1640s), Ranters (1650s), and utopian socialists attempted economic experiments that they believed would steer humanity into heaven on earth. Then, a hundred years later, new political traditions of the London Corresponding Society (1792–99) sought to reform Parliament so as to be responsive to working-class needs. All of this began generations before the IWW declared that the "working class and the employing class have nothing in common."[4] Toward the end of the IWW's first wave (1905–20), the Russian working classes would overthrow the tsar (1917). For several years until power was centralized, cooperative and communal activities flourishing in soviets (local councils) gave hope to the planetary working class, anarchists included.

The history of everyday resistance throughout the industrial and social factory systems, since the onset of planetary enclosure, entails a taxonomy of possible other worlds, of new societies in formation. Thus, this chapter follows the same general structure as those addressing slave and peasant guerrillas. Returning to the enclosures and then investigating the inception of the factory system will allow us to comprehend the basic functions of capitalism, which are still in operation today. Then, by looking at the struggles surrounding the capitalist crisis of the mid-1970s and the advent of neoliberalism, I will expound on the effects of resistance and rebellion. ("Neoliberalism" refers to an economic and political strategy of deregulating financial markets, removal of tariffs and trade barriers for business, privatization of state services, and massive government austerity.)[5] The passage from Keynesian state intervention in the economy (and relative labor peace) to neoliberalism coincides with the shift from the industrial to the social factory, hence a shift in the terrain of class struggle.[6] Lastly, counter-communities, forms of everyday resistance, and the generalized revolt against work move us toward the contemporary period when, I suspect, many of these guerrilla engagements are still operational. It is our task to read, inquire into, record, and circulate these struggles.

FROM PLANETARY ENCLOSURES TO THE FACTORY SYSTEM

Class struggle marks the period between the original enclosures and the cycle that led to the global uprisings of May 1968 and the series of general strikes and insurrections around the planet between 1968 and 1975.[7] In effect, the historical record of the entire modern era is "written in letters of blood and fire," as Karl Marx so fittingly reminds us.[8]

The violence of the enclosures coincides with a series of peasant wars that broke out in waves across Europe.[9] In response to these upheavals there were a series of "concessions: guarantees of rights, representative institutions, courts of appeal" that "constrained the ... paths of war making and state making."[10] Further, early states benefited from the accumulation of capital. Thus, the time of enclosure and immediately afterward was marked by "war making, protection [of certain classes], extraction [of resources], and state making."[11] The early merchant class, as a bourgeoisie in its infancy, was a "progressive" force against the power of the kingdoms, principalities, and empires that had dotted the European landscape for hundreds of years prior. And in time the bourgeoisie would supersede the aristocracy. Nevertheless, outside of these princely territories, and often clandestinely within them, a rich set of life practices and means of subsistence were flourishing. "War making and state making" was required to separate the European peasantry from the commons through the efforts of a "protected class" that lusted after resources and labor power. In effect, the displaced peasantry itself was enclosed by this infant bourgeoisie in the factories and cities of early industrial capitalism.

Evolving from prior forms, such as the "putting-out" (subcontracting) system and craft industries, the factory system by the late eighteenth century used landless peasants as unskilled workers. This division of labor imposed partitions within the working class between skilled and unskilled, between men, women, and children, and between those of various races and ethnicities. Centralizing the production process in one location allowed for increased surveillance of the workday and eventually required new energy sources to power machinery. From water power to the steam engine and finally electricity, capitalism's lust for labor was complemented by its hunger for energy—for wood, coal, oil, gas, and eventually uranium. Technological innovations allowed the factory owners to produce more goods with the same labor and in turn discipline the workforce by systematizing, mechanizing labor, and undermining wages. Of course, wages did not purchase the worker, only their labor power. Further, when crisis required layoffs, the capitalist mode of production could shed its workforce along with injured, ill, or aged workers. Civil and political society, managed by the state apparatuses, morphed to meet the requirements of the factory system. (Later Antonio Gramsci would refer to the relationship between civil-political and economic spheres as "Americanism and Fordism."[12]) At the point of production in the factory and (importantly) outside of it, "ordinary" working people revolted. These monumental shifts and rebellions came to a head in the People's Spring of 1848, a serious of upheavals of workers and peasants across Europe.

In response to the commotions in 1848, Marx and Friedrich Engels penned *The Manifesto of the Community Party*, famously calling the workers of the world to unite, and following this period they would be part of creating the First International in 1864. Joining the International four years later, Mikhail Bakunin and other collectivist anarchists would put forth a program for a "direct economical struggle against capitalism," and in the United States in 1869 the Knights of Labor would become one of the first labor organizations west of the Atlantic to organize industrial workers. Within ten years of the founding of these organizations, the bourgeoisie would attempt to violently repress the European and American working classes. These cycles of struggle would continue to mark the history of capitalism through to the present.

In the middle of the twentieth century, capitalism needed a stronger state to manage civil society and worker unrest. European democracies required fascism, the US required McCarthyism, and the Soviet Union needed Stalinism. The long century of the factory system would come to an end upon the smoldering barricades of May 1968. Henceforward capitalism extended the factory system into all of society. Commodities were no longer produced predominantly in fields and factories but in the entire social arena. The progeny of working-class militants shot in

Barcelona during the Spanish Civil War, the generation that followed those brought in front of the House Un-American Activities Committee, the generation whose elders died in Siberian gulags, would launch a cycle of planetary struggles in the late sixties concomitant with anticolonial struggles in the Third World. This turmoil would mark the passing from the modern world to the postmodern, from the New Deal to neoliberal capitalism, and from the industrial to the social factory. These shifts changed everything—and nothing.

WORKER GUERRILLAS AND NEOLIBERALISM

During the 1970s, international capitalism and the Keynesian state suffered irreparable crises of command over the working class, brought on by a multitude of conflicts. These entailed workers' councils, welfare rights efforts, student and antiwar movements, anticolonial movements, the US civil rights movement and Black Power, the feminist and lesbian/gay movements, and innumerable acts of everyday resistance by peasant and worker guerrillas. As capitalism attempted to reassert its dominance, the response to various crises (including food, energy, and financial crises) entailed attempts to decompose the working class and of re-imposing work. At the same time, the factory model was applied by capitalism to all of society, which launched new markets and arenas for accumulation. Not least, to discipline the working class effectively, extraordinary state violence was ramped up greatly, with mass incarceration on a domestic level in the US and counterinsurgency warfare on an international level as can be seen in US-funded anticommunist wars in Central America.

From a "work/energy crisis" to an "apocalypse," in George Caffentzis's exquisite words, "*our* problem is to see that capital's difficulties in planning and accumulating spring from its struggle against the refusal of work (the multi-dimensional subversion of the orderly transformation of energy into work). Thus, according to our decoding, through the noise of the apocalypse, we must see in the oil caverns, in the wisps of natural gas curling in subterranean abysses, something more familiar: the class struggle."[13] The New York City fiscal crisis was then applied across the planet as part of capital's strategy now referred to as neoliberalism. To grasp this fundamental shift in capitalist and state strategy we must turn to the movements and struggles immediately preceding these crises. What follows is a narrative of these cycles of struggle, and to tell this story I will move from one geographical location to another and often step back in time to illustrate how struggles in particular places unfolded.

Beverly Silver, in *Forces of Labor: Workers' Movements and Global-ization since 1870*, describes how capitalism sought cheaper and unor-ganized pools of labor in United Kingdom in the 1950s, France and Italy in the 1960s, Germany and Spain in the late 1960s, and South America, South Africa, and Korea in the 1980s.[14] At every point of development capitalism sought to escape the struggle of the working class on the local level while disciplining it on the global level through lower wages, com-petition between labor pools, and uneven development. As with cyclical slave rebellions the working class has periodically if briefly thrown off the yoke of capitalism: the People's Spring of 1848, the Paris Commune in 1871, workers' council movements (including the Russian soviets) from the early 1900s to the 1920s, antifascist resistance movements of the 1930s and 1940s, and the May 1968 upheavals, to name a few. These successive revolutionary manifestations were expressions of accumulat-ed resistance and rebellions.

Cycles of struggle take place on two general levels that meet in plac-es and flow together: the terrain of everyday life (everyday resistance) and the terrain of civil, political, and economic society (overt move-ments). Class struggle in the US has been notably violent, and sabotage, theft, arson, slowdowns, and other practices have been used to avoid the violence perpetrated by the state and the private thugs of capitalist enterprise. These acts have become part of the lexicon of tactics used by workers' organizations. The IWW, founded in 1905, is a perfect ex-ample of this. As an organization, it arose out of a set of preexisting associations and practices that developed in a rebellious counterculture that existed as a strong undercurrent in American life.[15] Louis Adamic maps the skirmishes between the US working class and powerful in-dustrialists in his 1931 book *Dynamite: The Story of Class Violence in America*, which shows how working-class organizing and resistance in all its forms was met with violence from capitalism and the state. One of the most interesting sections of the text is where Adamic discusses his own experiences working alongside an IWW member who was adept at slacking and sabotage at the job site. Here the extent of worker guerril-las fighting on the terrain of everyday life, becomes clear:

> In St. Louis ... I heard the story (which I later verified) of an incident
> that occurred one winter before the first world war when the city
> was full of starving and freezing unemployed workers who had come
> in from the camps and fields. The wobblies decided to force the city
> to take care of them. One day several hundred of them invaded the
> restaurants, ordered big meals, ate, and then presented their checks to

the cashiers, telling them to charge them to the mayor. Arrested, they made speeches in court that broke on the front page. The town got excited over the prospect of thousands heading for St. Louis to eat at the mayor's cost—for that was just what they did, out of jail or in. The city council then hastily passed an emergency bill to start municipal houses with free beds and meals. The "stunt" was a form of sabotage on the community, dramatic and humorous, which, frankly, appealed to me.

Indeed, not a few wobblies with whom I came into contact, though intensely serious, were genial, amusing and intelligent fellows, quite frank about their ideas and doings. They were freelance missionaries in the cause of the underdog to whom the end justified the means, with the self-imposed duty to harm the propertied classes as much as, and whenever, possible: *guerrilla* soldiers in the class war.[16]

What one can extract from such a statement is that the IWW was part of a set of practices, in which "freelance missionaries" would organize under the union banner when necessary and act as part of a guerrilla army when able. As the IWW developed its base of power (*potentia*) from the Western Federation of Miners to factories of New England and the forests of the Pacific Northwest, it was met with violent repression at every turn.[17] The nationalistic and anti-radical fervor of World War I brought on the Espionage Act of 1917 and the Sedition Act of 1918, used to justify mass arrests in 1919 and 1920 (the so-called Palmer Raids) and limit speech. This would be followed the Immigration Act of 1924 (greatly limiting US immigrants from southern and eastern Europe) and repression that would last through World War II and into the 1950s.[18] The state did not attempt to attack workers' organizations, it sought to decompose the working class as a whole. It was the political composition of the working class—union organization and working-class power—that prevented capitalists from lowering wages and disposing of workers at a whim. Thus, wages became "sticky downward" (unable to be reduced) as capitalists could no longer decrease wages and fire workers with each downturn of the business cycle. Union power, in part, led to the crash that would signal the arrival of the Great Depression.

The Depression notwithstanding, the working class continued to demand wage increases, income separated from work via welfare, and New Deal programs. The state unsurprisingly responded with violence. On the heels of "the bloody conflicts of 1934," which witness strikes in West Coast ports and Midwest factories, in December 1936 the United Auto Workers (UAW) strikes at the Flint, Michigan, General Motors (GM) plant illustrated the power of the class and its composition vis-à-vis capitalism. These strikes, which followed ones by UAW workers in Fisher Body plants in Kansas City and Atlanta as noted in Brecher, would develop into one of the largest upsurges of industrial worker militancy in US history.[19] During the UAW strikes, sabotage, slowdowns, and other forms of guerrilla warfare proliferated at the plants. These tactics contributed greatly toward winning these strike actions and recognition of the UAW's demands. The mid-1930s would mark the onset of manufacturing dominated by the big auto companies, and autoworkers won strike after strike in North America throughout the late 1930s.[20]

The US strikes of 1936–37 would be but one articulation of the struggle against the Fordist assembly line and Taylorism, a system that attempts to "scientifically" manage the assembly line by setting time limits for job tasks. According to Silvia Federici and Mario Montano, writing in the early 1970s under the pen name Guido Baldi, "The 'scientific organization of labor,' the technological leap of the Twenties, serves but one purpose: to destroy the specific articulation of the labor force which was the basis for the political re-composition of the working class during the first two decades of the century."[21] Fordism and Taylorism, however, failed to sufficiently discipline and decompose the working class globally. With the stick unsuccessful, all that was left was the carrot. The Keynesian state, named for British economist John Maynard Keynes, sought to link productivity and wages while bringing the working class into the very heart of capitalist production.[22] Pacifying the working class came in many guises: New Deal programs, the National War Labor Board, and, after World War II, the GI Bill (only accessible to whites), housing and infrastructure subsidies, access to higher education (and hence middle-class employment), labor-saving technologies in the home, and the advance of mass media in the form of radio and then television.[23]

The black struggle for dignity and equality under the law was given a boost by African American soldiers returning from World War II. Many of them would challenge racial injustice at home after fighting it abroad, sparking the civil rights movement. Bus boycotts, sit-ins, and other acts of refusal were organized and were accompanied by forms of everyday resistance, theft, sabotage, and the like. Describing the conflict in Birmingham, Alabama, historian of African American history Robin D. G. Kelley writes: "In the twelve months beginning September 1941, there were at least 88 cases of blacks occupying 'white' space on public transportation, 55 of which were open acts of defiance in which African-American passengers either refused to give up their seats or sat in the white section. But this is only part of the story; reported incidents and complaints of racial conflict totaled 176. These cases included at least 18 interracial fights among passengers, 22 fights between black passengers and operators, and 13 incidents in which black passengers engaged in verbal or physical confrontations over being shortchanged."[24] The activities Kelley lists were part of a larger movement to dismantle racism. As the movement progressed, this meant demanding not only jobs but also welfare and reparations for wages due—that is, access to wages that were not directly connected to the performance of imposed work. Additionally, African Americans in the prison system during the mid-twentieth century would set upon the guards, the most immediate human representatives of their oppression, in revolt after revolt, as waves of struggle circulated through the prisons.[25] Whites and blacks often participated in these rebellions together as their forebears at Harpers Ferry had. At every point of development this struggle would be met with violence from the state and from both the official and unofficial representatives of state power. For instance, a multiracial group of young Freedom Riders, who in May 1961 were seeking to integrate interstate busing by traveling from the North to the South, experienced extreme violence at the hands of these unofficial representatives. In collusion with Alabama police, white vigilantes, members of the Ku Klux Klan, firebombed the Freedom Riders' bus, attempted to trap the passengers inside, and then beat them after they escaped the bus. Violence was likewise used against autoworkers in the same Detroit plants that had been the site of the UAW strikes in 1936. After black workers organized into revolutionary unions there in the 1960s, they were met with violence dispensed by local and union racists, as recounted in Dan Georgakas and Marvin Surkin's *Detroit, I Do Mind Dying.*[26] As the civil rights movement surged into the Black Power movement, state-sponsored violence against it intensified with the implementation of the Federal Bureau of Investigation's Counter Intelligence Program (COINTELPRO). COINTELPRO targeted the Black Panthers, the American Indian Movement, and student movements by disrupting organizations and, at least in the case of the Panthers and AIM, murdering members.

While Black Power spread through the Detroit auto plants via the Detroit Revolutionary Union Movement (DRUM) and the League of Revolutionary Black Workers, student struggles and anticolonial movements were circulating around the planet.[27] In response, a number of nation-states launched campaigns of repression. On October 2, 1968, the Mexican state massacred dozens (or even hundreds) of university student demonstrators in Tlatelolco, Mexico City. On May 4, 1970, the US (in its apparatus of the National Guard) shot student antiwar protesters on the Kent State University campus in Ohio, which was echoed by fatal police shootings of black college students in Jackson, Mississippi, eleven days later. At least thirteen other students were murdered by police and federal agents on campuses from May 1967 to November 1972, not to mention those who were shot but did not die.[28] In August 1968 Soviet tanks entered Prague to quell student-worker uprisings and calls for democracy. The state rushes in where capitalism fears to tread.

All of these struggles preceding and following the May 1968 student uprising in France took place outside of factory walls and outside of previously existing, acceptable channels for political struggle. This was the shape of movements to come. Struggles emerging after 1968 took place outside factory gates in homes and school and streets. As Mariarosa Dalla Costa argues in *The Power of Women and the Subversion of the Community*: "The community ... is not an area of freedom and leisure auxiliary to the factory, but is integral to the capitalist way of producing, and increasingly becom[ing] regimented like a factory, ... a social factory."[29] In moving the class war to this territory (repeated state attacks on protesters turned class struggle into outright war), capitalism and the state followed the movement of the working class. Militants in factories and universities had brought the struggle to the streets and engaged civil society. It is through the lens of the social factory that the coalesced rebellions of students and workers of the time can be understood. "From Tokyo to Paris, London and Berlin," as Tariq Ali and Susan Watkins put it in *1968: Marching in the Streets*, the rebellion and outright war moved around the world: Moscow, Prague, New York, Havana, Washington, Sasebo (Japan), Athens, Hamburg, Saigon, and beyond.[30]

Against the social factory and from the conditions of their everyday lives, including those of housework and unpaid labor, women began to rebel. Writing in 1975 Barbara Ehrenreich and Deirdre English describe housework as "invisible" economically and politically. They write, "Housework is maintenance and restoration: the daily restocking of the shelves and return of each cleaned and repaired object to its starting point in the family game of disorder."[31] In reaction women constructed new lives outside and against the nuclear family and against the imposition of unpaid reproductive labor. Dalla Costa and the Wages for Housework Campaign were among the first to articulate the problem when they reasoned, "Housewives make up a hidden reserve work force: unemployed women work behind closed doors at home, to be called out again when capital needs them elsewhere.... The family under capitalism is a center of consumption and reserve labor, but a center also of production."[32] Women in recomposing their lives became guerrillas of desire as millions began to refuse housework, and this, as well as nearly a decade of overt rebellions, led to a crisis of reproductive labor that required capitalism, the state, and institutions in civil society to attack and seek to decompose the power of women through culture war, limits placed on contraception and abortion, and the clearly inadequate state interventions around violence against women and gender-nonconforming peoples. After suffering countless abuses at the hands of the police, the gay rights movement would launch itself from a small bar in Manhattan's Greenwich Village. From the June 28, 1969 Stonewall Riot, gay, lesbian, and transgender people began to challenge the heteronormativity that had hindered their lives and started to publicly criticize the processes of social reproduction that used the nuclear, heterosexual family as its mechanism of production and control.

Returning to workers' struggles, by 1972 the peak of strike activity would be over in the US. The early 1970s would also mark the onset of an offensive by capitalism. By the early 1980s the Professional Air Traffic Controllers Organization (PATCO) had been busted up by the Reagan administration (1981), improvements in education and the social safety net were rolled back (free tuition and welfare benefits, for instance), and extensive battles in a culture war against the status gained by women, gays and lesbians, and people of color were launched.

Throughout the nearly five hundred years of class struggle that I have described in this book, the dominant form of struggle has oscillated between guerrilla warfare and overt rebellion. These have often blended into the everyday lives of the participants. Thompson appreciated the complexity of class relations and wrote: "If we stop history at any given point, then there are no classes but simply a multitude of individuals with a multitude of experiences. But if we watch these [people] over an adequate period of social change, we observe patterns in their relationships, their ideas, and their institutions. Class is defined by [people] as they live their own history, and in the end, this is its only definition."[33] For Thompson class is relational, defined by and expressed collectively, philosophically, and organizationally through relationships within the working class itself and with the bourgeoisie (alongside it or against it). These class relations cannot be considered universally, nor can they be limited to overt rebellions and the official organizations of the Left. By reading the cycles of struggle and inquiring into class composition in certain periods and at specific geographical locations, class relations can be understood within the contexts they are operating within. Class composition is not determined by overt rebellions alone—strikes, riots, and burning of government offices. Rather, it is the relationships between resistance, rebellion, and everyday and overt struggles that lead to the rising power of the working class vis-à-vis capitalism and the state. Wobbly "freelance missionaries," "blacks occupying 'white' space," militants of DRUM, "unemployed women work[ing] behind closed doors at home," striking UAW members, and innumerable others have shared struggles and furthered the "contradictions of capitalism" as a result of this circulation and increasing working-class power. Likewise today such factors accumulate, leading to crisis, and then capitalism and the state responds.[34]

● ● ●

In 1971 President Richard Nixon, responding to inflation (devaluation of money leading to the increase in prices) and unemployment, took the US off the gold standard. That is, US currency in dollars was no longer to be pegged one to one to gold in the Central Reserve Bank. The reasons given were that Nixon's administration need to control inflation and unemployment in order to ensure long-term growth and the health of the capitalist order. In fact, the federal government increased control over the economy through management of the money supply and amplified instability in financial and labor markets. But the inflationary economy that developed in the late 1960s and early 1970s was the result of working-class struggle. For when workers demand more wages and housewives and others refuse to perform the work of social reproduction and the reproduction of labor power for free, the state and capital aspire to "regain control." This is done by depressing wages and interrupting the Keynesian productivity scheme (higher wages for higher productivity) through an increase in the cost of commodities across the economy.[35]

Undoubtedly, rising food and energy prices affect the working class and can undercut wage gains. But there is a secondary ill effect of the increase in food prices: it causes the working class to expend more resources to perform its own reproduction and causes stress in the household. On the other hand, energy prices affect all other commodities, so an increase in, say, heating oil or gasoline affects not only consumers but industry as well. Cheap energy allows capitalism to deploy technology and machines to undercut working-class power on the shop floor while increasing production.[36] The push toward increased development in certain sectors coupled with underdevelopment in others (especially noticeable in the inner city and the Rust Belt) has marked the neoliberal period.

New York City witnessed the erosion of its manufacturing sector in the two decades leading up to the fiscal crisis of the mid-1970s. At this point, capitalism began to develop new industries and considerably revamp and monetize others, each with corresponding new forms of work (including an increase in temporary work)—entailing service and care industries, information technology, education, and health care, for example. Here again we see the embryonic social factory. High union wages and class composition forced manufacturers to seek cheaper pools of labor as the city increasingly became a center for finance capital and what we now call "creative industries": advertising, mass media, and other cultural production. With high wages in the manufacturing sector, New York City's working class had made considerable gains, including wage increases and benefits for unionized public employees and increased payments to welfare recipients (led by the black-women-run National Welfare Rights Union). High school and public college students demanded free tuition and control over curriculum, and the City University of New York would have a free tuition policy from 1970 until the fall of 1976. Community members succeeded in forcing the city to spend money on everything from infrastructure to schools.[37] Despite the power of the working class, New York City politicians began cutbacks in city programs. Francis Fox Piven and Richard Cloward, wrote in *Radical America* at the time, in an article titled "The Urban Crisis as an Arena for Class Mobilization,"

> By the early 1970's, urban strife had subsided; a degree of political stability had been restored, in no small part as a result of the concessions granted in the 1960's. At the same time, however, the disparity between expenditures and revenues in the older cities widened dramatically, for the long-term economic trends that were eroding the manufacturing base of these cities accelerated rapidly under the impact of the recessionary policies of the Nixon-Ford administrations. As unemployment rose precipitously in the central cities, they experienced sharply declining municipal revenues, for much of these revenues [are] earned through sales and income taxes. Moreover, once the turmoil of the 1960's ebbed, the federal and state governments could reduce their grants-in-aid to the older central cities thereby worsening the disparities in city budgets even more. The situation thus became ripe for a mobilization of national and local business interests to force expenditures into line with revenues by cutting the cost of the populist politics in the cities.[38]

Confronting organized labor and cutting benefits of welfare recipients was neither sound policy for capitalism and the state nor was it going to be sufficient to decompose the working class. Massive social budget cuts were then taken up by other major US cities and then exported in the form of structural adjustment strategies. As David Harvey concludes, the "management of the New York fiscal crisis pioneered the way for neoliberal practices both domestically under Reagan and internationally through the IMF in the 1980s."[39] Austerity policy was an indirect strategy to accomplish this task. Ideological assault on the very notion of a social safety net was another. In the looming culture war of the 1980s and 1990s capitalists sought to undermine the solidarity and cohesion that had developed in working class, feminist, queer, black, brown, indigenous, and poor communities by reasserting white supremacy and hetero-patriarchy. This solidarity under attack was the result of forty years of struggle in everyday life and through overt organizing and rebellions.

To summarize the social factory as described thus far, capitalism and the state first followed the working class onto the social terrain. When struggles that originated in the auto factories of Detroit, Turin, and other industrial centers began to spread across the planet outside of the factory gates and outside the political channels of the state and parties—new possibilities blossomed.[40] With sectors of the working class struggling for wages and for better working conditions (something that had always taken place, though not at the level reached during this period), Americanism as the requisite sphere supporting Fordism was extended. Second, new forms of temporary, precarious office and service work emerged, under the logic of factory work but outside of the factory. At least initially these functioned as a part of an assembly line where workers perform timed job tasks. One only needs to observe baristas working at Starbucks to see this in action. And now the service economy has come to influence all other forms of labor. A plumber no long simply replaces a pipe, one is reviewed online after the fact and required to provide a positive experience for the customer in addition to fixing a leak. Increasingly in the overall economy, not only physical commodities are exchanged but so are affects—feelings and sensations—as plumbers, fast food workers, flight attendants, child-care providers, massage therapists, nurses, and others serve the emotional needs of consumers. Scholars often refer to this type of work as immaterial or affective. Meanwhile demands of the previous cycles of struggle are recuperated and redeployed by capitalism. For instance, flexible work schedules are now common but without the reassurances and stability needed for one to plan a life or pay bills.

A third stage of the development of the social factory has been capitalists' attempt to address the crisis of social reproduction, as increasing numbers of women started refusing traditional roles thanks to the new women's movement of sixties and seventies. As Federici noted, "The clearest evidence that women have used the power of the wage to reduce their unpaid labor in the home has been the explosion of the service sector in the '70s. Cooking, cleaning, taking care of children, even problem solving and companionship have been increasingly 'taken out of the home' and organized on a commercial basis."[41] This led to a shift in capitalism, creating new markets along with the expansion of service work. What began as a demand for gender equality and pay for the work of reproductive labor power was commodified. A highly exploited labor force of domestic workers in Europe and the US, frequently immigrant women of color, has served to fill a niche created initially by feminist demand and then captured by capitalism. The social factory has not replaced the industrial factory, it has augmented it. Industrial manufacturing clearly still takes place, although production has been increasingly automated and factories moved to regions with low wages—often out of the country entirely. Initially manufacturing was shifted to the Global South, where displaced peasants have flooded into cities and urban slums as a result of their land being enclosed. But, increasingly, regions of the US now have sufficiently low wages for manufacturing.

With the onset of the social factory, class struggle continued, as did the onslaught of neoliberalism. It wasn't until 1981, with the firing of the PATCO strikers, that a larger revenge against trade unions and other working-class organizations was unleashed. Capitalism attempted to reorganize the working class on a global scale, often using time-tested strategies: massive new enclosures of land previously held in common or used for subsistence agriculture, violent and repressive regimes in the Global South, the threat of nuclear war and the use of low-intensity warfare, and the reorganization of production and social reproduction. During this time, in the 1980s, the working class was on the defensive, the women's movement was institutionalized, unions were attacked, ghettoization and police violence dampened revolts among people of color, and new forms of work began to appear (e.g., precarious and temporary). Meanwhile working-class struggle left the direct field of conflict by creating new forms of activity and life, manifest, for example, in punk rock and rap music.[42] The women's movement too was not eliminated but manifest itself, in part, in the cultural productions of a new generation of feminists. Uncovering the still untold, or at least under-told, story of radical movements in the US since the late 1970s will aid us in grasping the strengths and pitfalls of contemporary movements. (The next chapter will grapple with this.) While cliché, it is true: the struggle continues.

CREATING COUNTER-COMMUNITIES

To exhaustively describe the creation of counter-communities in the industrial and social factory would be a monumental task. An attempt thus requires a degree of theoretical abstraction. As we have seen, the history of the working class is one of cyclical struggle, at times intense. Capitalist technological and spatial development and overt and covert state repression are capitalist attempts to decompose working-class power. Forms of everyday resistance throughout the industrial and social factory require, as we have seen, solidarity, communication, and mutual aid. These activities intersect with the everyday practices of those struggling in the industrial and social factory. To use a metaphor drawn from guerrilla practice the world over, counter-communities are the mountains from which the guerrillas of desire descend in order to strike at the forms of power that are capturing their activities, their labor power, their very essence and energy.

Solidarity

As any union organizer will tell you, without solidarity on the shop floor a campaign is not winnable. What is true for union organizing is likewise the case for everyday resistance. This is part of the reason why capitalism has used the division of labor in addition to other authoritarian methods to dominate and control the working class—by dividing it internally through the likes of racism, heteropatriarchy, nationalism, and religious chauvinism. The innumerable effects in civil and political society are well known. In the factory system of the Global North a division of labor allocated skilled and unskilled labor to specific populations, and this form of domination was consolidated in the Fordist production line. In 1947 an American autoworker using the name Paul Romano (actually Phil Singer) collaborated with a then-unknown Chinese American militant writing under the "party name" of Ria Stone (Grace C. Lee, latter Boggs) on a pamphlet titled *The American Worker*. Attending to the division of labor in Detroit auto plants, Romano observed, "The wage scales and classification in the shop are extremely numerous. It is a continual battle to reach a higher classification and more money, with one worker competing against another. Much anger is generated between workers and against the company over upgrading or promotions to new jobs. Every time a new job is open, a bitter wrangle takes place. It is not predominantly a question of the nickel raise involved, as it may seem on the surface, but a desire for recognition and a change for exploitation of one's own capabilities."[43] Romano points to a number of key issues. First, with "numerous" pay rates and job categories, the capitalist mode separates workers into production units and wage hierarchies. Second, the divisions in the plant pit workers against each other, although there is "much anger" directed at the company as well. Third, workers are not simply looking for a "nickel raise" but what scholar Geoff Mann calls increases in the "qualitative aspect of the wage" (that is, the substantive improvements that increases in wages actually and symbolically offer).[44] This final issue illustrates how workers are invested in their productive capacities, which capitalism captures and acts upon like a vampire. At times, workers have qualitative aspirations and gain recognition when engaged in the process of production. It is when workers confront capitalist and neoliberal logic and develop solidarity and a collective will and imagination that they begin to overcome the imposition of work.

On this matter, Romano continues, "At lunch time, workers will often discuss how a job could be done more efficiently from beginning to end. They will talk about what stock to use, how to machine it, how to do certain operations on various machines with various set-ups. But they never get a chance to decide how and why things should be done. However, if they can't use all they know, they try and use some of it."[45] These ordinary conversations illustrate both a longing for control over production and a sense of solidarity that develops within the factory system and for that matter within all of capitalist production. Workers must cooperate with each other to accomplish job tasks, and here is the beginning of capitalism's downfall: a counter-community, based on cohesion and trust, within, against, and beyond capitalism.

Cooperative relationships at the point of production can result in expressions of solidarity and commonality. In Studs Terkel's *Working: People Talk about What They Do All Day and How They Feel about What They Do* there are interviews with garbage collectors Nick Salerno and Roy Schmidt. Salerno remarks, "I got a good crew, we get along together, but we have our days." Schmidt comments, "Maybe we'll pull into an alley and they'll take five minutes for a cigarette break. We might chew the fat about various things—current events, who murdered who (laughs), sensational stories. Maybe one of the fellas read an article about something that happened over in Europe. Oh, once in a while, talk about the war [Vietnam]. It has never been a heated discussion with me."[46] While it would be amusing to believe that there is a secret conspiracy of garbage men going on in alleys, these testimonials describe ongoing interactions and the sense of solidarity amongst those on the job.

Martin Glaberman and George Rawick comment in "The American Working Class," "After they enter a factory, workers find out about one another: who is glib and good at negotiating, who is strong and brave and good at blocking a plant gate or beating up a scab, who is astute as a tactician, who is a public speaker, etc."[47] This knowledge is based upon the relationships workers have with one another, and to act upon these notions—to beat up a scab, for instance—a strong sense of solidarity is required. Often individual workers are responsible for stronger bonds on the job, when identifiable leaders emerge organically or militants create opportunities for relationships to develop. This solidarity was particularly cogent in the feminist movement where consciousness-raising groups allowed women to discuss private problems collaboratively. Federici writes: "Women have always found ways of fighting back, or getting back at [men], but always in an isolated and private way. The problem, then, becomes how to bring this struggle out of the kitchen and bedroom and into the streets."[48] With Wages for Housework and similar campaigns women aimed at reclaiming two important and intertwined goods, "to take back our time, which happens to be our lives; to take back the wealth which we have created with generations of unpaid labor."[49] Moving women from the isolation of the kitchen or bedroom toward the collectivity of "the streets" required increasing trust and cohesion among women. This does not develop without vibrant communication and ongoing, mounting acts of mutual aid.

Communication

A network of communication exists throughout the industrial and social factory for sharing tactics and keeping conversations out of earshot of the boss. Worker guerrillas meet in bars, churches, union and community halls, alleys, break rooms, and backrooms, discussing conditions on the job and strategies to resist the imposition of more work. These networks have their own rhythms, languages, and even songs. Paul Willis's classic book on British schoolchildren, *Learning to Labor: How Working Class Kids Get Working Class Jobs*, concludes that the habits and behaviors adopted during their teenage years determine and then follow working class kids into their working lives. The language of the schoolyard finds its way, even if morphed, onto the factory floor. Willis writes, "The distinctive form of language and highly developed intimidatory humour of the shopfloor is also very reminiscent of the counter-school culture. Many verbal exchanges on the shopfloor are not serious or about work activities. They are jokes, or 'pisstakes,' or 'kiddings' or 'windups.' There is a real skill in being able to use this language with fluency: to identify the points on which you are being "kidded" and to have appropriate responses ready in order to avoid further baiting."[50]

Every work site, industry, and region has its own terms for teasing workmates, or nicknames to differentiate individuals. At the metal fabricator where I worked for five years there was Black Kev, White Kev (me), Pops, Hot Carl, Boss (who wasn't the boss but acted like it), Von the Truck Whisperer (who could accurately determine how much product could fit on a flatbed), and many I have forgotten. These linguistic strategies produce bonds between workers and mask communication channels for counter-planning and other forms of everyday resistance.

What are now expletives and monikers were once work songs, which themselves sprang from slavery. Slave songs morphed into songs of black workers, men and women. Robin D. G. Kelley comments regarding tobacco workers in the South, "Singing in unison not only reinforced a sense of collective identity in these black workers but the songs themselves—most often religious hymns—ranged from veiled protests against the daily indignities of the factory to utopian visions of a life free of difficult wage work."[51] These songs have always been part of working-class culture and expressed the experiences and dreams of those who sang them. A working-class language developed that was used in the working and community lives of the industrial and social proletariat. This common tongue often provided a way to conceal everyday resistance from authorities and generate the social cohesion necessary for overt rebellion.

Mutual aid

In a sense, the working class is continuously engaged in communication and mutual aid. In *Facing Reality*, which contributed the opening epigraph to this chapter, James, Boggs, and Castoriadis commented that "there is no need for these shop floor organizations to be formally organized. As soon as the men in a department know one another and go through the work together, they are organized."[52] They continue later in the text, "In the factories, workers develop methods and forms of co-operation, of mutual help and solidarity, of organization, which already anticipates socialist relations. Here also the task of a revolutionary organization is, first, to recognize these forms, to explain the significance of them, and to let itself be guided by them in what it is doing and in what it is saying."[53] By reading these activities of cooperation as well as the struggles, as *Facing Reality*'s authors suggest, a whole set of practices come into view.

These practices are as old as they are new. Thompson noted that as peasants entered the cities and factories following the enclosure of their lands they "remembered village rights, of notions of equality before the law, of craft traditions." And innovative forms of mutual aid emerged with subsequent periods and stages of capitalism. While cooperatives, credit unions, and benevolent societies are among the best known overt forms, collaborative storehouses and armories, traffic in illegal goods, and "autoreduction" movements are a selection of examples that have functioned, and undoubtedly still function, in everyday life. "Autoreduction," two authors summarize, "is the act by which consumers, in the area of consumption, and workers, in the area of production, take it upon themselves to reduce, at a *collectively* determined level, the price of public services, housing, electricity; or in the factory, the rate of productivity."[54] For instance, in Turin, Italy in the autumn of 1974 social movements sought to decrease consumer prices after "spontaneous, unorganized" reductions took place. From and through these points of activity, we find linkages with other counter-communities and life activities outside of the factory walls. In dance halls, clubs, grog shops, bars, churches, parks, on street corners, and in innumerable other spaces, ways of organizing life emerge and acts of resistance are planned. It has been these languages, spaces, acts of mutual aid, and solidarity that have created a culture of silence and counter-morality that have served as support network and metaphorical arms supplier for the guerrillas of desire throughout the industrial and social factory.

A MULTIPLICITY OF EXPRESSIONS, A MYRIAD OF FORMS

As we have seen previously under slavery and in peasant politics, guerrillas take on multiple appearances and use a myriad of ways to resist the imposition of work. In the industrial and social factory, the specter of theft returns, as do sabotage, slowdowns, wildcat strikes, and exodus. To this list we will add counter-planning (reorganizing the process of production and reproduction) and the act of refusing the discipline of the union and other official Left organizations. Exploring the individual expressions of these forms will lead us toward consideration of the generalized revolt against work. Moreover, since the period addressed in this chapter comes immediately before our present day, close attention should be given to the forms described here as they might very well be circulating in our own workplaces, communities, and lives.

Theft
Worker guerrillas have often pilfered the commodities they have produced along with raw materials, machines, and tools. Supplies have

regularly disappeared from factories, construction sites, and offices before heading for the black market or the personal use of the guerrilla who smuggled them out. As Kelley offered about his own experiences, "Like virtually all my fellow workers, I liberated McDonaldland cookies by the boxful, volunteered to clean 'lots and lobbies' in order to talk to my friends, and accidentally cooked too many Quarter Pounders and apple pies near closing time, knowing full well that we could take home whatever was left over."[55] Often proletarians have directly stolen back the product of their own labor, and at times individual thefts were an overt tactic in a protracted class struggle. "Proletarian shopping" was the term used by the Italian *autonomia* movement for mass expropriation of goods or the "autoreduction" of prices intended to follow after a group of militants would conduct a sit-in at an establishment and demand lower prices on goods. Without access to the means of subsistence and survival outside the wage relation, proletarians requiring or yearning for goods will steal them. To prevent such activity inside and outside of the factory, a whole set of disciplinary procedures were created to deter and, if necessary, punish offenders. The statutes forged in the phase of enclosure, with the gallows as ultimate representation of such punishment, were enforced when moral and religious prohibitions against theft failed. Public executions of "such groups belong[ing] to the labouring poor or the class of proletarians" were instructive.[56] Theft, be it at the point of production or in the community at large, has historically been dealt with through a set of surveillance and disciplinary mechanisms particular to a time and location. To map out the boundless thievery throughout the industrial and social factory is an impossible task. Yet prevention methods have developed along with technological capitalism from guards and checkpoints outside of the factory gates to surveillance cameras and body scanners in offices, fast food establishments, and public squares. My purpose here is to draw out general categories, such as theft, so that we can consider their ramifications for resistance and rebellion in our own contexts, our own times.

Sabotage

Often when capitalism would attempt to increase productivity by deploying new technologies, speed up the line, or expand the working day, sabotage would take place. Such acts would have distinctive targets and diverse levels of secrecy depending on whether they took place in a factory, office, or home. In the latter, housewives often "sabotaged" their products by providing alternatives and other forms of reproduction to their families outside of the capitalist command of reproductive labor.

That is, when a homemaker opened possible paths for her working-class children beyond what capitalism expected of them, challenged traditional gender rolls (by encouraging girls to take initiative and lead and involving boys in cooking and cleaning), or rejected unwanted sexual advances by a predatory husband, she disrupted the production of a base commodity for capitalism: labor power. As women left the home periodically, responding to the expanding labor market, to take on a second job, a paid one, they often used sabotage (as Kelley relates in the next sentence). Kelley comments: "There is evidence of household workers scorching food or spitting in food, damaging kitchen utensils, and breaking household appliances, but employers and white contemporaries generally dismissed these acts as proof of black moral and intellectual inferiority."[57] Here Kelley calls our attention to the racial component in sabotage, and how black guerrillas in the industrial and social factory were, like their enslaved forbears, assumed to be feeble or ill as they resisted the conditions they were forced to live under. In our view, it is with this very activity that they maintained their dignity and humanity.

Sabotage in industrial settings was often organized as part of a larger campaign or circulated through factory circuits. To counter speedups or in response to grievances, wrenches would be thrown into the works or products would be rendered unusable. There was a long history of this activity in auto plants, one of the key commodities and areas of production during the twentieth century. Bill Watson states, "In several localities of the plant, organized acts of sabotage began.... Such things were done as neglecting to weld unmachined spots on motor heads; leaving out gaskets to create a loss of compression; putting in bad or wrong-size spark plugs; leaving bolts loose in the motor assembly; or, for example, assembling the plug wires in the wrong firing order so that the motor appeared to be off balance during inspection. Rejected motors accumulated."[58] As these rejected motors accumulated, so did the experiences and acts of the worker guerrillas. These simple acts could bring entire assembly lines to a halt or make clear the intent of the workers without risking a strike or other overt action. Clandestine, often individual acts of sabotage would accrue, forcing capital to capitulate to the demands of the workforce and often shift capacity by increasing production, hiring additional workers, or surveilling workers to prevent damage to commodities and the means of production.

Counter-planning
The reorganization of production and reproduction is the reorganization of the imposition of work itself. Here on the terrain of everyday

life among sectors of the working class, a counterplan is implemented to more effectively accomplish work tasks or to create needed break times, to create power outside of management.[59] To Watson's counter-planning on the shop floor, Federici contributes counter-planning from the kitchen, and to this we can add counter-planning in the office, café, or retail store. "It is the freedom to organize their work as they please," writes Watson, "combined with all sorts of details, such as smoking on the job, the condition of the restroom, not working when it is too hot, which pass under the title of 'local grievances.'"[60] These local grievances are justification used by worker guerrillas throughout the industrial and social factory. Initial gripes amass into collective grievances, which in turn sparks further action.

This ability to reorganize production is paramount for the daily survival of the working class in the factory, where the discipline of the work regime is ever-present. Work is reorganized to create free time or to protect fellow workers. On this matter, James, Boggs, and Castoriadis reflect:

> In one department of a certain plant in the United States, there is a worker who is physically incapable of carrying out his duties. But he is a man with a wife and children, and his condition is due to the previous strain of his work in the plant. The workers in that department have organized their work so that for nearly ten years he has had practically nothing to do. They have defied all efforts of the foreman and supervision to discharge him, threatening to throw the whole plant into disorder if any steps are taken to dismiss the invalid. That is the socialist society.[61]

This "socialist society" also takes place in the home, where housewives are under a different work regime. Whereas the process of domestic work is not generally monitored, social pressure and the direct imposition of work by capitalism is pervasive there. Historically this has meant pressure on women's entire lives, with little escape other than through resistance. Today it means pressure on the lives of all who work both inside and outside the home.

Housewives reorganize their reproductive work in a series of ways to create free time for other activities and opportunities to connect with other friends. With the women's movement of the 1960s and 1970s, housewives increasingly defied the imposition of reproductive work by their husbands and society and opened the door for women to define their own lives. While Watson is specifically referring to the industrial factory, his comments certainly apply to the social factory as well, when he says, "The seizing of quantities of time for getting together with friends and the amusement of activities ranging from card games to reading or walking around the plant to see what other areas are doing is an important achievement for laborers."[62] It is in these quantities of time, these moments of escape that the working class begins to construct new lives and new ways of being.

Slowdowns and wildcat strikes

As the launch of a strike approached, and as part of the periodic outbreaks of everyday resistance, worker guerrillas would often slow or shut down the production process. Workers on the assembly line also work to rule, following the rules so as to deliberately slow the rate of work, thus decreasing the rate of production. This is a direct form of struggle against the imposition of Fordism or speedups. Speaking about southern tobacco farmers, Kelley writes: "When black women stemmers had trouble keeping up with the pace, black men responsible for supplying tobacco to them would pack the baskets more loosely than usual."[63] Heightened communication and solidarity are needed to perform such acts. Likewise with slowdowns, which, unlike theft and sabotage, require a certain degree of cooperation among workers. The timing of slowdowns—such as during a peak harvest or the holidays (at retail establishments), as contracts are being renewed, or after the firing of a fellow worker—conveys workers' disgruntlement without overt rebellion.

A slowdown carried to its logical end becomes a shutdown. Slowdowns and shutdowns take place before the strike and on the terrain of everyday life. Watson comments, "The shutdown is radically different from the strike; its focus is on the actual working day. It is not, as popularly thought, a rare conflict. It is a regular occurrence, and, depending on the time of year, even an hourly occurrence.... The shutdown is nothing more than a device for controlling the rationalization of time by curtailing overtime planned by management."[64] Here the concept of the shutdown, and we can include slowdown here too, intersects with a larger set of actions centered around counter-planning the workday. The shutdown and the slowdown allow the working class to control the pace of work, and the specific attributes they express depend on the direct, immanent conditions that confront particular workers.

As a strike against a company's bureaucracy and command structure, the wildcat strike began to circulate as an organized form of working-class defiance. "Wildcats are a constant defiance and rejection of the capitalist system and of the union bureaucracy which has tied its fortunes to capitalism," James, Boggs, and Castoriadis write. From wildcats and neighboring struggles a new organizational form, one that was direct rather than representational, developed: that of the workers' council.[65] Accordingly, Anton Pannekoek views "council organization" as

> a real democracy, the democracy of labor, making the working people master of their work.... The activity of the councils, put in action by the workers as the organs of collaboration, guided by perpetual study and strained attention to circumstances and needs, covers the entire field of society. All measures are taken in constant intercourse, by deliberation in the councils and discussion in the groups and the shops, by actions in the shops and decisions in the councils.... All social power is vested in the hands of the workers themselves. Wherever the use of power is needed against disturbances or attacks upon the existing order it proceeds from the collectivities of the workers in the shops and stands under their control.[66]

Councils coordinated the self-activity of the working class on the terrain of everyday life. As Michael Hardt and Antonio Negri summarize, "The great power of the workers' councils resides in the fact that they activated and utilized already existing relationships among workers in the factories: the same circuits of communication that function in production were repurposed in the political structures of the councils."[67] In the 1960s in France, Italy, and Germany these workers' councils developed links with the growing student movement, while in the US they often intersected with (and at times were defined by) Black Power, as in the Dodge Revolutionary Union Movement (DRUM) and League of Revolutionary Black Workers. It was in these struggles that "revolt against work" was fully articulated as a political concept and as a framework for the working-class movement. The working-class movement against work and organizational forms developed in the industrial factory (such as workers' councils) would emerge in the social factory (autoreduction movements, Wages for Housework campaign). It would take a complete decomposition of the working class and massive, violent political repression to reimpose capitalist command.

Against the official organizations of the Left

While unions were initially one of the institutions expressing working-class needs and desires, by the mid-1950s it was clear that the union had become a blunt tool, often used to impose capitalist work discipline. As my purpose here is to foster understanding of the activity of the guerrillas of desire and not the entirety of union history, I'll jump to the general revolt of the working class against certain business unions.

Rank-and-file revolts targeted union collusion with management, the state, or both. The state sought, quite successfully at times, to decompose the industrial unions and radical organizations that arose in the US during the late nineteenth and early twentieth centuries. Using legal and extralegal means, the state raided offices, arrested syndicalists (revolutionary unionists who believe in workers control of production), deported immigrants associated with radical organizations, and, through local police and with the tacit support of the Department of Justice, even physically assaulted those suspected of planning worker revolts. Trade unions and the "loyal opposition" (left progressives loyal to the state and capitalism), out of fear or opportunism, compromised with the state and were incorporated within its framework. By signing no-strike pledges and working on the Council of National Defense and other so-called war boards, as the American Federation of Labor unions did, unions were effectively part of the US government's efforts in World War II.[68] Additionally, with the development of Keynesianism, increases in wages became tied to production: wages wouldn't increase unless production increased. Hence the working class now had a vested interest in production, which resulted in the overproduction of commodities that would periodically throw capitalism into crisis. It was the unions too that would be required to control the workforce—by disciplining workers through fines, access to work, and in part through the contracts they signed to make good on the Keynesian "deal." Since World War II, Rawick writes: "In return [for wage increases and keeping up with increases in productivity] unions have had to insure industrial peace by disciplining the workers and curtailing their demands on all issues save money and fringe benefits.... The CIO unions became through the process the political weapons of the State against the working class."[69] As part of their prostration before the state, unions expelled syndicalists, socialists, communists, and anarchists. The de-radicalization of the union movement was part of its arrangement with the state. In the new political environment it was enmeshed in power relationships it had helped to forge.

By the mid-1950s, a series of strikes, union-led and not, began to spread across the planet, but this time the working class defined itself against capitalism, the state, and the union—all of the mechanisms that attempted to discipline it. Often these strikes took place informally in everyday life, a terrain that allowed for abandoning the union form and the creation of other organizational bodies, such as workers' councils.

Sabotage, slowdowns, work stoppages, and eventually strikes all developed in response to the attempt to decompose the working class and prevent its further political recomposition. In this context, "strikes" took place against the unions. In *Facing Reality* James, Boggs, and Castoriadis describe such a strike by workers and how it is part of a larger phenomenon: "In the U.S. Rubber Plant in Detroit during the 16 months prior to April 1956, there were on average two wildcat stoppages a week. The Rubber Union is powerless to stop them. That is the abiding situation in thousands of plants all over the United States. It is no secret."[70] In this particular example, we see the working class counter-planning beyond the immediate conditions of the factory and toward a general revolt against the unions. At this time new forms of working-class organization developed and participated directly in the class struggle that would carry the class through May 1968 to the high point of union activity, at least in the US: the early 1970s. A series of wildcat strikes would shake the foundations of both capital and the union itself, and workers' councils were organized. In recent history, democratic caucuses within unions, advocacy organizations, workers' centers, and solidarity networks have coexisted as the formal, overt expression of working-class rebellion in the US. Each of these initiatives expresses the discontent among American radicals and working people for how undemocratic unions have become or operate in the absence of unions, with some critical of other official organizations of the Left as well. The rousing rejection of the nonprofit industrial complex, business unions, and even left-leaning religious organizations, by the working class is in part a manifestation of the limitations these enterprises place on working-class self-activity.

Exodus

The working class has also sought to escape the work regime. The massive human migrations unleashed by capital contain two contradictory elements: the process of enclosure and forced migration on one hand, and the attempt of the working class to flee harsh working conditions on the other. One of the clearest examples is the migration of African Americans from the South to the North from 1910 to 1970. As Isabel Wilkerson, author of the remarkable *The Warmth of Other Suns: The Epic Story of America's Great Migration*, pronounced,

> From the early years of the twentieth century to well past its middle age, nearly every black family in the American south, which meant nearly every black family in America, had a decision to make. There

were sharecroppers losing at settlement. Typists wanting to work in an office. Yard boys scared that a single gesture near the planter's wife could leave them hanging from an oak tree. They were all stuck in a caste system as hard and unyielding as the red Georgia clay, and they each had a decision before them. In this, they were not unlike anyone who ever longed to cross the Atlantic or Rio Grande.[71]

The black working class sought to reconstruct their lives in the North and West and in the process racially reorganized and politically recomposed the entire US. A similar process took place in Italy during the 1950s and 1960s when southern Italians, seen as racially different from their northern counterparts, migrated to northern factories in search of work. In both countries, these migrations launched major urban rebellions. Additionally, migration from the Global South to the Global North has illustrated and continues to illustrate ways in which workers seek to improve their conditions. Too often this migration has been viewed as forced movement, as migrants leaving areas with low wages and state violence rather than an attempt at massive reorganization of the class. It is in exodus, in fleeing as their peasant and slave counterparts did before them, that the guerrillas of desire throughout the industrial and social factory have often sought to create new forms of life against all the institutions and relations of power that contain and capture their activity.

GENERALIZED REVOLT AGAINST WORK

The activities of the guerrillas of desire throughout the industrial and social factory can only be properly understood when considering the context in which they occur, as was the case with the actions of these guerrillas' enslaved and peasant kin. By abstracting from this perspective and looking historically at activity against capitalism and the state, we can see the guerrillas as a sector of the working class refusing work in everyday life. To understand this revolt against work, it is important to look at both the productive sphere, a well-mined area, and reproduction, which is far less frequently discussed and often ignored. Dalla Costa writes that women "must refuse housework as women's work, as work imposed upon us, which we never invented, which has never been paid for, in which [men] have forced us to cope with absurd hours, 12 and 13 hours a day, in order to force us to stay at home."[72] Viewing the working class broadly to include slaves and peasants as well as students, homemakers, immigrants, and factory and office workers reveals the breadth of struggle and generalized revolt against work that continues to be imposed.

The cycle of struggle that began with the wildcat strikes and rebellions by people of color across the planet, from the civil rights movement to anticolonial struggles, forced capitalism to invent new commodities (a service economy) and cultivate new forms of work (precarious, temporary, and affective). Workers in this new economy have faced different life rhythms, and a new chronological sense has developed beyond the capitalist time clock. This has presented a new challenge but also opportunities for immensely rich and substantive self-activity. In this regard, Kelley describes the daily lives of black worker guerrillas since the emergence of the American labor movement in the 1880s:

> For a worker to accept reformist trade union strategies while stealing from work, to fight streetcar conductors while voting down strike action in the local, to leave work early in order to participate in religious revival meetings or rendezvous with a lover, to attend a dance rather than a CIO mass meeting was not to manifest an "immature" class consciousness. Such actions reflect the multiple ways black working people live, experience, and interpret the world around them. To assume that politics is something separate from all these events and decisions is to balkanize people's lives and thus completely miss how struggles over power, autonomy, and pleasure take place in the daily lives of working people.[73]

The complexity of resistance calls attention to the importance of everyday life as a site of struggle but also the need for inquiry, intervention, and theorization. The act of creating concepts is similar to that of creating metaphors, but they have different purposes and take place at different levels of abstraction. The purpose of the metaphor of the guerrillas of desire—as slave, peasant, and worker guerrillas—is to describe prevailing and potential struggles taking place on the terrain of everyday life. Connecting these struggles to dreams and desires can allow one to see how these struggles keep guerrillas from being completely dominated by capital and the state. It is to the concept of everyday resistance, and its relevance for contemporary revolutionary organizing, that we must now turn.

PART III

7

ON ORGANIZING

GUERRILLAS IN THE CONTEMPORARY PERIOD. LEFT COMMUNITY-BASED ORGANIZATIONS. RISE OF NONPROFITS, DECLINE OF UNIONS. AFFINITY GROUPS AND COLLECTIVES. ORGANIZERS TO COME, ORGANIZATIONS "ALL THE WAY DOWN."

> The question of the future of the revolution is a bad question because, in so far as it is asked, there are so many people who do not *become* revolutionaries, and this is exactly why it is done, to impede the question of the revolutionary-becoming of people, at every level, in every place.[1]
>
> —Gilles Deleuze in conversation with Claire Parnet,
> *Dialogues*

While Long Island's Modern Times Collective was initially caught in the whirlwind that was the counter-globalization movement, by August 2000 it increasingly focused locally. These endeavors included hosting long-term community dialogues (regular public discussions without predetermined topics or ends), active solidarity with a network of day labor workers' centers, and amassing resources (e.g., space, funds, art and printing supplies, and books) for use by the collective's members and constituents.[2] An excommunicated reverend along with a former guerrilla with the Farabundo Martí para la Liberación Nacional (Farabundo Martí National Liberation Front, El Salvador), both well studied in the pedagogy of Paolo Freire, trained the collective to facilitate community discussions.

Dialogues were held in large, open church halls with participants facing each other around a circle. Those who partook often described their desire to produce a "life worth living" and to situate their lives within the ecosystems of Long Island: coastal forest, pine barren, grasslands, estuary, and beach. Questions emerged: How will food be cultivated? What agriculture will this require? How will fruits and vegetables get picked? To address human needs, those assembled began to figure out labor processes and collective projects. Time spent in dialogue is unlike time spent awaiting the alarm bell or watching the time clock. Often these conversations ended organically, as those in the circle instinctively understood matters to be temporarily settled and knew that unaddressed and under-addressed questions would find their way into subsequent sessions. New participants would join these circles to talk about an occasion when they had refused an imposition—of work, compulsory schooling, family obligations, gender identity norms, assumptions about sex and sexuality—or bourgeois expectations. These refusals typically had required mutual aid in the form of accomplices, affinity, a sense of trust, and an awareness of solidarity and commonality.

In the previous chapters of this book, everyday forms of resistance were drawn from the historical record. This chapter will examine organizing strategies that hinder or further the amplification and circulation of these practices.

On organizing

In the first two years of the twenty-first century, New York-based social anarchist and then nonagenarian Sidney Solomon, a mentor of mine, would argue that anarchism was always organized. Social anarchists as part of the oddly named Vanguard Group in the 1930s would "draw a circle to mark that we believed in organization," he would say.[3] And organization requires *organizing* or at least implies it. Historical and contemporary approaches to organizing vary widely. This can be framed as consciousness-raising, unionization, or building community. Organizations from ACORN (which developed out of the National Welfare Rights Organization) and business unions (that is, trade unions that function as commercial and protectionist agents rather than organized expressions of working class power) to anarchist collectives and the IWW assume that they are to serve one central purpose: to organize the unorganized, agitate those who aren't agitated, and then educate the uneducated. (Some see this reversed: educate, agitate, and organize).[4] The results of such approaches diverge, as do the ideologies that justify and reinforce their methods.

Forms of everyday resistance and the narratives thus far noted serve as initial counter-arguments to the assumption that organizations are chiefly to educate, agitate, and organize. The overview in this chapter is not a comprehensive, all-encompassing analysis of possible approaches to organizing. I argue that organizing today and in the future must be attuned to everyday resistance, "reading the struggles," and the ongoing self-activity of the autonomous, broadly defined working class. A critical examination of historical and contemporary approaches taken by the Left and radicals in North America during the past forty years will provide a useful synopsis of overt rebellion against neoliberal capitalism. Organizing strategies vary widely among Left community-based organizations, business unions, nonprofits, self-referential affinity groups, and prefigurative anarchist collectives.

As a necessary aside, I view all forms of collective activity as organized, from the temporary affinity group used for a single clandestine action to a formal political collective, from a single Food Not Bombs feeding to an integrated set of community-based social services, from a casual slowdown on the job to a city-wide general strike. The difference between individual and collective actions can sometimes be difficult to distinguish, as Francis Fox Piven and Richard Cloward note in *Poor People's Movements: Why They Succeed, How They Fail*: "Strikes and riots are clearly forms of collective action, but even some forms of defiance which appear to be individual acts, such as crime or school truancy or incendiarism, while more ambiguous, may have a collective dimension, for those who engage in these acts may consider themselves to be part of a larger movement. Such apparently atomized acts of defiance can be considered movement events when those involved perceive themselves to be acting as members of a group, and when they share a common set of protest beliefs."[5] In turn, a movement is a collection of organizations and initiatives with shared practices and objectives. The questions before us are these: Does the scale and type of organization accomplish the tasks set forth by participants? Does the initiative correctly combine spontaneity and organization so as to be medicines rather than poisons? Can militants, organizers, and organic, working-class intellectuals become apt at "reading the struggles?" As part of a collective endeavor, can a new type of organizer inquire about, record, circulate, amplify, and intervene in the new society as it emerges?

GUERRILLAS IN THE CONTEMPORARY PERIOD

The slave, peasant, and worker guerrillas described in the previous chapters created counter-communities through solidarity, communication, and mutual aid while expressing a myriad of forms of resistance, from theft and sabotage to exodus and assassination. Recording this activity is an important undertaking, and understanding its role in creating crises within capitalism and the state is paramount for furthering these crises toward a revolutionary situation. Everyday resistance and overt rebellion cause capitalism to go into crisis, and both are factors in revolutionary transformation. Although everyday resistance is not the only cause of crisis, it is the one factor in which organizers and revolutionaries can have a direct impact through the reading, recording, circulation, and amplification of the new society in formation.

Documenting and understanding historical forms of resistance can illuminate present struggles and power relations but alone cannot substitute for a substantive and engaged analysis of working-class struggle. Further, to suggest that radicals can identify a singular revolutionary subject or predict the next upheaval before "reading the struggles" ignores the multitudinous nature of working-class self-activity and insurrection. There are no revolutionary prophets. Those who claim to be are charlatans, vanguardists, and authoritarians.

Everyday resistance is a politics by other means.[6] Another means to politics suggests new ways of detecting resistance in the present, aligning ourselves with it, as James, Boggs, and Castoriadis say, and producing knowledge about these struggles.[7] Organizers will need to produce and circulate their own knowledge, their own understanding of resistance and rebellion.

Increasingly, since the onset of neoliberal regimes of work and the rise of the service economy, workers' cooperative capacities are central to the production process. Capitalism in effect is the "labor problem" that is solved by capturing these capacities. Neoliberal capitalism has developed increasingly ingenious ways of seizure including just-in-time production and the temporary, service, and so-called sharing economies. Thus, still developing forms of everyday resistance will require sharp, perceptive contemporary militants to uncover and further them.

Let us look at this less abstractly. While working at a coffee shop it might sometimes be fun to interact with customers and workmates, but the same positive and outgoing attitude is required when one is having a terrible day. Emotional regimes of work are increasingly expected in jobs previously defined as material and manual—work done by the likes of plumbers and hairdressers. Now these workers aren't simply providing a service but an experience. Work refusal in these instances is not simply a method of maintaining one's productive capacities and physical energy but the preservation of emotional and mental well-being. Preserving one's self is difficult in care industries—the work done by nurses, in-home caregivers, health aides, day-care and social workers—as well. The Madrid-based feminist collective Precarias a la Deriva (loosely translated as Precarious Women Workers Adrift) once asked: "What is a care strike?"[8] Answering, they suggested that a reorganization of care, an interruption of the imposition of care work, will place this necessary activity on our political horizons. As with the Wages for Housework Campaign a generation before them, Precarias is calling attention to a form of work that is often devalued, gendered, and highly exploitative. Care work, as with housework, is necessary for capitalist accumulation and the production of its most important commodity: labor power.

Even as capitalism has sought to monetize care and housework it has undercut the working class's ability to reproduce itself though stagnating wages, increasing rents and commodity prices, a decrease in welfare payments, and destruction of unions. This seems contradictory as capitalism requires the reproduction of labor power for continued commodity production. If capitalism can attack the working class in the sphere of reproduction, then the class is easier to exploit in sphere of production. Workers need to show up ready to work, but they need not be well fed. Capitalists certainly don't want them to be able and willing to take risks such as committing acts of resistance or getting involved in union organizing.

Co-opting demands from the previous period—for flexible work and time off—capitalism has developed a veritable industry of temporary or contingent types of work, what European and South American social movements call precarious labor. Temporary agencies have sprung up to serve companies in need of on-call employees, workers who are immediately released upon the completion of a project. Manpower, Inc., and Robert Half International, for laborers and office workers respectively, are just two well-known companies of hundreds of such outfits. Periodicals such as *Processed World* and the *Temp Slave* zine chronicled the upsurge of temporary office workers who, per Chris Carlsson and Adam Cornford, understood "the collective power of information handlers to subvert the circulation of capital."[9] As office work, personal computers, and other new information technologies became increasingly central to capitalist production in the United States and Europe, it could be said that there was a shift from Fordist to post-Fordist production.

Identifying guerrillas of desire in offices, across coffee shop counters, and in Uber and Lyft cabs is beyond the scope of this work and is best done in situ. Concepts, comprehensive strategies, and books such as this one can narrow one's focus and aid in detecting precise forms of refusal, mutual aid, and self-activity. Theory is not a substitute for engaged, collective research and organizing. The role of textual interventions is to sharpen our analytical tools, our conceptual lenses. Nevertheless, to rethink the revolutionary project in our contemporary period we must, as Friedrich Nietzsche would suggest, "have the courage for an *attack* on [our] convictions!!!"[10]

LEFT COMMUNITY-BASED ORGANIZATIONS

Forefather of modern community organizing Saul Alinsky has entered contemporary popular discourse through being demonized by the Right rather than due to celebration by the Left. Alinsky committed the crime of empowering poor people and people of color, the "have-nots," to take away the power of the "haves." He launched citizens' groups, forged coalitions with civil and religious leaders, and sought to improve living conditions through pressure campaigns. The official organizations of the Left—political parties, unions, nonprofits, left-leaning religious groups, community-based organizations, and foundations—have largely abandoned his central charge of organizing poor people to act in their own self-interest. The Left has seemingly given up organizing altogether, unless it serves the immediate needs of a political campaign or contract renegotiation.

Meanwhile Alinsky is inadequate for understanding and furthering resistance and rebellion for three principal reasons. First, he personifies complex relations of power in adversarial figures—slumlords, bosses, or elected officials. Second, his conception of organizing is based upon making demands of the state for resources and recourse rather than building community-based institutions and demanding that the state pay for them. Third, Alinsky's descendants view working-class and poor communities as apathetic and unorganized. Since each of these attributes are still present in Left and even radical communities they are worth examining.

In the Alinsky model the community rallies against an enemy, a figure who represents power itself. This idea should be challenged. It is not simply the slumlord that holds or hordes power over tenants but an entire regime of accumulation, property ownership, state subsidies, unenforced regulations, real estate and business associations, nonprofit mediators, and the sheriff, who is the slumlord's last resort when subtler forms of coercion have failed and eviction has become indispensable. A wicked landlord cannot simply be replaced with a benevolent one. Although publicly shaming a landlord is an important part of a housing justice campaign, the property owner is part of a larger set of power relations. The personification of power lends credence to the terrible idea that one can read the face of power and then effectively speak truth to it. Much of the contemporary Left continues to believe that speaking the truth in itself has power, even after years of screaming themselves hoarse to no avail. Slumlords, bosses, and elected officials do not respond to truth, they respond to force. It is the role of organizers to clarify the individual and combined functions of landlords, bosses, and bureaucrats as part of a campaign to abolish them.

Nevertheless, Alinsky points to a common theme that is essential for all organizing when he suggests that "the potential organizer's personal experience" should always be used "as the basis for teaching."[11] It is the personal experiences and everyday resistance of potential organizers that are always drawn upon during a process of becoming a revolutionary. But this begs a question: what is the role of the teacher in Alinsky's model? The responsibility of Alinsky's teacher was to incorporate potential organizers into a preconceived organizational form (a citizens' group) and belief system (Left, progressive). Then the potential organizer is taught how to work within existing models and political systems to make demands of these systems for resources. As a result, potential organizers' experiences, reflections, and drives that thrust beyond the confines of the existing order are used by the state for its own renewal (that is, reform and minor redistribution of resources rather than new social relations). Moreover, prolonged contact with institutional and political machinations of the state (what Piven and Cloward call "structuring institutions") limits the possibilities for refusal and mutual aid.

As a potential organizer becomes part of an Alinskyite organization another question appears: what is the role of the organizer? Wade Rathke, ACORN founder, in developing his organizing model from Alinsky's earlier conception wrote in 1973, "The organizer is the key component in developing an un-organized and apathetic community into a viable organization."[12] Rathke's conception epitomizes a type of organizer, one who cannot recognize the already existing forms of struggle taking place in working-class communities. Other Alinsky-inspired models repeat similar mistakes. The authors of the Midwest Academy manual propose, "If organizers encounter people who seem apathetic, it is because we haven't been able to convince them that organizing is one way to get what they need. In fact, we usually don't know what they need because we don't understand their self-interest."[13] Such a statement makes assumptions about poor and working-class people. Apathy could be the result of repeated ineffectual attempts to go through legal and official channels individually and collaboratively or previous promises by Left organizers that went unfulfilled. Additionally, people who have figured out easier alternatives to directly address their needs are simply apathetic to outside agitation.

With the onset of neoliberalism Alinsky, the Industrial Areas Foundation, the Midwest Academy, and neighboring approaches enacted by ACORN arguably improved or preserved the material conditions of working-class and poor people during a period of crisis, austerity, and repression. (The contribution of anarchists and other radicals was marginal, as important as it was.) During the initial years of the social factory these organizations struggled to maintain their footing on violently shifting ground. Alinsky and his ilk created narrowly focused organizations rather than larger social movements with all their complexity and possibility for working-class and poor people. And the further we have traveled since the 1972 publication of Alinsky's *Rules for Radicals*, the deeper the Alinsky school has been incorporated into the political machinations of the state; such incorporation requires co-opting community discontent for political campaigns.[14] For instance, ACORN gave up its independence, was linked to the "progressive" Working Families Party and played a role in electing local and national Democratic Party candidates. The ACORN-Working Families strategy focused on building the left wing of the Democratic Party as the party itself and the larger society moved rightward.

Arguably, while Alinskyite community organizing approaches have had a considerable impact on contemporary methods, the rise of nonprofits and the decline of unions has more fundamentally changed the possibilities for organizing working-class and poor peoples.

RISE OF NONPROFITS, DECLINE OF UNIONS

Since the 1970s the neoliberal state has instituted policies of "deregulation, privatization, and [withdrawn] from many areas of social provision" as it has reflected "the interests of private property owners, businesses, multinational corporations, and financial capital."[15] As services have been privatized, austerity measures instituted, unionized workers demobilized and unions decertified, and the field of social services left fallow, a nonprofit sector has continued to develop in the arenas abandoned by the state. Regardless of its stated purposes, the sector has regulated the discontent of working-class and poor peoples, and it continues to do this. Struggle is managed through the nonprofit industry, and nonprofits mitigate demands made of the state for public resources.[16] How is this accomplished?

As Jeffery Barry and David Arons of Left-center think tank the Brookings Institute write, "The modern welfare state has largely been subcontracted to nonprofits.... Government provides a significant portion of the financial resources but by subcontracting the actual administration of programs to nonprofits, it is able to take advantage of the dedication, imagination, and private fund-raising capacity of these public-spirited organizations."[17] This subcontracting reflects how the federal government has increasingly abandoned Great Society programs, ideals, and standards. In effect, the government has privatized social services (to the nonprofit sector) and then expected civil society to raise funds to address the shortfall between need and limited government contracts. Further, citizens are providing a subsidy to the state in the form of volunteer work and financial contributions for services the state should be delivering. Nonprofit social services are not as accountable to public pressure campaigns or demands of individual recipients as government-provided services are, and hence it is a conservative force.

The nonprofit sector emerged during the 1970s. Then during the Reagan presidency, the dismantling of state services entered an accelerated phase. Nonprofits served to lubricate the process of privatization. Subsequently, beginning in the mid-1980s and continuing into the present, the nonprofit sector as a whole has increased dramatically (see figure 1). Compared to 1975, when 82,000 nonprofits accounted for $54 billion in annual revenue, in 1985 there were 107,000 nonprofits with annual revenue totaling $268 billion.[18] By 2012, these numbers reached 280,000 tax exempt organizations with $1.73 trillion in annual revenue.

FIGURE 1. SOURCE: INTERNAL REVENUE SERVICE

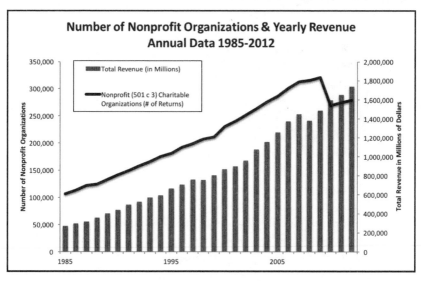

Gerald Ford didn't simply say that New York should "Drop Dead," as the *New York Daily News* headline shouted on October 30, 1975, but also that the unionized government workforce and the services it provided should as well. Government employment is now around 15.5 percent, down from its peak at 20 percent of the overall workforce in the early 1970s. The past four decades have been witness to the massive decline of unionized, waged government jobs in social services. These have been replaced by low-waged, non-union jobs in nonprofit fiefdoms. By 1997 "an estimated 52 percent of federal, state, and local government funds for social services went to nonprofits."[19] As of 2001, "approximately half of all nonprofits [were] involved in health care (11 percent) or human services (37 present)."[20] These trends, as with the growth of the sector, have continued into the present.

Nonprofits not only develop in relation to the "volunteer society" proposed by Reaganites and their Democratic Party confederates. They also become avenues to launder money for conservative and liberal causes, avenues used by wealthy donors who apply their dollars to social initiatives rather than allow them to be taxed. Some nonprofit organizations are administrators of poverty, thus preventing substantive structural change that would allow poor and working class people from obtaining direct control over the necessities of life. The control that nonprofit service providers have over the populations they serve is particularly stark when considering housing. The Team Colors Collective, of which I am part, suggests that nonprofits managed the housing crisis that erupted in 2008, although this could be said about nonprofit housing policy in general. We argue,

> Anger towards housing insecurity is frequently channeled through non-profits, and in the non-profit narrative.... When a personal crisis—such as a particular default or eviction—is overcome, the non-profits funded with the government's generous hand take the credit for standing up to or negotiating with a landlord or lender. In a certain way, these organizations ensure that the class offensive on the part of the state, capital, and non-profit bureaucrats is seen as an *all-in-this-together* effort supporting renters and homeowners. But when emergency rental assistance programs run out of funding, when court-mandated mediation attempts fail, or when the mortgage-holder *still* cannot pay their re-financed balance, the blame is placed on misfortune or the irresponsibility of tenants and homeowners, rather than the coordinated management of misery. *Neoliberal discourse requires that the blame always fall on the individual.*[21]

Nonprofits share numerous facets with neoliberal capitalism. Narratives of personal failure (couched as moral responsibility) are applied by the managers of our misery to those receiving social services.

As with contemporary capitalism's need for financialization (increased role and power of financial institutions in the economy), demands cannot be made of nonprofits for resources directly. Financialization and nonprofits are mechanisms to avoid demands. As the Midnight Notes Collective remarks, "The main function of the financialization of capital was to buffer accumulation from working class struggle by putting it beyond its reach and by providing a hedge against it by making it possible for capitalists to bet against the success of their own investments, hence providing insurance in any eventuality."[22] Nonprofits buffer public funding from working-class demands, while making it possible to discipline the class by excluding troublesome individuals from needed programs, closing or relocating services, or by aligning themselves with the needs of funders over those accessing services. Ultimately nonprofits, as with business unions, have served as managers of discontent during a period of stagnating wages, increased incarceration, and generalized war on the poor.

As nonprofits ascended, unions declined and with them the frequency and intensity of strikes. It has been said that the strike is the ultimate expression of the power of the working class, and this is one measure of working-class power vis-à-vis capitalism. Since the mid-1970s there has been a remarkable decrease in work stoppages. Charting the number of strikes involving one thousand or more workers since World War II, there was a peak in 1952, then again in 1969 and 1974, with a decline in frequency during the late 1970s.[23] Since this period the mass strike has never recovered its prominence (see figure 2). Subsequently, after the 2008 economic crisis there have been less than twenty strikes a year in the US involving one thousand or more workers. And it is not just the number of strikes that have decreased but their extent and arguably their efficacy as well, since business unions backtracked on concessions won from employers (wages, benefits, and retirement packages). Shorter and smaller strikes have replaced the larger workplace actions witnessed earlier. (I am not suggesting that longer, bigger strikes are better than smaller, shorter ones. Rather, it is an open question if unions, with decreased membership rosters and thinner strike funds, could hold up in a lengthy strike action against a multinational corporation with extensive assets.) While the decline of the strike can partly be attributed to the decrease in overall unionization, there are several other factors (including how public-sector union workers, such as teachers, are legally prohibited from striking). Unions have abandoned strikes for negotiated settlements and transactional relationships (services provided in exchange for union dues) with the rank and file. Capitalism responded to prior working-class struggle by decentralizing the workplace, special-izing tasks, and isolating "teams" of workers in the process. Corporate franchising separates larger blocks of workers into disconnected units. Additionally, deindustrialization, automation, and outsourcing jobs overseas directly attacked the industries with the highest rates of union-ization and worker militancy. With fewer workplaces of one thousand or more workers, fewer mass strike actions are taking place. Along with the decrease in strikes the present period has been witness to the decline of union density in the overall workforce.

FIGURE 2.SOURCE: BUREAU OF LABOR STATISTICS

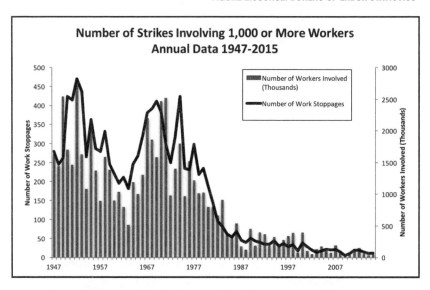

The period since the mid-1970s has been marked by considerable decrease in the percentage of the workforce that is unionized, declining from over 25 percent in the late 1970s to fewer than 15 percent in 2000. Since 2008 the rate has fallen steadily to 11.1 percent in 2014, and this percentage was maintained in 2015. Currently "public-sector workers [have] a union membership rate (35.3 percent) more than five times higher than that of private-sector workers (6.7 percent)."[24] Of course it is teachers and other public-sector unions that have come under the most scrutiny and attack recently. Business unions have been in decline since joining the National War Labor Board at the onset of World War II.[25] While there was a period of labor peace during the late 1950s and early 1960s, working-class self-activity peaked again through militant workplace actions outside of the official organizations of the Left during the late 1960s and early 1970s. Labor action coincided with the black freedom struggle, student antiwar movement, and planetary upheavals during this period. But from the late 1970s to the present, unions have shifted their focus away from organizing.[26]

At its finest, union organizing begins from two important assumptions: workers are the experts about their workplace, and "there are common problems and there are collective solutions."[27] Further, workplace organizing often begins with identifying militant leadership at the center of mutual aid networks and workers who have directly or indirectly refused orders of the boss, both of which build respect and recognition among workmates. Meanwhile business unions have receded from external organizing and instead have relied on contract negotiations, corporate pressure campaigns, lobbying, and legislative avenues. This confluence of factors has led to labor's decline and seeming inability to recover.

Along with the emergence of nonprofits, union decline, and development of neoliberalism, increasing social atomization and the loss of public space has marked the past forty years. We are "bowling alone," as illustrated by the disappearance of civic and social organizations while mutual activities of sports leagues, neighborhood associations, and religious groups have sharply decreased in the US.[28] Basically, the organized public sphere has been superseded by new online publics. The latter lack the social cohesion, embodied interaction, density of relationships, and cooperative impulse of the former. Meanwhile, public spaces—parks, squares, street corners—are being enclosed, public resources are becoming privatized, and "the right to be seen, to be heard, and to directly influence the state and society" itself is disappearing.[29] Without civil and social organizations, religious groups, and militant unions—that is, the societies that produce and weave the social fabric—individuals directly face the omnipresent power of the state and the blunt force of neoliberal capitalism.[30] Power is armed. It has always been armed. The question is whether we are going to go to our mountains and prepare to fire back.

AFFINITY GROUPS AND COLLECTIVES

As a result of the turbulent shifts at the end of the 1970s, radical movements have become increasingly cultural in nature. Consequently, they are often without formal organizational structures, recording devices (newsletters, newspapers, journals, and the like) and a method of determining if "the dose makes the poison."[31] In *Political Protest and Cultural Revolution*, the seminal text on the anti-nuke movement, Barbara Epstein argued in 1991 that "the attraction of cultural revolution, and the idea that culture is a substitute for strategy, has been an important current in the movements of the sixties and beyond" when "the critique of culture has come to be seen as in itself political practice."[32] That is, the customs and behavior of radicals within their own habitually insular and self-referential communities (as subcultures) replaced direct engagement with political institutions (state apparatuses and local governments) and economic institutions (business unions, corporations, etc.). The idea was that if the dominant American culture is criticized and in turn moves in a more liberatory direction, then the political and economic realms will as well. A few examples of this cultural turn are in order.

Several key texts, appearing decades apart, have shaped the contemporary radical imagination, and each contains arguments and concepts that were incorporated into notions of organizing. Initially out of step with their contemporaries, "The Tyranny of Structurelessness" (1970), "Anti-Mass: Methods of Organization for Collectives" (circa 1970–71), and "Give Up Activism" (2001) have each contributed to contemporary conceptions of radical politics.[33] That is not to say that any one of these texts serve a central, key, or unique role.[34] But these three were important to the cultural and tactical discussions that marked the counter-globalization movement and many formulations since.

Written as a direct response to the elitism of male-dominated radical movements of the 1960s, Jo Freeman's "The Tyranny of Structurelessness" is concerned with the inability of feminist consciousness-raising groups to move beyond the limitations of their organizing model. According to Freeman, "the basic problem didn't appear until individual rap groups exhausted the virtues of consciousness-raising and decided that they wanted to do something more specific. At this point they usually floundered because most groups were unwilling to change their structure when they changed their task."[35] The inability of consciousness-raising groups to take on new, structured configurations prevented them from advancing. While Freeman identifies structurelessness as a problem, Cathy Levine, in a subsequent article, claims the opposite. Levine believes that structure is offered by Freeman "as a solution to the strategic stalemate, as if structure would give us theoretical insight or relief from personal anxieties."[36] Tyrannies of structure and structurelessness continue to haunt our conversations about strategy. Rather we should ask: which organizational form is appropriate for the tasks before us with the dynamics and relationships that exist within current and possible future participants? Such an answer cannot be decided a priori. One's worldview, beliefs, or political doctrine cannot decide the appropriate form of organization independent of, or prior to, the task the organizational form will address.

"Anti-Mass" reads as if it could be an indirect response to Freeman's proposal (likely both are simply responses to debates taking place at the time) and directly addresses the cultural turn in radical politics. The pamphlet's anonymous authors view "the mass" as an undifferentiated social body produced by consumer capitalism so as to pacify the population. "The mass is unconscious of its social existence," they conclude, "because it is organized by Coca-Cola and IBM."[37] According to the "Anti-Mass" authors, a mass is unconscious, while a class is conscious. Since mass-based organization cannot lead the masses, the collective—as a small, leaderless group—must lead the class. Further, they define self-activity quite differently than the autonomist tradition does: "Self-activity is the reconstruction of the consciousness (wholeness) of one's individual life activity. The collective is what makes the reconstruction possible."[38] Putting definitional differences aside, if a collective is required for self-organization to occur, for consciousness to develop, then everyday resistance would require the collective to be politically meaningful and effective. Besides, the measure of working class self-activity, resistance, and rebellion (as argued throughout the book) is its composition, not its level of correct political consciousness.[39] In operation, "Anti-Mass" sets up a straw argument in its notion of mass to couch its vanguardism under an anarchist label.

Finally, "Give Up Activism" criticizes the role of the activist or militant as "a specialist or expert in social change." Since the anonymous author views specialization as being rooted in capitalism's division of labor and alienation, a revolutionary struggle "will involve the breaking out of all preconceived roles and the destruction of all specialism."[40] At first glance "Give Up Activism" appears to be a rebuttal of the vanguardism of "Anti-Mass" and its ilk, but it contains an undercurrent of anti-intellectualism while equating specialization with authoritarianism. A slight digression is required to explore this problem further.

While classical anarchism differentiated its criticism of authoritarianism in society from the idea of authority within an organization, contemporary radicals connect the two.[41] The 2009 book *Black Flame: The Revolutionary Class Politics of Anarchism and Syndicalism* addressed the matter by offering that "the broad anarchist tradition accepted a measure of coercion. This is a key issue, ignored by approaches that reduce anarchism to individualism and antistatism, or define anarchism as an opposition to any constraints on any individual."[42] Our current notion of anti-authoritarianism, outside *Black Flame*'s deceptively narrow conception of the "broad anarchist tradition," developed in part as a rejection of the coercive nature of revolutionary movements. Positions of authority in revolutionary organizations held by white, cisgendered heterosexual men, predominantly middle-class, not only essentially excluded participation by most of humanity but also severely impeded revolutionary possibilities. Hence, we should be wary of replicating relations of power within organizations, while being clear about the difference between authoritarianism and authority.

The inability of contemporary radicals to understand the difference between authoritarianism in society and authority in an organization is the result of the conflation of means and ends, what is now referred to as prefiguration. This is a consequence of anarchism going through a pacifist period during the 1940s through to the 1970s.[43] Authoritarian means result in authoritarian ends, fair enough. But rejecting expertise, knowledge, and specialized roles is not a critique of power relations within an organization or in society. When a seasoned militant cautions that a particular course of action proposed by a new activist should be reconsidered, the response is too often "you're authoritarian," or some variant thereof. Subcultural notions of antiauthoritarianism have been extended to those with any form of experience, hence expertise and knowledge. Thus, forms of everyday resistance cannot be inquired about, recorded, circulated, amplified, or intervened in without being impeded at times by this prohibition. "Give Up Activism" requires caution as it reinforces these subcultural notions.

Along with Freeman, Levine, and the anonymous authors of "Anti-Mass" and "Give Up Activism," contemporary radicals express concern about reproducing hierarchies and dominant relations of power in revolutionary organizations. In effect, while they are apprehensive about replicating capitalist divisions of labor, and rightly so, they equate any form of specialization with authoritarianism. Such a presumption is based on the oversimplified notion that since divisions of labor under capitalism are gendered, for instance, then specialization of labor is, as a result, always gendered. It would be nonsensical to presume that there would be no specialized human activities in a postrevolutionary society. If we look at daily necessities, it is clear that some specialization will be required. How will food, shelter, energy, transportation, education, child care and elder care, medicine and health care, cultural and productive activities, and social events be produced and organized? How are such activities distributed without replicating racialized, gendered, ageist, and ableist divisions of labor? These are open questions. Will each receive according to one's need and have the opportunity to produce according to one's ability while making fully participatory, directly democratic decisions in the institutions and organizations required to produce such daily needs in common? These are practical questions. Common projects that emerge out of everyday resistance practices will require a rejection of authoritarianism that limits revolutionary possibilities along with a recognition of the authority (ability, knowledge, proficiency, and influence) that develops inherently from engaging in cooperative activities.

Contemporary approaches

The contemporary period—wherein movements are "fluid, open, and constantly shifting across the terrain"—is difficult to decipher.[44] Contemporary revolutionaries rely on organizational arrangements such as affinity groups and collectives, but how these positions have been interpreted and deployed diverge widely. In the abstract, "affinity group" or "collective" as a designation simply refer to a level of formality. Clandestine cells created for a singular underground direct action are affinity groups, whereas closed organizations requiring prescribed membership duties and dues are collectives.

Putting collectives aside momentarily, the affinity group model requires further scrutiny. The model utilized by the Federación Anarquista Ibérica during the Spanish Revolution of 1936–39 required affinity groups to link up as part of a larger organizational body. Currently affinity groups defined by social networks and friendship groupings find their immediate predecessors in the counter-globalization movement. Nowadays affinity groups have internal affinity, but, unlike in revolutionary Spain, those participating in them have scant relationships with the neighborhoods, workplaces, and communities in which they are part. Furthermore, the external relationships are too often temporary and limited to a specific direct action or street mobilization. Without ongoing actions and spokescouncils (a collection or cluster of affinity groups) to coordinate demonstrations, affinity groups have often been isolated and lacked common purpose.

As for the collective, routinely it is viewed as a way to prefigure a new society. Prefiguration is a watered-down version of utopianism and is based in the simple claim that means should reflect ends. Social movement historian Chris Dixon identifies four types of "prefigurative praxis" as they appear in movement contexts: countercultural lifestyles, counter-institutions, interorganizational horizontalism, and "creating and practicing more egalitarian modes of interacting within movement contexts."[45] With the exception of counter-institutions, each of these attributes are as vague as they are commonly held. When applied historically, prefiguration allows us to identify the form and function of counter-institutions. But to propose that prefiguration is an operational concept—that by "creating and practicing more egalitarian modes of interacting" we will move toward a revolutionary society—borders on magical thinking.

Conceptually prefiguration is ambiguous, and politically and organizationally it is disastrous. I believe prefiguration fails to provide us with a useful understanding of the world for four main reasons. First, it justifies self-referential beliefs and insular subcultural movements while assuming that every "good" act, no matter how ineffectual, is a win since it prefigures another world.[46] Second, it cannot properly account for everyday resistance, for acts that are not *consciously* prefiguring a new world. For instance, there are numerous accounts of slaves maiming or killing themselves. While self-harm and suicide can reflect a desire for a new society, it is not a recording of the new society as such. There are some acts of resistance that do not or should not prefigure a new world. Third, prefiguration ignores the complex relationship between individual and social change: as the social order changes, so do individuals, and as individuals change, so does the social order. Behaviors prefigured now might not apply in a year, much less in a new society. Fourth, the overemphasis on means-ends congruence discounts the course of revolutionary struggle. Strategies, organizational forms, and ways of being that exist under capitalism and the state will be fundamentally different in a post-revolutionary society. Prefigurative politics draws our attention away from the close and careful examination of the composition of the working class since it maintains the false claim that our counter-institutions, lifestyles, and organizations connect the utopian future to the idealistic present.

Instead of viewing actions as prefigurative, they should be honored in their own right and understood as part of a continuum: from clandestine to aboveground, everyday to overt, democratic to undemocratic, liberatory to repressive, effective to ineffective, circulatory to stagnant, structured to structureless, formal to informal, historical to unhistorical and superhistorical.[47] Resistance and rebellion are simultaneously affective and material and theoretical.

The question is not whether an act is prefigurative. The questions are these: In which ways is an action emancipatory? What are its limitations? Where and why did it emerge (in context with numerous forces, desires, ideas), and what were its effects? What did it *do* affectively, materially, and theoretically? The idea that how we live now should reflect how we live following a revolutionary change is a fair and noble one, even when it does not allow for radicals to move from the present into this new world.

Currently affinity groups and collectives, in addition to Left community-based organizations, nonprofits, and business unions, are ill equipped to orient themselves toward resistance taking place in everyday life. Just as stale ideas, concepts hastily adopted into anarchist or autonomist theory from other traditions, and fixed theoretical structures restricted revolutionary thinking, the possibilities for revolutionary organizing have been constrained. False dichotomies such as spontaneous and organized, underground and aboveground, pre-political and political, and unconscious and conscious are imposed on working-class self-activity, as is the dualism of resistance versus institution-building. Most importantly, a priori ideological conceptions prevent "reading the struggles"—making sense of politics—in any substantive and productive way.

Contemporary revolutionary organizing, defined broadly to include all organizational forms from the temporary clandestine cell to the formal nonprofit, are predicated on the assumption that working-class and poor people are neither organizing nor resisting. To paraphrase voices common in contemporary movements, either we will need the spark of an insurrection or the patient educational process of a social anarchist study group to generalize revolutionary struggle across the population. Everyday resistance suggests that a generalized revolt against work already exists and that it is the role of organizers to inquire into, amplify, circulate, and propagate the refusal of work and practices of mutual aid expressed by the working class. In doing so, everyday resistance and overt rebellion as factors in revolution become increasingly perceptible, other possibilities for politics appear, and a new front opens in the struggle against capitalism and the state.

ORGANIZERS TO COME, ORGANIZATIONS "ALL THE WAY DOWN"

In perusing organizing manuals from Labor Notes (the Labor Education and Research Project), the War Resisters League, Service Employees International Union, the IWW, and other organizations already mentioned, it's remarkable how nearly none of them answer a simple question: where do organizers (and organizations) come from? Nearly all begin—and continue as the War Resisters League manual does—with the first chapter serving to provide an ideological justification for the organization's politics only be trailed by "Organizing a Local Group" as the second chapter.[48] The Labor Notes manual, *A Troublemakers Handbook*, starts by suggesting that organizers initiate organizing by asking questions and listening to the answers. Fair enough. This is then followed by a guide to mapping one's workplace.[49] Only fifty-two words in the handbook are dedicated to finding "the natural leaders." In Eric Mann's *Playbook for Progressives: 16 Qualities of the Successful Organizer*, part 1 is titled "The Job Description" and subsequent chapters are titled "The Foot Soldier," "The Evangelist," "The Recruiter," and "The Group Builder."[50] These titles suggest that organizers are born fully formed. Nonprofits and business unions often hire organizers directly out of college instead of from the communities and shop floors where they will be operating. So Mann's job titles—foot soldier, evangelist, recruiter, group builder—are apropos. Each of these manuals continue by describing coalition building, working with different fully formed constituencies, and mounting media strategies. Rarely is there a section on developing conversations and dialogues. None address how to inquire into existing modes of informal organizing or methods of survival in any substantive manner.

There is an approach not yet described that I will refer to as organizations "all the way down." What are the integral elements of an organization? Where are its precursors? Who told the hallowed stories that predate its formation? What experiences and encounters has the organizer emerged from? Where have these been recorded, and how can those of us acting in common amplify, circulate, and propagate these experiences and expressions? What are the constituent elements, forces, relationships, materials, needs, and desires that came together and allowed this organization to emerge? A response to these queries would require militants to investigate the constituent elements, forces, relationships, materials, needs, and desires that *could* emerge and are in fact emerging. Becoming attuned to the taxonomy of struggle, to everyday resistance in this manner, in turn requires a new type of organizer.

Organizers to come will develop out of personal experiences marked by the refusal of work and practices of mutual aid. They will use analyses of the rich and substantive history of revolutionary movements in addition to staging encounters with one another that will produce, circulate, and accumulate knowledge. These organizers will always be growing, always becoming facilitators, ethnographers, inventors of culture and custom, and coordinators of collective life. Community dialogues are just one method of uncovering everyday resistance. To this we can add assemblies, surveys, inquiries, engaging public performances, and other means. It is from these processes that the principles that will define a new society will emerge.

Gilles Deleuze and Felix Guattari illustrate the process of revolutionary becoming by using the metaphor of the wasp and the orchid.[51]

In the life cycles of these organisms the wasp pollinates the orchid, while the orchid provides sustenance to the wasp. Each needs the other. The wasp in returning to its nest performs a dance to alert the colony as to the location of the orchid. The orchid emits electrical fields to communicate with and attract the wasp. Wasps and orchids map one another. They have previously co-evolved, and they will continue to evolve together. They become different together because of this relationship. Revolutionary becoming functions identically. Becoming a revolutionary requires encounters with the affective, material, and theoretical aspects of the world—of everyday resistance and overt struggle. Correspondingly, becoming a revolutionary requires confronting the limits imposed by capital, the state, and the social order. It requires confrontation. In this sense, as Silvia Federici argues, "power educates."[52]

The role of the organizer is to further the revolutionary becoming of those with whom they engage. I am not suggesting that relationships happen naturally, spontaneously, or by simply following a whim. Encounter is an intensive and inventive process, and one does not simply conclude the process. Just as we do not stop learning during the course of our lives, organizers do not earn their designation by reading a manual, and militants do not become revolutionary by bestowing that label upon themselves. Similarly, there is no difference between organizers to come and the guerrillas of desire. The organizer and the guerrilla are points on a continuum. The role of this new type of organizer is defined by one's inquiry into everyday resistance. The organizer's task is to assist with the emergence and growth of this resistance, to amplify and circulate its struggles and the knowledge those struggles produce. This task is our task, and in the process we "recognize the new society, align ourselves with it, and record the facts of its existence."[53] In this sense the organizer will be attentive toward addressing needs (such as constructing Survival Pending Revolution programs along the lines of those of the Black Panther Party, which provided free breakfast, medical care, and access to urban farms) and desires (to learn, to commune, to be productive). Finally, organizers to come must delineate between the desire to repress and the desire to liberate, between *potestas* and *potentia*.

Our capitalist and statist enemies are clear: the "organizers of [our] boredom" (to reference Raoul Vaneigem) prefer cannibalism, a scorched earth, and the Rapture to the possibility of giving up a miniscule portion of their ill-gotten luxuries.[54] It is too simple to say that the Germans were duped by fascism. It is too easy to claim that white Americans are stupid and thus voted against their interests while placing their hope in the authoritarian abyss of the Trump regime. *Potestas* and *potentia* appear as impulses in everyday life and can become imperatives.[55] Uncovering *potestas* and aiding *potentia* will require interventions into the everyday lives of guerrillas struggling and organizing. How to intervene and what kind of intervention is required cannot be answered in the abstract. Rather, the organizer must be able to distinguish between liberatory and repressive impulses and what needs and desires these impulses satisfy. This task, as with the many tasks of the organizers to come, is a collective endeavor—one we must undertake in common.

8

CONCLUSION: TO MAKE A REVOLUTION POSSIBLE

The task of the revolutionary is to produce new kinds of relationships between human beings. Such a generative process begins in the actually existing struggles of the working class: in everyday resistance, the refusal of work, mutual aid, and self-activity. Correspondingly, the revolutionary is an organizer who encounters, records, amplifies, and circulates the new society as it appears in these struggles. These ideas and proposals will not be proven independent of the struggles they illuminate and certainly not in texts such as this one. Only as part of a living, experimental revolutionary project can contemporary radical movements in the United States begin to construct forms of organization and ways of life appropriate for liberating the working class from the imposition of work in all its guises.

I have set out to challenge existing paradigms, theoretical and organizational. Evidence of everyday resistance in prior times and in our own period is at the center of this challenge. In this book I have attempted to accomplish four things: first, to illustrate linkages between theorists and scholars attuned to practices of everyday resistance; second, to argue that everyday resistance is a factor in revolution; third, to initiate reconsideration of both the anarchist tradition and the autonomist current; and fourth, to recommend useful concepts (everyday resistance, crises of capitalism, social factory, workerism, state as apparatus, *potestas* and *potentia*) and metaphors (guerrillas of desire, a world where many worlds fit) for revolutionary theory and mobilization. Accounting for everyday resistance necessitates all four of these charges.

I have strived to demonstrate how everyday resistance, as one factor among many, creates crises in capitalism. Further, in concert with overt rebellion, everyday resistance is part of a constellation of actions that can lead to "working class victory (revolutionary defeat of capital[ism])."[1] Through acts of everyday resistance the working class attempts to "annihilate the forces of the State, destroy the State-form."[2] And the state responds. Not only must the state attempt to provide for the smooth operation and continued reproduction of a particular mode of production (historically capturing escaped slaves, taxing peasants, disciplining students and workers, and ensuring continued divisions of labor), it also needs to manage the welfare of the population (which it does by policing, controlling territory, monopolizing violence, administering resources unequally, and unevenly delivering educational and health services) and intervene in civil society in order to ensure cooperation—and loyal opposition—from the academy, unions, nonprofit organizations, and religious and professional associations. I have attempted to demonstrate how the working class is autonomous from capitalism, the state, and the relations of power that flow through and animate these systems.

In a similar fashion, I have suggested a framework—a taxonomy— for examining everyday resistance in the present and in situ. I have proposed two general classifications (creating counter-communities and "a multiplicity of expressions, a myriad of forms") with specific but adaptable sub-categories (solidarity, communication, and mutual aid in the former; theft, sabotage, feigning illness, suicide, slowdowns and strikes, exodus, arson, and assassination, among others, in the latter). These theories require field-testing, measurement, fine-tuning, and further inquiry. Investigating class composition and working-class self-activity, with the intent of amplifying and circulating this activity, requires a willingness to experiment and adapt.

There is much to be done, theoretically and in practice. An intellectual project that could, in part, reinvigorate the revolutionary tradition for our current age will begin with inquiry. Movement historian Andrew Cornell suggested in his recent book *Unruly Equality: U.S. Anarchism in the 20th Century*, "Broadly speaking, [between 1916 and 1972] the anarchists tended to theorize from their own experiences rather than investigating the ways in which groups of people occupying different subject positions experience power."[3] Arguably, even by incorporating intersectional feminism, critical race, and queer theory into anarchism, contemporary radicals haven't sufficiently developed ways of understanding that struggle and revolutionary subjectivity cannot be reduced to a singular or a priori position or personality.

Approaches from Autonomist Marxism—"reading the struggles" and the search for revolutionary subjectivities—is a possible, and in my mind necessary, corrective.

A reading of contemporary struggles demands further investigation. To produce knowledge as part of a revolutionary endeavor one should begin with a political reading of working-class self-activity. Such a reading should attempt to identify the particular attributes of struggle in a specific context and how collaborative and collective initiatives might intervene. There is a need for oral and amateur historians, folklorists, archival researchers, keen observers, wool weavers, seed sowers, and wanderers. Organizers have important roles in uncovering everyday resistance through staging community dialogues and other assemblies, conducting surveys and inquiries, engaging public performances, and other means. For the textually and historically minded, further research is needed on the specific role that working-class self-activity has in forcing capitalism into crisis, from the economic crises of 1857 to the present, including the 2008 housing and financial crisis. Moreover, the refusal of work is just one form of resistance among many. How this refusal combines with other forms of resistance—against the likes of white supremacy, settler colonialism, heteropatriarchy—has not been sufficiently addressed by autonomists. Finally, *Guerrillas of Desire* has focused on the sphere of production in relation to the sphere of reproduction. A subsequent text that centers on the domestic sphere, on the reproduction of labor power, is required to fully account for the resistance against capitalism.

Tomorrow's revolutionaries will rely on new forms of organization designed to address particular needs, tasks, and purposes. Hence, new ways of becoming revolutionary, of being an organizer, are essential. Organizers to come will no longer think from the level of the organization on up to coalitions, federations, and networks. Rather, these organizers will investigate the organization all the way down to its constituent parts, desires, and relations of power. All the well-meaning plans and collectives will be for naught if revolutionaries cannot recognize working-class self-activity, methods of struggle, and modes of organizing life among the working class. Becoming revolutionary is a process of becoming other than what capitalism and the state apparatus has *made* us—a process concomitant with collective self-making within the confines of present society. As the society changes, so does the individual; as individuals change, so does the society. Consequently, this "becoming other" is against purity, against homogeneity, against utopian impulses, against prefiguration and martyrdom and celebrity. It is those who inhabit the small, nearly imperceptible moments who are the harbingers of refusal and resistance, rebellion, and possible revolution. Thus, the new society exists in the refusal of work and the embrace of mutual aid and working-class self-activity. A new society begins, in part, in everyday resistance.

NOTES

Chapter 1. Introduction: Guerrillas of Desire

1   Silvia Federici, "Wages against Housework," in *Revolution at Point Zero: Housework, Reproduction, and Feminist Struggle* (Oakland: PM Press, 2012), 21.

2   Autonomist Marxism as it is presently conceived can be distinguished by three general positions. First, it considers the working class to be the primary antagonist in the class struggle rather than simply reactive to capitalist command. Autonomist Marxism views the working class as functioning autonomously from both capital and the official organizations of the class. Second, Autonomist Marxism sees working-class struggle as the cause of crisis under capitalism, directly confronting the assumption and argument that economic crisis is caused solely or predominately by overproduction, tendency of the rate of profit to fall, or capitalist competition. Third, and finally, Autonomist Marxism can be delineated from orthodox Marxism and other radical traditions by its use of Marxian categories such as self-activity, self-valorization, cycles of struggle, the reproduction of labor-power (unwaged housework), an expanded concept of the working class (that includes students, housewives, peasants, and workers in the social factory in addition to the industrial proletariat), and attention to the refusal of work.

3   Frances Fox Piven and Richard A. Cloward, *Poor People's Movements: Why They Succeed, How They Fail* (New York: Vintage Books, 1979), xxiii.

4   Karl Marx and Friedrich Engels, *The Communist Manifesto*, Samuel Moore, trans. (New York: Penguin Books, 1985), 84.

5   Informal conversation with the author, circa early 2000s. It is important to note that I am drawing on two tributaries that make up the current of Autonomist Marxism. The first emphasizes the refusal of work, while the second focuses on the commons. Initially these were viewed as separate

ways, but since the 1990s they have increasingly been articulated together.

6   See Institute on Race and Poverty, *Racism and the Opportunity Divide on Long Island* (Minneapolis: Institute on Race and Poverty, 2002), http://racialequitytools.org/resourcefiles/irp.pdf; Conor Cash, "Decomposition and Suburban Space," *Affinities: A Journal of Radical Theory, Culture, and Action* (Winter 2010), http://ojs.library.queensu.ca/index.php/affinities/article/view/6151.

7   Peter Linebaugh, *The Magna Carta Manifesto: Liberties and Commons for All* (Berkeley: University of California Press, 2008), 45–46.

8   Thomas Buechele, conversation with author, November 4, 2015.

9   Stanley Aronowitz, "On Narcissism," in *The Crisis in Historical Materialism: Class, Politics, and Culture in Marxist Theory* (New York: Praeger, 1981), 294–95. Emphasis added. It is from this fragment, this notion, that this book's title is drawn.

10   Sam Dolgoff, "The Rural Collectivist Tradition," in *The Anarchist Collectives: Workers' Self-management in the Spanish Revolution 1936–1939* (Montreal: Black Rose Books, 1990), 20.

11   While broadly attributed to Margaret Mead, the source of this well circulated quote is unclear. See "Frequently Asked Questions about Mead and Bateson," Institute for Intercultural Studies, http://www.interculturalstudies.org/faq.html.

12   The absurdity of naming the conference after a Monty Python catchphrase was not lost on conference organizers.

13   As part of our preparations for these community dialogues, collective members read Paulo Freire's *Pedagogy of the Oppressed* (New York: Continuum, 1997).

14   "Let us not love in word, neither in tongue; but in deed and in truth." 1 John 3:18 (King James version).

15   I have expanded upon the notion of anarchist principles in two readily available articles. Kevin Van Meter, "Freely Disassociating: Three Stories on Contemporary Radical Movements," *Perspectives on Anarchist Theory*, June 8, 2015, http://anarchiststudies.org/2015/06/08/freely-disassociating-three-stories-on-contemporary-radical-movements-by-kevin-van-meter; Kevin Van Meter, "Insurgent Islands: A Continuing Conversation on Anarchism with Principles," *Perspectives on Anarchist Theory*, November 9, 2016; https://anarchiststudies.org/2015/11/09/insurgent-islands-a-continuing-conversation-on-anarchism-with-principles-by-kevin-van-meter.

16   George Caffentzis has used the phrase "reading the struggles" in numerous public presentations over the past two decades (I can attest to this). See also Caffentzis, *In Letters of Blood and Fire: Work, Machines, and the Crisis of Capitalism* (Oakland: PM Press, 2013). I riff here on Kropotkin, whose *Mutual Aid* begins, "Two aspects of animal life impressed me most during

the journeys which I made in my youth in Eastern Siberia and Northern Manchuria." Peter Kropotkin, *Mutual Aid: A Factor of Evolution* (London: Freedom Press, 1993), 12.

17   Luis Brennan kindly suggested this necessary aside. Conversation with the author, circa February 2017.

18   Guido Baldi (Silvia Federici and Mario Montano), "Thesis on Mass Worker and Social Capital," *Radical America* 6, no. 3 (May 1972): 3–21.

19   Scholar Vinay Gidwani describes theoretical concepts as "a sense-making machine." Conversation with the author, circa May 2015.

20   The roots of this book, *Guerrillas of Desire*, as an organizing and intellectual endeavor, go back not only to the early days of the counter-globalization movement, as documented here, but also to research conducted during my undergraduate and graduate studies. The initial result of my studies took the form of a master's thesis titled "The Silent Guerrillas." I have used a new title for this book not simply to distinguish it from the thesis but also for an additional political reason. The term "silent" perhaps connotes that guerrillas are restraining themselves, but in fact they are only silent at times before state bureaucrats and bosses. Kevin Van Meter, "The Silent Guerrillas: Under Slavery, In Peasant Politics, and throughout the Industrial and Social Factories" (master's thesis, 2014, City University of New York).

21   It is important to note that I am repurposing Durruti's quote here. He was arguing about building barricades, and I am speaking about digging though the dust of history and ideology to find everyday resistance. Once this is dug up, barricades will certainly be needed. Buenaventura Durruti quoted in Abel Paz, *Durruti in the Spanish Revolution*, Chuck Morse, trans. (Oakland: AK Press, 2006), 478, 536, 537.

22   CUNY professor Forrest Colburn, who has written about everyday peasant resistance, once remarked to me circa 2004 that the highest compliment an author can receive is that one's writing is embedded with "human qualities."

23   Kira Smith kindly suggested marrying the goals of the book to reading strategies. Conversation with the author, circa February 2017.

Chapter 2. Recognizing the New Society

1   Martin Glaberman and Seymour Faber, *Working for Wages: The Roots of Insurgency* (New York: General Hall, 1998), 8.

2   C.L.R. James, Grace C. Lee (Grace Lee Boggs), and Pierre Chaulieu (Cornelius Castoriadis), *Facing Reality* (Detroit: Bewick Editions, 1974), 125.

3   James C. Scott, *Weapons of the Weak: Everyday Forms of Peasant Resistance* (New York: Yale University Press, 1985); George Rawick, *From Sundown to Sunup* (Westport, CT: Greenwood, 1972); James, Lee, and

Chaulieu, *Facing Reality*; Federici, *Revolution at Point Zero*. See also Anna Grimshaw, ed., *The C.L.R. James Reader* (Hoboken, NJ: Wiley-Blackwell, 1992).

4   James, Lee, and Chaulieu, *Facing Reality*, 166.

5   David Roediger, "Black Freedom and the Slave Narrative: An Interview with George Rawick," in *Listening to Revolt: The Selected Writings of George Rawick*, ed. David Roediger and Martin Smith (Chicago: Charles H. Kerr, 2010), 73.

6   Rebecca Solnit, *A Paradise Built in Hell: The Extraordinary Communities that Arise in Disasters* (New York: Penguin Books, 2009); Andrej Grubacic and Denis O'Hern, *Living at the Edges of Capitalism: Adventures in Exile and Mutual Aid* (Oakland: University of California Press, 2016).

7   Chris Dixon, *Another Politics: Talking Across Today's Transformative Movements* (Oakland: University of California Press, 2014), 85.

8   George Orwell, "Notes on the Way," in *My Country Right or Left, 1940–1943*, ed. Sonia Orwell and Ian Angus (Boston: David R. Godine, 1968), 16. Emphasis in original.

9   The English language shackles our comprehension with the prefix "self." The prefix *auto*, as in *autovalorizzazione* (auto-valorization), might be preferable. In the English language "self" connotes "individual," as in "self-advancement," "self-interest," and "self-made," and so "self-activity" may tend to be construed as entailing the ego—an individual worker, citizen, consumer, or voter. "Auto" more typically refers to spontaneity or an internal drive. For instance, "automobile" refers to a vehicle propelled by the internal combustion engine of the machine itself. Whatever the name, what the concepts of auto-activity, auto-valorization, auto-management, and auto-organization in turn describe is the autonomous unfolding of activity, value, coordination, and organization. Each concept points to levels of internally determined emergences that animate *potentia* and are directed by said internal forces and principles. Harry Cleaver, "Kropotkin, Self-Valorization, and the Crisis of Marxism," *Anarchist Studies* 2, no. 2 (1994): 119. For more on the question of translating "auto" as "self," see Harry Cleaver, "H. Cleaver on Self-Valorization in Mariarosa Dalla Costa's 'Women and the Subversion of the Community' (1971)," https://la.utexas.edu/users/hcleaver/357k/HMCDallaCostaSelfvalorizationTable.pdf.

10   Peter Kropotkin, *Mutual Aid: A Factor of Evolution* (London: Freedom Press, 1993), 234.

11   Ibid., 231.

12   Pierre Clastres, *Archeology of Violence*, trans. Jeanine Herman (New York: Semiotext(e), 1994), 88. See also Pierre Clastres, "Copernicus and the Savages," "Exchange and Power: Philosophy of the Indian Chieftainship," and

"Society Against the State," in, *Society Against the State*, trans. Robert Hurley (New York: Zone Books, 1987).

13 Harry Cleaver, *Reading* Capital *Politically* (Leeds: Anti/Theses; San Francisco: AK Press, 2000), 18.

14 George Rawick, "Working-class Self-Activity" in *Radical America*, 3, no. 2 (1969): 23–31.

15 Cleaver, "Kropotkin, Self-Valorization, and the Crisis of Marxism," 123.

16 Steve Wright, *Storming Heaven: Class Composition and Struggle in Italian Autonomist Marxism* (London: Pluto Press, 2002), 3. Emphasis in original.

17 Robert Graham, *We Do Not Fear Anarchy, We Invoke It: The First International and the Origins of the Anarchist Movement* (Oakland: AK Press, 2015), 51–52.

18 Ibid., 59.

19 Michael Bakunin, "Principles and Organization of the International Brotherhood," in *Michael Bakunin: Selected Writings*, ed. Arthur Lehning (London: Jonathan Cape, 1973), 81, noted in Graham, *We Do Not Fear Anarchy*, 75.

20 Paul Buhle, *Marxism in the United States: A History of the American Left*, 3rd. ed. (New York: Verso 2013), 35.

21 Quoted in Graham, *We Do Not Fear Anarchy*, 75.

22 Buhle, *Marxism in the United States*, 75.

23 Andrew Cornell, *Unruly Equality: U.S. Anarchism in the 20th Century* (Oakland: University of California Press, 2015), 121.

24 Karl Marx, *Capital*, vol. 1, trans. Ben Fowkes (New York: Penguin, 1990), 873.

25 Ann Lucas de Rouffignac, *The Contemporary Peasantry in Mexico* (Westport, CT: Praeger, 1985), 25.

26 Karl Marx and Friedrich Engels, *The Communist Manifesto*, trans. Samuel Moore (New York: Penguin Books, 1985), 83.

27 Cleaver, *Reading* Capital *Politically*, 82.

28 Marx, *Capital*, vol. 1, 125.

29 Geoffrey Ingham, *Capitalism* (London: Polity, 2008), 53. Additionally I recommend a book that draws upon Ingham: Geoff Mann, *Disassembly Required: A Field Guide to Actually Existing Capitalism* (Oakland: AK Press, 2013).

30 Harry Cleaver in discussion with Massimo De Angelis, July 1993. Published as "An Interview with Harry Cleaver," https://la.utexas.edu/users/hcleaver/InterviewwithHarryCleaver.html.

31 Peter Marshall, *Demanding the Impossible: A History of Anarchism* (Oakland: PM Press, 2010), 3.

32 Peter Kropotkin, *The State: Its Historic Role* (London: Freedom Press, 1997), 10.

33 Ibid.; emphasis in original.

34 Murray Bookchin, "Anarchism, Power, and Government," *New Compass*, http://new-compass.net/articles/anarchism-power-and-government.

35 Nestor Makhno, *The Struggle Against the State and Other Essays*, ed. Alexandre Skirda, trans Paul Sharkey (San Francisco: AK Press, 1996), 56.

36 Janet Biehl with Murray Bookchin, *The Politics of Social Ecology: Libertarian Municipalism* (Montreal: Black Rose Books, 1998); Antonio Negri, "Constituent Republic," in *Revolutionary Writing: Common Sense Essays in Post-Political Politics*, trans. Werner Bonefeld (Brooklyn: Autonomedia, 2003).

37 Gilles Deleuze and Felix Guattari, *Nomadology: The War Machine* (New York: Semiotext(e), 1986), 111.

38 The phrase "higher powers," the relations of power ordained by God, and the state apparatus in which God's ordination is secularized have biblical origins, as one might suspect. In the King James version of the Bible, Romans 13:1–2 declares, "Let every soul be subject unto the higher powers. For there is no power but of God: the powers that be are ordained of God. Whosoever therefore resisteth the power, resisteth the ordinance of God: and they that resist shall receive to themselves damnation." Secular states have adopted Machiavelli's maxim, that "armed prophets have conquered, and unarmed prophets have come to grief" and ascribed to Thomas Hobbes's belief that natural and civil powers are best "united by consent, in one person [or, in modern parlance, one governing body] ... that has the use of all their Powers depending on his will; such as is the Power of a Common-wealth." These "powers that be" require the threat, says Hobbes, of "Warre; and such a warre, as is of every man, against every man" and salvation in civil obedience and the social contact. Niccolò Machiavelli, *The Prince*, trans. George Bull (New York: Penguin Books, 1995), 19; Thomas Hobbes, *Leviathan*, ed. C.B. MacPherson, (New York: Penguin Books, 1981), 150, 185.

39 Michel Foucault, "Subject and Power," in *Beyond Structuralism and Hermeneutics*, 2nd. ed., ed. Hubert L. Dreyfus and Paul Rabinow (Chicago: University of Chicago Press, 1983), 211.

40 Glaberman and Faber, *Working for Wages*, 8.

41 Marx, *Capital*, vol. 1, 125.

42 Cleaver, *Reading* Capital *Politically*, 82.

43 It should be noted that I am speaking about capitalist production in an abstract, ideal way. Furthermore, this immediate process of production does not address financial commodities or financialization.

44 Marx, *Capital*, vol. 1, 342.

45 Deuteronomy 12:23.

46 For Mario Tronti, exploitation is necessary since "the conditions of capital are in the hands of the workers" as "there is no active life in capital without the living activity of labor power," hence "the capitalist class ... is in fact subordinate to the working class." Mario Tronti, "The Strategy of Refusal," in *Autonomia: Post-Political Politics* (Los Angles: Semiotext(e), 2007), 31.

47 Marx, *Capital*, vol. 1 1, 376–77.

48 Antonio Negri, *Marx Beyond Marx: Lessons on the Grundrisse* (Brooklyn: Autonomedia; London: Pluto, 1991), 72; Marx, *Capital*, vol. 1, 341. Negri is also referring to Karl Marx, *Grundrisse*, trans. Martin Nicolaus (New York: Penguin Books, 1993), 282–89.

49 Silvia Federici, "The Reproduction of Labor Power in the Global Economy and the Unfinished Feminist Revolution," in *Revolution at Point Zero*, 93. Federici is referring to Marx, *Capital*, vol. 1, 376–77.

50 Cleaver, *Reading* Capital *Politically*, 83–84. Emphasis in original.

51 The phrase "black proletariat" is from W. E. B. Du Bois, *Black Reconstruction* (New York: Harcourt, Brace and Company, 1935. For an autonomist take on the matter, see Ferruccio Gambino's "W. E. B. Du Bois and the Proletariat in *Black Reconstruction*," Libcom.org, https://libcom.org/library/w-e-b-du-bois-proletariat-black-reconstruction-ferruccio-gambino. Historian of slavery and capitalism John Ashworth suggests, "We may define class relationally in terms of the relationship between two groups at the point of production, where one group is seeking to appropriate to itself some or all of the labor of the other. On this definition slaves and slaveholders comprise classes." John Ashworth, *Slavery, Capitalism, and Politics in the Antebellum Republic*, vol. 1, *Commerce and Comprise, 1820–1850* (New York: Cambridge University Press, 1995), 13.

52 Ann Lucas de Rouffignac, *The Contemporary Peasantry in Mexico* (Westport, CT: Praeger, 1985), 55.

53 Glaberman and Faber, *Working for Wages*, 13; Zerowork Collective, "Introduction to Zerowork 1," in *Midnight Oil: Work, Energy, War 1973-1992*, ed. Midnight Notes Collective (New York: Autonomedia, 1992), 111–12. Emphasis in original.

54 Joanna Brenner, "Class," in *Keywords for Radicals: The Contested Vocabulary of Late-Capitalist Struggle*, eds. Kelly Fritsch, Clare O'Connor, and AK Thompson, (Chico: CA: AK Press, 2016), 80.

55 Ibid., 85.

56 Stanley Aronowitz, *How Class Works: Power and Social Movement* (New Haven: Yale University Press, 2003), 62.

57 Kathi Weeks, *The Problem with Work: Feminism, Marxism, Antiwork Politics, and Postwork Imaginaries* (Durham: Duke University Press, 2011), 94.

58 Antonio Negri, "Potentialities of a Constituent Power," in *Labor of Diony-sus: A Critique of the State-Form* (Minneapolis: University of Minnesota Press, 1994), 273.

59 Friedrich Engels, *The Condition of the Working Class in England*, trans. David McLellan, (New York: Oxford University Press, 1993), 96; Karl Marx, *Capital*, vol. 1, 794.

60 As Cleaver offered, "The struggle against the imposition of work has been central to the history of the making of the working class, from the initial resistance to the original imposition of work in the period of primitive accumulation through the long centuries of resisting and avoiding the expansion of work time (longer, harder hours) to the more recent aggressive struggles to reduce work time and liberate more open-ended time for self-determined activity." Harry Cleaver, "Theses on Secular Crisis in Capitalism: The Insurpassability of Class Antagonisms," paper presented at Rethinking Marxism Conference, Amherst, Massachusetts, November 13, 1992; https://la.utexas.edu/users/hcleaver/secularcrisis.html.

61 Zerowork Collective, "Introduction to Zerowork 1."

62 Harry Cleaver, "Marxian Categories, the Crisis of Capital and the Constitution of Social Subjectivity Today," in *Revolutionary Writing: Common Sense Essays in Post-Political Politics*, ed. Werner Bonefeld (Brooklyn: Autonomedia, 2003), 43. Originally published in *Common Sense* ("Journal of the Edinburgh Conference of Socialist Economists"), no. 14 (1993): 32–55.

63 Nick Dyer-Witheford, *Cyber-Marx: Cycles and Circuits of Struggle in High-Technology Capitalism* (Urbana: University of Illinois Press, 1999), 66. Emphasis in original.

64 Toni Negri, "Archeology and Project: The Mass Worker and The Social Worker," in *Revolution Retrieved: Selected Writings of Marx, Keynes, Capitalist Crisis and New Social Subjects, 1967–83* (London: Red Notes, 1988), 209.

65 E. P. Thompson, *The Making of the English Working Class* (New York: Vintage Books, 1966), 9–11.

66 Henry Ford, quoted by Willis Thornton, *New York World-Telegram*, July 24, 1933.

67 Barbara Ehrenreich and John Ehrenreich, "The Professional-Managerial Class," in *Between Labor and Capital*, ed. Pat Walker (Boston: South End Press, 1979).

68 Anton Pannekoek, *Workers Councils* (Oakland: AK Press, 2002), 8.

Chapter 3. From Concept to Metaphor

1 Harry Cleaver, discussion with the author, January 8, 2006.

NOTES

2   Ibid.

3   Ibid.

4   Ibid.

5   Kristian Williams, "The Other Side of the COIN: Counterinsurgency and Community Policing," in *Life during Wartime: Resisting Counterinsurgency*, ed. Kristian Williams, Will Munger, Lara Messsersmith-Glavin (Oakland: AK Press, 2013).

6   Cleaver interview.

7   Antonio Gramsci, "The Intellectuals," in *Selections from the Prison Notebooks*, ed. and trans. Quintin Hoare and Geoffrey Nowell Smith (New York: International Publishers, 1971), 5–14.

8   Further reflections from this interview and a thorough treatment of the history of Autonomist Marxism in the United States will be addressed in a subsequent book.

9   Tasos Sagris, A.G. Schwarz, and Void Network. eds., *We Are an Image from the Future: Greek Revolt of December 2008* (Oakland: AK Press, 2010); Dimitris Dalakoglou and Antonis Vradis, eds., *Revolt and Crisis in Greece: Between a Present Yet to Pass and a Future Still to Come* (Oakland: AK Press, 2011).

10 Invisible Committee, *The Coming Insurrection* (Los Angles: Semiotext(e), 2009).

11 "Obedience Stopped, Life Is Magical," chapter 4 in Sagris, Schwarz, and Void Network, *We Are an Image from the Future*.

12 Gregor Kritidis, "The Rise and Crisis of the Anarchist and Libertarian Movement in Greece, 1973–2010," in *The City Is Ours: Squatting and Autonomist Movements in Europe from the 1970s to the Present*, ed. Bart van der Steen, Ask Katzeff, Leendert van Hoogenhuijze (Oakland: PM Press, 2014).

13 Michael Schmidt and Lucien van der Walt, *Black Flame: The Revolutionary Class Politics of Anarchism and Syndicalism* (Oakland: AK Press, 2009).

14 Quoted in Didier Eribon, *Michel Foucault*, trans. Betsy Wind (Cambridge, MA: Harvard University Press 1991), 282.

15 Dan Berger, *Outlaws of America: The Weather Underground and the Politics of Solidarity* (Oakland: AK Press, 2006), 272–78.

16 Ibid., 272–73.

17 Shin'ya Ono, "A Weatherman: You Do Need a Weatherman to Know Which Way the Wind Blows," in *Weatherman*, ed. Harold Jacobs, ed. (Ramparts Press, 1970), 132, http://www.sds-1960s.org/books/weatherman.pdf.

18 Karin Ashley, et al., "You Don't Need a Weatherman to Know Which Way the Wind Blows," *New Left Notes*, June 18, 1969), http://www.sds-1960s.org/sds_wuo/weather/weatherman_document.txt.

19 Peggy McIntosh, "White Privilege: Unpacking the Invisible Knapsack," 1989, National SEED Project, http://nationalseedproject.org/white-privilege-unpacking-the-invisible-knapsack. These reflections were greatly improved by reading Douglas Williams, "Privilege," in *Keywords for Radicals: The Contested Vocabulary of Late-Capitalist Struggle*, ed. Kelly Fritsch, Clare O'Connor, and AK Thompson (Oakland: AK Press, 2016).

20 Michael Staudenmaier, *Truth and Revolution: A History of the Sojourner Truth Organization, 1969–1986* (Oakland: AK Press, 2012), 325.

21 Ibid., 93 (for a full rendition of this conflict, see 91–94).

22 John Zerzan, introduction to *Against Civilization* (Los Angles: Feral House, 2005), 3.

23 Murray Bookchin, "What Is Social Ecology?," in *The Modern Crisis* (Philadelphia: New Society Publishers, 1986), 59–60.

24 Deleuze and Guattari argue that "all concepts are connected to problems without which they would have no meaning and which can themselves only be isolated or understood as their solution emerges. We are dealing here with a problem concerning the plurality of subjects, their relationship, and their reciprocal presentation." This passage from *What Is Philosophy?*, their last collaborative endeavor, draws our attention toward the activity being abstracted. If the phenomena did not exist or did not appear to exist, there would be no need to conceptualize it. Human communication and sociability requires the creation of concepts, and the task of revolutionary theory in particular and philosophy in general is to describe human existence. Deleuze and Guattari continue to describe the threefold "nature of the concept:" "first, every concept relates back to other concepts, not only in its history but in its becoming or its present conditions. Every concept has components that may, in turn, be grasped as concepts"; second, these components create an internal "consistency of the concept"; third, "each concept will therefore be considered as a point of coincidence, condensation, or accumulation of its own components." These components are identifiable and (of course) do not exist alone and only as themselves. Gilles Deleuze and Felix Guattari, *What Is Philosophy?* (New York: Verso, 1994), 16, 19–20.

25 Cleaver interview.

26 Martin Glaberman and Seymour Faber, *Working for Wages: The Roots of Insurgency* (New York: General Hall, 1998), 11.

27 Friedrich Nietzsche, *The Will to Power*, trans. Walter Kaufmann and R.J. Hollingdale, ed. Walter Kaufmann (New York: Vintage Books, 1968), 220. Emphasis in original.

28 James C. Scott and Marty Glaberman and Seymour Faber used taxonomies of struggle in their own endeavors. See James C. Scott, "Everyday Forms of

Resistance," in *Everyday Forms of Peasant Resistance*, ed. Forrest D. Colburn (Armonk, NY: M.E. Sharpe, 1989), 3–33; Glaberman and Faber, "War on the Job," in *Working for Wages*, 59–96.

29 Spinoza, *Ethics*, trans. G. H. R. Parkinson (New York: Oxford University Press, 2000).

30 George Orwell, "Politics and the English Language," in *George Orwell: In Front of Your Nose, 1945–1950*, ed. Sonia Orwell and Ian Angus (Jaffrey, NH: David R. Godine, 2000), 130.

31 Gilles Deleuze and Michel Foucault, "Intellectuals and Power: A conversation between Michel Foucault and Gilles Deleuze," in *Language, Counter-Memory, Practice: Selected Essays and Interviews by Michel Foucault*, ed. Donald F. Bouchard (Ithaca, NY: Cornell University Press, 1980).

32 Donald Davidson, "What Metaphors Mean," in *On Metaphor*, ed. Sheldon Shacks (Chicago: University of Chicago Press, 1979), 29.

33 Subcomandante Marcos is the masked spokesman for the armed Mayan resistance movement called the Zapatista Army of National Liberation, based in Mexico's southernmost state of Chiapas, popularly known as the Zapatistas or by their Spanish acronym EZLN. Marcos, a pen name, is an author of countless communiqués and a dozen books, including the collection from which I draw from here: Marcos, *Our Word Is Our Weapon: Selected Writings of Subcomandante Marcos*, ed. Juana Ponce de León (New York: Seven Stories Press, 2001), 18.

34 The phrase "to make a revolution possible" is directly influenced by the Zapatistas and the Midnight Notes Collective. Here I borrow it from my collective work with Team Colors. Team Colors Collective, *Wind(s) from Below: Radical Community Organizing to Make a Revolution Possible* (Portland, OR: Eberhardt Press, 2010).

Chapter 4. Under Slavery

1 George Rawick, *From Sundown to Sunup* (Westport, CT: Greenwood, 1972), 95.

2 Raymond A. Bauer and Alice H. Bauer, "Day to Day Resistance to Slavery," *Journal of Negro History* 27, no. 4 (October 1942): 388–419;

3 John Hope Franklin and Loren Schweninger, *Runaway Slaves: Rebels on the Plantation* (New York: Oxford University Press, 1999), 2.

4 Mary Ellison, "Resistance to Oppression: Black Women's Response to Slavery in the United States," *Slavery and Abolition* 4, no. 1 (1983): 56–63.

5 Herbert Aptheker, "Slave Guerrilla Warfare" *To Be Free: Studies in American Negro History* (New York: International Publishers, 1969), 11.

6 Rawick, *The American Slave*, 96.

7   Herbert Aptheker, *American Negro Slave Revolts* (New York: International Publishers, 1994).

8   Kristian Williams, *Our Enemies in Blue: Police and Power in America*, 3rd ed. (Oakland: AK Press, 2015), 64–65. See also Sally Hadden, *Slave Patrols: Law and Violence in Virginia and the Carolinas* (Cambridge, MA: Harvard University Press, 2003).

9   Eugene Genovese, *From Rebellion to Revolution: Afro-American Slave Revolts in the Making of the Modern World* (Baton Rouge: Louisiana State University Press, 1979), 1–2.

10 David Williams, *I Freed Myself: African American Self-Emancipation in the Civil War Era* (New York: Cambridge University Press, 2014); Richard Hart, *Slaves Who Freed Themselves: Blacks in Rebellion* (Kingston, Jamaica: University of the West Indies Press, 2002); C.L.R. James, *The Black Jacobins: Toussaint L'Ouverture and the San Domingo Revolution* (New York: Vintage Books, 1989).

11 James Oakes, "The Political Significance of Slave Resistance," *History Workshop* 22, (Autumn 1986): 89–107.

12 "Voyages," Trans-Atlantic Slave Trade Database, http://www.slavevoyages .org/assessment/estimates.

13 The great treaties and juridical documents of the Western world are not chronicles of peace but trace the forms of the state that arise during war. This history begins in the Treaty of Westphalia (rise of modern nation-state), continues with Treaty of Tordesillas (wherein Spain and Portugal divided South America in two), followed by the constitutions of the great Republics (American and French), the Berlin Conference (wherein the Western nations divided Africa), and the 1945 Yalta Conference (dividing the world in two by the United States, allied with the United Kingdom, and the Soviet Union). Although the agreements listed here determined territorial rule across the globe, these treaties between nation-states provided the legal justification for the discipline and control of unruly multitudes, as well as weaker nations, and the monopoly on violence within those weaker nations and territories. Although modern developments have followed this general pattern, reinforcing state sovereignty in some instances while undermining it in other agreements (including the United Nations Charter, the Hague and Geneva Conventions, the Non-Proliferation Treaty, and Universal Declaration of Human Rights), the latter thrust is the result of many in the international community demanding peace and human rights.

14 Stuart B. Schwartz, "Indian Labor and New World Plantations: European Demands and Indian Responses in Northeastern Brazil," *American Historical Review* 83, no. 1 (February 1978): 46.

15 Schwartz, "Indian Labor and New World Plantations."

16   Ibid., 59.

17   Stuart B. Schwartz, *Slaves, Peasants, and Rebels: Reconsidering Brazilian Slavery* (Champaign: University of Illinois Press, 1996), 103.

18   Cedric J. Robinson, *Black Marxism: The Making of the Black Radical Tradition* (Chapel Hill: University of North Carolina Press, 2000), 125.

19   Edgar F. Love, "Negro Resistance to Spanish Rule in Colonial Mexico," *Journal of Negro History* 52, no. 2 (April 1967): 89–103.

20   Darold D. Wax, "Negro Resistance to the Early American Slave Trade," *Journal of Negro History* 51, no. 1 (June 1966): 1–15.

21   Ian Baucom, "Specters of the Atlantic," *South Atlantic Quarterly* 100, no. 1 (Winter 2001): 61–82.

22   James, *The Black Jacobins*, 9.

23   Howard Zinn, *A People's History of the United States* (New York: Harper Collins, 1995), 178.

24   John Ashworth, *Slavery, Capitalism, and Politics in the Antebellum Republic*, vol. 1, *Commerce and Comprise, 1820–1850* (New York: Cambridge University Press, 1995), 6.

25   Black and militant white scholars began unearthing slave narratives in the 1930s, and the influence of this continues into the present (with such recent feature films as *Free State of Jones* and the 2016 *Birth of a Nation*, the latter based on the story of Nat Turner). While academic sources will provide much of the narrative that follows, as it did for the sections above, a key consideration for slave guerrillas is the role of everyday resistance, in concert with overt rebellion, in the political, economic, and moral crises that led to the Civil War. Much of the historiography of the second bloodiest conflict ever on US soil (the genocide of indigenous peoples being the first) has focused on the Emancipation Proclamation, rural southern agriculture versus urban northern industry, conflict over slavery in newly chartered states, states' rights, or some combination of various catalyzing events (the Missouri Compromise and "Bleeding Kansas," the publication of *Uncle Tom's Cabin*, the Dred Scott decision, John Brown's raid, and Lincoln's election, for example). Moreover, the period surrounding the US Civil War is among the closest examined in human history, with chronicles of micro-periods (e.g., the economic crisis of 1857 and Reconstruction), particular commodities (cotton and free vs. slave labor), and political changes (abolitionism, the Confederacy, and black representation in government. As late as 1974, historian Eric Foner criticized the scholarly consensus by arguing that there needed to be greater consideration given to the role of the abolition movement in the causes of the Civil War. But without reference to Aptheker, Rawick, or other chronicler of slave resistance, slave subjectivity is absent from the lacunae he mentions. Foner

asserted, "We need to know more about how the slaves themselves were affected by, and perceived, the vast changes which took place in the South in the fifty years preceding secession—the ending of the slave trade, the rise of the cotton kingdom, and the expansion of slavery southward and westward." This is a mere mention, without proposal regarding how to go about answering this question. Any succinct summary of the period is hampered by the extent of the available material. Even a Marxian analysis of the "Antebellum Republic" is barely contained within two hefty successive volumes, with author John Ashworth decrying that "black resistance is virtually ignored by historians who write about the origins of the Civil War." Today's standard introductory histories of slavery and the Civil War, somewhat as a result of the black liberation movement, are required to at least acknowledge slaves' subjectivity and their role in ending chattel slavery, even if direct linkages between breaking tools on the plantation and the demise of the slavocracy are not demarcated. Contemporary texts, including *American Slavery: A Very Short Introduction*, incorporate passages such as this: "The most oppressed were never completely powerless: they could assert their objections by withholding their labor by pretending to be sick, or by breaking the tools necessary for carrying out the owner's tasks." In effect, it is now common to argue that slaves were agents of their own emancipation. Eric Foner, "The Causes of the American Civil War: Recent Interpretations and New Directions," *Civil War History* 20, no. 3 (September 1974), 210–11; Ashworth, *Slavery, Capitalism, and Politics in the Antebellum Republic*, vol. 1, 5; Heather Andrea Williams, *American Slavery: A Very Short Introduction* (New York: Oxford University Press, 2014), 51.

26 Robinson, *Black Marxism*, 75.

27 Brian Holden Reid, *The Origins of the American Civil War* (New York: Longman, 1996), 200.

28 Max Grivno, *Gleanings of Freedom: Free and Slave Labor along the Mason-Dixon Line, 1790–1860* (Urbana: University of Illinois Press, 2011), 128.

29 Williams, *I Freed Myself*, 40.

30 Ibid., 48.

31 Genovese, *From Rebellion to Revolution*, 113.

32 Genovese, *From Rebellion to Revolution*, 69. Genovese's claim is confirmed by Aptheker, who states: "There is evidence to demonstrate that the years of the Civil War witnessed considerable activity on the part of militant fugitive slave outlaws frequently operating together with the guerrilla bands formed by deserters from the Confederate Army." Aptheker, *American Negro Slave Revolts*, 360.

33 Rawick, *From Sundown to Sunup*, 96. See also Aptheker, *American Negro Slave Revolts*, 359; Williams, *I Freed Myself*, 5.

34 Ashworth, *Slavery, Capitalism, and Politics in the Antebellum Republic*, vol. 1, 6. Note also Aptheker's assertion that "there was much disaffection and unrest amongst slaves, frequently advancing to the form of conspiracy and rebellion. Unquestionably the conflict itself, particularly as its anti-slavery nature became more manifest, was of prime importance in bringing this about." However, he continued, "direct evidence of this ... is available in only a few cases." Aptheker, *American Negro Slave Revolts*, 94.

35 Bernard Mandel, *Labor, Free and Slave: Workingmen and the Anti-Slavery Movement in the United States* (Urbana: University of Illinois Press, 2007), 23–24.

36 Ashworth is clear on this point: "The class conflict that existed between slave and master, though enormously important, was not of itself enough to unravel the southern social fabric. It would be quite wrong to assume that the South in 1860 was on the verge of a servile rebellion or that the resistance of the slaves, without outside pressure from the North, was sufficient to destroy slavery in the region." John Ashworth, *Slavery, Capitalism, and Politics in the Antebellum Republic*, vol. 2: *The Coming of the Civil War, 1850–1861* (New York: Cambridge University Press, 2007), 3.

37 Karl Marx, *Capital*, vol. 1, 414.

38 Du Bois, *Black Reconstruction in America*, 15.

39 Rawick, *From Sundown to Sunup*, 113.

40 Bauer and Bauer, "Day to Day Resistance to Slavery," 396.

41 Gerald Horne, *Confronting Black Jacobins: The U.S., the Haitian Revolution, and the Origins of the Dominican Republic* (New York: Monthly Review Press, 2015).

42 Rawick, *From Sundown to Sunup*, 107.

43 Ibid.

44 Rawick, *From Sundown to Sunup*, 32–51; Aptheker, *American Negro Slave Revolts*, 56–59, 67.

45 John G. Akin, *A Digest of the Laws of the State of Alabama* (Alabama Department of Archives and History, 1833), 398, http://www.archives.alabama .gov/teacher/slavery/lesson1/doc1-10.html.

46 Genovese, *From Rebellion to Revolution*, 6–8, 28–32, 42–48.

47 Aptheker, *American Negro Slave Revolts*, 59.

48 Rawick, *From Sundown to Sunup*, 97.

49 Alex Lichtenstein, "That Disposition to Theft, with Which They Have Been Branded: Moral Economy, Slave Management and the Law," *Journal of Social History* 21, no. 3 (Spring 1988): 418–19.

50 John Hope Franklin and Loren Schweninger, *Runaway Slaves: Rebels on*

the Plantation (New York: Oxford University Press, 1999), 90.

51 Lichtenstein, "That Disposition to Theft," 414.

52 Ibid., 423.

53 Aptheker, *American Negro Slave Revolts*, 141.

54 Bauer and Bauer, "Day to Day Resistance to Slavery," 402.

55 C.G. Parsons, *Inside View of Slavery, or, A Tour among the Planters* (Boston: John P. Jewett, 1855), 94.

56 Bauer and Bauer, "Day to Day Resistance to Slavery."

57 Wax, "Negro Resistance to the Early American Slave Trade," 13.

58 Bauer and Bauer, "Day to Day Resistance to Slavery", 409.

59 Slave suicide as a trope is a challenging concept. See Richard Bell, "Slave Suicide, Abolition and the Problem of Resistance," *Slavery and Abolition* 33, no. 4 (2012): 525–49.

60 Bauer and Bauer, "Day to Day Resistance to Slavery," 414.

61 Aptheker, *American Negro Slave Revolts*, 142–43.

62 Bauer and Bauer, "Day to Day Resistance to Slavery," 391–92.

63 Ibid., 404.

64 Rawick, *From Sundown to Sunup*, 30.

65 Bauer and Bauer, "Day to Day Resistance to Slavery," 399.

66 Rawick, *From Sundown to Sunup*, 116.

67 Ibid., 30.

68 Ibid., 111.

69 Frederick Douglass, *My Bondage and My Freedom* (New Haven: Yale University Press, 2014), 223.

70 Stephanie M. H. Camp, "'I Could Not Stay There': Enslaved Women, Truancy and the Geography of Everyday Forms of Resistance in the Antebellum Plantation South," *Slavery and Abolition* 23, no. 3 (2002): 1–20; Stephanie M. H. Camp, *Closer to Freedom: Enslaved Women and Everyday Resistance in the Plantation South* (Chapel Hill: University of North Carolina Press, 2004), 36, 50.

71 Lichtenstein, "That Disposition to Theft," 419.

72 James, *The Black Jacobins*, 20.

73 Schwartz, *Slaves, Peasants, and Rebels*.

74 Ibid., 108.

75 Ibid., 118.

76 Ibid., 122, 124.

77 Aptheker, *American Negro Slave Revolts*, 143.

78 Ibid.

79 Michael Hardt and Antonio Negri, *Empire* (Cambridge, MA: Harvard University Press, 2000), 123.

80 Rawick, *From Sundown to Sunup*, 95.

NOTES

Chapter 5. In Peasant Politics

1   Scott, *Weapons of the Weak*, xv.

2   Ibid., 241.

3   Scott, "Everyday Forms of Resistance," in Colburn, *Everyday Forms of Peasant Resistance*, 11. See also Jim Scott (James C. Scott), "Everyday Forms of Peasant Resistance," in *Everyday Forms of Peasant Resistance in South-East Asia*, ed. James C. Scott and Benedict J. Tria Kerkvliet (Totowa, NJ: Frank Cass, 1986); Benedict J. Tria Kerkvliet, "Everyday Politics in Peasant Societies (and Ours)," in *Journal of Peasant Studies* 36, no. 1 (2009): 227–43.

4   Pierre Clastres, *Society against the State* (New York: Zone Books, 1987), 193.

5   De Rouffignac, *The Contemporary Peasantry in Mexico*, 55.

6   As Marc Edelman suggests, I have reverted to the contemporary activist definitions. Marc Edelman, "What Is a Peasant? What Are Peasantries? A Briefing Paper on Issues of Definition," prepared for the first session of the Intergovernmental Working Group on a United Nations Declaration on the Rights of Peasants and Other People Working in Rural Areas, Geneva, July 15–19, 2013.

7   Via Campesina, "Declaration of Rights of Peasants—Women and Men," 2009, http://www.viacampesina.net/downloads/PDF/EN-3.pdf.

8   Sidney W. Mintz argued, in the inaugural issue of the *Journal for Peasant Studies*, that there is a "need for middle-range definitions of peasantries and of peasant societies: definitions that fall somewhere between real peasant societies 'on the ground,' so to speak, and the widest-ranging level of definitional statement, adequate to describe all of them. Hence there is no intention here to qualify the genuine need for definition, but to make a step toward bridging the gap between the realities of the daily life of peasant people on the one hand, and the highest level of definitional abstraction on the other." While Mintz provides a "heterogeneous" definition he still viewed peasants and farmers as fundamentally different categories. According to him and other social scientists, peasants subsist, farmers work. Sidney W. Mintz, "A Note on the Definition of Peasantries," *Journal of Peasant Studies* 1, no. 1 (1973): 91–106.

9   Harry Cleaver, "Internationalization of Capital and Mode of Production in Agriculture," *Economic and Political Weekly* 11, no. 13 (March 27, 1976): A2–A5, A7–A16.

10 Peter Linebaugh, "Karl Marx, the Theft of Wood, and Working Class Composition: A Contribution to the Current Debate," in *Stop, Thief! The Commons, Enclosures, and Resistance* (Oakland: PM Press, 2014), 55, originally published in *Crime and Social Justice* 6 (Fall/Winter 1976), 5–16.

11   Karl Marx, editorial in supplement to *Rheinische Zeitung* 307 (November 3, 1842), Marxists Internet Archive, http://marxists.catbull.com/archive/marx/works/1842/10/25.htm#p1.

12   Linebaugh, "Karl Marx, the Theft of Wood, and Working Class Composition," 52.

13   Ibid.

14   Scott, *Weapons of the Weak*, 35.

15   James C. Scott, *Seeing Like a State: How Certain Schemes to Improve the Human Condition Have Failed* (New Haven: Yale University Press, 1998).

16   Laura Stokes, *Demons of Urban Reform: Early Witch Trials and Criminal Justice, 1430–1530* (New York: Palgrave Macmillan, 2011).

17   Silvia Federici correctly criticized Karl Marx and Michel Foucault for ignoring the plight of women as they defended the proletarians, gleaners of the woods, mentally ill, and "criminal element." Silvia Federici, *Caliban and the Witch: Women, the Body and Primitive Accumulation* (New York: Autonomedia, 2004), 103.

18   Steve Stuffit, *Radical Brewing: Work, Energy, Commoning and Beer* (Bristol Radical History Group, 2009).

19   Midnight Notes Collective, "Introduction to the New Enclosures," *Midnight Notes*, 10 (1990).

20   Harry Cleaver, "Food, Famine, and the International Crisis," *Zerowork*, no. 2 (Fall 1977). John H. Perkins, *Geopolitics and the Green Revolution: Wheat, Genes, and the Cold War* (New York and Oxford: Oxford University Press, 1997).

21   Vandana Shiva, *The Violence of the Green Revolution: Third World Agriculture, Ecology and Politics* (Atlantic Highlands, NJ: Zed Books; Penang, Malaysia: Third World Network, 1991), 46–47.

22   Ibid.

23   Harry Cleaver, "The Contradictions of the Green Revolution," *American Economic Review* 62, no. 2 (May 1972), 177–86.

24   Philip Mattera, "National Liberation, Socialism, and the Struggle against Work: The Case of Vietnam," *Zerowork*, no. 2 (Fall 1977); Cleaver, "Food, Famine, and the International Crisis."

25   Scott, "Everyday Forms of Resistance," 26.

26   Nathan Brown, "The Conspiracy of Silence and the Atomistic Political Activity of the Egyptian Peasantry, 1882–1952," in Colburn, *Everyday Forms of Peasant Resistance*, 109.

27   Steve Hindle, *On the Parish? The Micro-Politics of Poor Relief in Rural England, c. 1550–1750* (New York: Oxford University Press, 2004).

28   Stokes, *Demons of Urban Reform*.

29   Scott, "Everyday Forms of Resistance," 8.

30 Scott, *Weapons of the Weak*, xvi.

31 Scott, "Everyday Forms of Resistance," 24.

32 Scott, *Weapons of the Weak*, 22.

33 Michael F. Jiménez, "Class, Gender and Peasant Resistance in Central Colombia, 1900–1930," in Colburn, *Everyday Forms of Peasant Resistance*, 128–29.

34 De Rouffignac, *The Contemporary Peasantry in Mexico*, 116.

35 Ibid.

36 Jiménez, "Class, Gender and Peasant Resistance in Central Colombia," 131.

37 Romachandra Guha, "Saboteurs in Forest: Colonialism and Peasant Resistance in the Indian Himalaya," in Colburn, *Everyday Forms of Peasant Resistance*, 68.

38 Brown, "The Conspiracy of Silence and the Atomistic Political Activity of the Egyptian Peasantry," 98.

39 Jacek Kochanowicz, "Between Submission and Violence: Peasant Resistance in the Polish Manorial Economy of the Eighteenth Century," in Colburn, *Everyday Forms of Peasant Resistance*, 47.

40 Gavin Smith, "The Fox and the Rooster: The Culture of Opposition in Highland Peru," *This Magazine* 19, no. 1 (April 1985), 10.

41 Kochanowicz, "Between Submission and Violence," 45.

42 Scott, *Weapons of the Weak*, 248–49.

43 Ibid., 259.

44 Forrest D. Colburn, "Foot Dragging and Other Peasant Responses to the Nicaraguan Revolution," in *Everyday Forms of Peasant Resistance*, 181–82.

45 Ibid., 178.

46 Smith, "The Fox and the Rooster."

47 Kochanowicz, "Between Submission and Violence," 52.

48 Jiménez, "Class, Gender and Peasant Resistance in Central Colombia," 129.

49 Guha, "Saboteurs in Forest," 74.

50 Brown, "The Conspiracy of Silence and the Atomistic Political Activity of the Egyptian Peasantry," 101.

51 Notes from Nowhere, eds. *We Are Everywhere: The Irrespirable Rise of Global Anticapitalism* (New York: Verso Books, 2003), 162.

52 Kochanowicz, "Between Submission and Violence," 49.

53 Ibid.

54 Frank Dikötter, *Mao's Great Famine: The History of China's Most Devastating Catastrophe, 1958–1962* (New York: Bloomsbury, 2011).

55 Daniel Kelliher, *Peasant Power in China: The Era of Rural Reform, 1979–1989* (New Haven: Yale University Press, 1992), 242.

56 Ibid.

57 Ibid., 239.

58   Colburn, "Foot Dragging and Other Peasant Responses," 180.

59   David Zweig, "Struggling over Land in China: Peasant Resistance after Collectivization, 1966–1986," in Colburn, *Everyday Forms of Resistance*, 164.

60   Scott, *Weapons of the Weak*, 44.

61   Brown, "The Conspiracy of Silence and the Atomistic Political Activity of the Egyptian Peasantry," 105.

Chapter 6. Throughout the Industrial and Social Factory

1   James, Lee, and Chaulieu, *Facing Reality*, 5.

2   Federici, *Caliban and the Witch*, 31.

3   Thompson, *Making of the English Working Class*, 194.

4   Preamble to the IWW Constitution, https://iww.org/culture/official/preamble.shtml.

5   The importance of the New York City fiscal crisis to capitalist strategy on a planetary scale, as well as to early neoliberalism, has been well documented by David Harvey in *A Brief History of Neoliberalism* (New York: Oxford University Press USA, 2007) and Eric Lichten in *Class, Power and Austerity: The New York City Fiscal Crisis* (South Hadley, MA: Bergin and Garvey, 1986).

6   Harry Cleaver, "Karl Marx: Economist or Revolutionary?," in *Marx, Schumpeter and Keynes: A Centenary Celebration of Dissent*, ed. Suzanne W. Helburn and David F. Bramhall (Armonk: M.E. Sharpe, 1986), 121–46.

7   For a summary of the upheavals of 1968, see Tariq Ali and Susan Watkins, *1968: Marching in the Streets* (New York: Free Press, 1998).

8   Marx, *Capital*, vol. 1, 875.

9   See chapters 1 and 2 in Murray Bookchin, *The Third Revolution: Popular Movements in the Revolutionary Era*, vol. 1 (New York: Cassell, 1996).

10   Charles Tilly, "War Making and State Making as Organized Crime," in *Bringing the State Back In*, ed. Peter Evans, Dietrich Rueschemeyer, and Theda Skocpol (Cambridge: Cambridge University Press, 1985), 183.

11   Ibid.

12   Antonio Gramsci, *Selections from the Prison Notebooks* (New York: International Publishers, 2010), 277–318.

13   George Caffentzis, "The Work/Energy Crisis and the Apocalypse," in *Midnight Oil: Work, Energy, War, 1973–1992*, ed. Midnight Notes Collective (Brooklyn: Autonomedia, 1992), 215–71. Emphasis in original. See also Kolya Abramsky, ed., *Sparking a Worldwide Energy Revolution: Social Struggles in the Transition to a Post-Petrol World* (Oakland: AK Press, 2010).

14   Beverly J. Silver, *Forces of Labor: Workers' Movements and Globalization since 1870* (New York: Cambridge University Press, 2003).

15 Fred Thompson and Patrick Murfin, *The I.W.W.: Its First Seventy Years, 1905–1975* (Chicago: Industrial Workers of the World, 1976); Salvatore Salerno, *Red November, Black November: Culture and Community in the Industrial Workers of the World* (Albany: State University of New York Press, 1989). For the relationship between the IWW and culture in the 1960s, see Franklin Rosemont and Charles Radcliffe, eds., *Dancin' in the Streets! Anarchists, IWWs, Surrealists, Situationists and Provos in the 1960s, as Recorded in the Pages of the Rebel Worker and Heatwave* (Chicago: Charles H. Kerr, 2005).

16 Louis Adamic, *Dynamite: The Story of Class Violence in America* (1931; repr., New York: Chelsea House, 1958), 380–81. Emphasis added.

17 Eric Thomas Chester, *The Wobblies in Their Heyday: The Rise and Destruction of the Industrial Worker of the World in the World War I Era* (Santa Barbara, CA: Praeger, 2014).

18 On the role of the IWW in free speech fights, see John Duda, ed., *Wanted: Men to Fill the Jails of Spokane Fighting for Free Speech with the Hobo Agitators of the Industrial Workers of the World* (Chicago: Charles H. Kerr, 2009). On the relationship between anti-immigrant sentiment and anti-radical fervor, see Cornell, *Unruly Equality*, 53–79.

19 For the period leading up to and including the strikes, see Jeremy Brecher, *Strike!*, revised, expanded, and updated ed. (Oakland: PM Press, 2014), 169, 146–207.

20 Ibid.

21 Baldi, "Thesis on Mass Worker and Social Capital," 3–21.

22 Cleaver, "Karl Marx: Economist or Revolutionary."

23 Ira Katznelson, *When Affirmative Action Was White: An Untold History of Racial Inequality in Twentieth-Century America* (New York: W.W. Norton, 2006).

24 Robin D. G. Kelley, "We Are Not What We Seem: Rethinking Black Working-Class Opposition in the Jim Crow South," *Journal of American History* 80, no. 1 (June 1993): 104.

25 Dan Berger, *Captive Nation: Black Prison Organizing in the Civil Rights Era* (Chapel Hill: University of North Carolina Press, 2014).

26 Dan Georgakas and Marvin Surkin, *Detroit, I Do Mind Dying* (Boston: South End Press, 1998).

27 Ibid.

28 Ward Churchill and Jim Vander Wall, *The COINTELPRO Papers* (Boston: South End Press, 1990), 220–21, cited in Kristian Williams, *Our Enemies in Blue: Police and Power in America*, 3rd ed. (Oakland: AK Press, 2015), 297–98.

29 Mariarosa Dalla Costa, *The Power of Women and the Subversion of the*

Community (London: Falling Walls Press, 1972), 65.

30 Ali and Watkins, *1968*, 19.

31 Barbara Ehrenreich and Deirdre English, "The Manufacture of Housework," in *Capitalism and the Family* (San Francisco: Agenda, 1978), 8.

32 Dalla Costa, *The Power of Women and the Subversion of the Community*, 64.

33 Thompson, *The Making of the English Working Class*, 11.

34 The causes of the crises of capitalism are diverse and well-debated. By arguing that the crises are the result of working-class struggle is to claim a position within these debates. While Harvey and I differ considerably in regard to the weight given to particular causes of capitalist crisis, his book on the contradictions of capitalism provides a useful summary of these complex phenomena. David Harvey, *Seventeen Contradictions and the End of Capitalism* (New York: Oxford University Press, 2014).

35 Harry Cleaver, *Reading* Capital *Politically*, 74.

36 Caffentzis, "The Work/Energy Crisis."

37 See Lichten, *Class, Power and Austerity*, esp. pp. 82–94; "When Tuition at CUNY Was Free, Sort Of," http://www1.cuny.edu/mu/forum/2011/10/12/when-tuition-at-cuny-was-free-sort-of. For the history of the National Welfare Rights Union, see Felicia Kornbluh, *The Battle for Welfare Rights: Politics and Poverty in Modern America* (Philadelphia: University of Pennsylvania Press, 2007).

38 Francis Fox Piven and Richard Cloward, "The Urban Crisis as an Arena for Class Mobilization," *Radical America* 11, no. 1 (January–February 1977): 11. See also Harvey, *Brief History of Neoliberalism*, 44–48; William Tabb, *The Long Default: New York City and the Urban Fiscal Crisis* (New York: Monthly Review Press, 1982).

39 Harvey, *Brief History of Neoliberalism*, 48.

40 Nick Dyer-Witheford, *Cyber-Marx: Cycles and Circuits of Struggle in High-Technology Capitalism* (Urbana: University of Illinois Press, 1999), 75–76.

41 Silvia Federici, "The Restructuring of Housework and Reproduction in the United States in the 1970s," in *Revolution at Point Zero: Housework, Reproduction, and Feminist Struggle* (Oakland: PM Press, 2012), 49.

42 Benjamin Holtzman, Craig Hughes, and Kevin Van Meter, "DIY and the Movement beyond Capitalism (in the United States)," in *Constituent Imagination: Militant Investigation / Collective Theorization*, ed. David Graeber, Stevphen Shukaitis, and Erika Biddle (Oakland: AK Press, 2007).

43 Paul Romano (Phil Singer) and Ria Stone (Grace C. Lee), *The American Worker* (Detroit: Bewick Editions, 1972), 35.

44 Geoff Mann, *Our Daily Bread: Wages, Workers, and the Political Economy*

of the American West (Chapel Hill: University of North Carolina Press, 2007).

45   Romano and Stone, *American Worker*, 36.

46   Interviews with Nick Salerno and Roy Schmidt in Studs Terkel, *Working: People Talk about What They Do All Day and How They Feel about What They Do* (New York: MJF Books, 2004), 103–5.

47   Martin Glaberman and George Rawick, "The American Working Class," in *Listening to Revolt: The Selected Writings of George Rawick*, 87.

48   Federici, "Wages against Housework," in *Revolution at Point Zero*, 18.

49   Wendy Edmond and Suzie Fleming, "If Women Were Paid for All They Do," in *All Work and No Pay: Women, Housework, and the Wages Due*, ed. Wendy Edmond and Suzie Fleming (Bristol, UK: Falling Wall Press, 1975), 12.

50   Paul Willis, *Learning to Labor: Why Working Class Kids Get Working Class Jobs* (New York: Columbia University Press, 1981), 55.

51   Kelley, "We Are Not What We Seem," 75.

52   James, Lee, and Chaulieu, *Facing Reality*, 31.

53   Ibid., 91.

54   Eddy Cherki and Michel Wieviorka, "Autoreduction Movements in Turin," in *Autonomia: Post-Political Politics*, ed. Sylvère Lotringer (Los Angles: Semiotext(e), 2007), 72. Emphasis in original.

55   Robin D. G. Kelley, *Race Rebels: Culture, Politics, and the Black Working Class* (New York: Free Press, 1996), 1.

56   Peter Linebaugh, *The London Hanged: Crime and Civil Society in the Eighteenth Century* (New York: Cambridge University Press, 1992), 111.

57   Kelley, "We Are Not What We Seem," 91.

58   Bill Watson, "Counter-Planning on the Shop Floor," *Radical America* 5, no. 3 (May–June 1971): 77.

59   Brecher, *Strike!*, 206.

60   Watson, "Counter-Planning on the Shop Floor," 80

61   James, Lee, and Chaulieu, *Facing Reality*, 107.

62   Watson, "Counter-Planning on the Shop Floor," 80.

63   Kelley, "We Are Not What We Seem," 90.

64   Watson, "Counter-Planning on the Shop Floor," 80.

65   James, Lee, and Chaulieu, *Facing Reality*, 23.

66   Anton Pannekoek, *Workers' Councils* (Oakland: AK Press, 2003), 48.

67   Michael Hardt and Antonio Negri, *Declaration* (Argo-Navis, 2012), 91.

68   Paul Buhle, *Taking Care of Business: Samuel Gompers, George Meany, Lane Kirkland, and the Tragedy of American Labor* (New York: Monthly Review Press, 1999).

69   George Rawick, "Working Class Self-Activity," *Radical America* 3, no. 2 (March–April 1969): 30.

70 James, Lee, and Chaulieu, *Facing Reality*, 21.

71 Isabel Wilkerson, *The Warmth of Other Suns: The Epic Story of America's Great Migration* (New York: Random House, 2010), 8.

72 Dalla Costa, *The Power of Women and the Subversion of the Community*, 87.

73 Kelley, "We Are Not What We Seem," 112.

Chapter 7. On Organizing

1 Gilles Deleuze and Claire Parnet, *Dialogues* (New York: Columbia University Press, 1987), 147. Emphasis in original. For a slightly different translation, see Gilles Deleuze and Claire Parnet, "Politics," in *On the Line*, trans. John Johnson (New York: Semiotext(e), 1983), 113–14.

2 For additional information on these community dialogues and their political significance, see Kevin Van Meter, "Insurgent Islands: A Continuing Conversation on Anarchism with Principles."

3 Sidney Solomon, conversations with the author, circa 1998–99.

4 Initially the "A" in ACORN stood for Arkansas. For ACORN's development out of the National Welfare Rights Organization, see Felicia Kornbluh, *The Battle for Welfare Rights: Politics and Poverty in Modern America*, 168–169.

5 Piven and Cloward, *Poor People's Movements*, 4.

6 Michel Foucault, *"Society Must Be Defended": Lectures at the Collège de France, 1975–1976* (New York: Picador, 2003), 16.

7 James, Lee, and Chaulieu, *Facing Reality*, 125

8 Precarias a la Deriva concluded: "It seems a paradox, if, because the strike is always interruption and visibilization and care is the continuous and invisible line whose interruption would be devastating. But all that is lacking is a change of perspective to see that … there is no paradox: the caring strike would be nothing other than the interruption of the order that is ineluctably produced in the moment in which we place the truth of care in the center and politicize it." Precarias a la Deriva, "A Very Careful Strike—Four Hypothesis," in *The Commoner: A Webjournal for Other Values*, no. 11 (Spring 2006), 42, http://www.commoner.org.uk/11deriva.pdf.

9 Chris Carlsson and Adam Cornford, "Talking Heads," in *Bad Attitude: The Processed World Anthology*, ed. Chris Carlsson with Mark Leger (New York: Verso, 1990), 8; Jeff Kelly, ed. *Best of Temp Slave* (Madison, WI: Garrett County Press, 1997).

10 Nietzsche quoted in Walter Kaufmann, *Nietzsche: Philosopher, Psychologist, Antichrist* (Princeton: Princeton University Press, 1974), 354.

11 Saul Alinsky, *Rules for Radicals: A Pragmatic Primer for Realistic Radicals* (New York: Vintage Books, 1972), 64.

12 Wade Rathke, "ACORN Community Organizing Model," *Wade Rathke: Chief*

Organizer Blog, http://chieforganizer.org/wp-content/uploads/2011/06/ ACORN-Organizing-Model.pdf. For the relationship between Alinsky and ACORN, see Arlene Stein, "Between Organization and Movement: ACORN and the Alinsky Model of Community Organizing," *Berkeley Journal of Sociology* 31 (1986): 93–115.

13 Kim Bobo, Jackie Kendall, and Steve Max, *Organizing for Social Change: Midwest Academy Manual for Activists* (Santa Ana, CA: Seven Locks Press, 2001), 8.

14 This notion can be found in ibid., 6: "Direct action is not the only form, or the only 'correct' form, of organizing. Electoral, union, social service, public interest, advocacy, educational, and legal organizing all play a role in advancing progressive goals. The principles of direct action have applications in many other kinds of organizing, particularly electoral campaigns, advocacy, and union organizing."

15 David Harvey, *A Brief History of Neoliberalism* (New York: Oxford University Press, 2005), 3, 7.

16 INCITE! Women of Color Against Violence, *The Revolution Will Not Be Funded: Beyond the Non-Profit Industrial Complex* (Boston: South End Press, 2009).

17 Jeffery Berry and David Arons, *A Voice for Nonprofits* (Washington, DC: Brookings Institution Press, 2003), 3. See also Steven Rathgeb Smith Michael Lipsky, *Nonprofits for Hire: The Welfare State in the Age of Contracting* (Cambridge, MA: Harvard University Press, 1998); Elizabeth T. Boris and Eugene C. Steuerle, eds., *Nonprofits and Government: Collaboration and Conflict* (Washington, DC: Urban Institute Press, 2006).

18 Alicia Meckstroth and Paul Arnsberger, "A 20-Year Review of the Nonprofit Sector, 1975–1995," *Internal Revenue Service, Statistics of Income Bulletin* 18 (1998): 149–69, https://www.irs.gov/pub/irs-soi/20yreo.pdf; Internal Revenue Service, Statistics of Income Division, "SOI Bulletin Historical Table 16," https://www.irs.gov/uac/SOI-Tax-Stats-Historical-Table-16. Note that this data set "exclude[s] private foundations and most religious organizations" and "organizations with receipts under $25,000 were not required to file."

19 Elizabeth T. Boris, et al. "Human Service Nonprofits and Government Collaboration: Findings from the 2010 National Survey of Nonprofit Government Contracting and Grants," Urban Institute, October 7, 2010, http://www.urban.org/research/publication/human-service-nonprofits -and-government-collaboration-findings-2010-national-survey -nonprofit-government-contracting-and-grants/view/full_report.

20 Berry and Arons, *A Voice for Nonprofits*, 4–5.

21 Team Colors Collective, *Wind(s) from below: Radical Community*

Organizing to Make a Revolution Possible (Portland, OR: Team Colors Collective and Eberhardt Press, 2010), 42–43. Emphasis in original.

22 Midnight Notes Collective and Friends, *Promissory Notes: From Crisis to Commons* (Jamaica Plain, MA: Midnight Notes, 2009), 7.

23 "Work Stoppages Involving 1,000 or More Workers, 1947–2015," US Department of Labor, Bureau of Labor Statistics, https://www.bls.gov/news .release/wkstp.t01.htm. See also Doug Henwood, "A Working Class Disarmed," *LBO News from Doug Henwood*, April 2, 2014; http://lbo-news .com/2014/04/02/a-working-class-disarmed.

24 "New Release: Union Members—2014," US Department of Labor, Bureau of Labor Statistics, ww.bls.gov/news.release/archives/union2_01232015. pdf, shows similar trends. See also John Schmitt, "Union Membership Trends 1948–2012," *No Apparent Motive*, http://noapparentmotive.org/ blog/2013/01/25/union-membership-trends-1948-2012.

25 Paul Buhle, *Taking Care of Business: Samuel Gompers, George Meany, Lane Kirkland, and the Tragedy of American Labor* (New York: Monthly Review Press, 1999).

26 Stanley Aronowitz, *The Death and Life of American Labor: Toward a New Worker's Movement* (Brooklyn: Verso, 2014); Steve Early, *Save Our Unions* (New York: Monthly Review Press, 2013); Kim Moody, *US Labor in Trouble and Transition: The Failure of Reform from Above, the Promise of Revival from Below* (New York: Verso, 2007).

27 Dan La Botz, *A Troublemaker's Handbook: How to Fight Back Where You Work—and Win!* (Detroit: Labor Notes, 1991), 4–5.

28 Robert D. Putnam, *Bowling Alone: The Collapse and Revival of American Community* (New York: Simon & Schuster, 2001).

29 Don Mitchell, *The Right to the City: Social Justice and the Fight for Public Space* (New York: Guilford Press, 2003), 132.

30 Retort, *Afflicted Powers: Capital and Spectacle in a New Age of War* (New York: Verso, 2005).

31 "If the dose makes the poison": a translation from the Latin phrase "sola dosis facit venenum," attributed to Paracelsus, the founder of taxonomy. Friedrich Nietzsche considers the difference between medicine and poison to be one of measurement. It is in the Nietzchean sense that I use this phrase. Friedrich Nietzsche, "On the Uses and Disadvantages of History for Life," in *Nietzsche: Untimely Mediations*, ed. Daniel Breazeale, trans. R. J. Hollingdale (Cambridge: Cambridge University Press, 1997).

32 Barbara Epstein, *Political Protest and Cultural Revolution: Nonviolent Direct Action in the 1970s and 1980s* (Berkeley: University of California Press, 1991), 18.

33 Jo Freeman, "The Tyranny of Structurelessness," in *Quiet Rumours: An*

Anarcha-Feminist Reader, 3rd. ed., ed. Dark Star (Oakland: AK Press, 2012); *Anti-Mass: Methods of Organization for Collectives* (New York: Anok and Peace Press, n.d.); "Give Up Activism," *Do or Die*, no. 9, 160–61, http://eco-action.org/dod/no9/activism.htm. Additional influential titles include Ward Churchill, *Pacifism as Pathology: Reflections on the Role of Armed Struggle in North America*, new ed. (Oakland: PM Press, 2017); Hakim Bey, *Temporary Autonomous Zone* (Brooklyn: Autonomedia, 1991); Murray Bookchin, *Social Anarchism or Lifestyle Anarchism: An Unbridgeable Chasm* (Oakland: AK Press, 1995).

34 Other influences on the movements of the late 1990s and early 2000s included tree-sits in the Pacific Northwest, anti-road actions in Europe, republished material from the Situationist International, and communiqués of the Ejército Zapatista de Liberación Nacional.

35 Freeman, "The Tyranny of Structurelessness," 68.

36 Cathy Levine, "The Tyranny of Tyranny," in *Quiet Rumours: An Anarcha-Feminist Reader*, 3rd ed., ed. Dark Star (Oakland: AK Press, 2012), 79.

37 *Anti-Mass*, 1.

38 Ibid., 10.

39 Zerowork Collective, "Introduction to Zerowork 1," in *Midnight Oil: Work, Energy, War 1973–1992*, ed. Midnight Notes Collective (New York: Autonomedia, 1992), 112.

40 "Give Up Activism."

41 Kristian Williams and Andrew Cornell greatly added to my understanding of the difference between anti-authority and anti-authoritarian.

42 Michael Schmidt and Lucien van der Walt, *Black Flame: The Revolutionary Class Politics of Anarchism and Syndicalism* (Oakland: AK Press, 2009), 67.

43 While there were prefigurative elements in classical anarchism, this tendency became more pronounced with anarchism's encounter with nonviolence. One of the central tenets of nonviolence is that to create a nonviolent society we must act nonviolently toward one another as well as our adversaries. This confluence of means and ends was transposed from nonviolence to all political proposals by adherents. Hence means prefigure ends. Cornell, *Unruly Equality*.

44 As the Team Colors Collective wrote in 2010, "We call this cycle of struggle a period of *whirlwinds*. They are dissimilar to fires that erupt out of a definable mix of elements with specific targets and accurate generalities; rather, winds are caused by pressures that vary in different locales, constructed from particularities and, at times, incommunicable singularities. Fires burn until the oxygen or fuel runs out, whereas winds are fluid, open,

and constantly shifting across the terrain. Fires carry a creative and destructive urge, extinguishing what exists to make way for something new; winds search for what is common and articulate the common in new ways as they circulate." Team Colors Collective, "Sowing Radical Currents in the Ashes of Yesteryear: The Many Uses of a Whirlwind," in *Uses of a Whirlwind: Movement, Movements, and Contemporary Radical Currents in the United States* (Oakland: AK Press, 2010), 9.

45 Chris Dixon, *Another Politics: Talking Across Today's Transformative Movements*, 85.

46 Team Colors Collective, "Abandoning the Chorus: Checking Ourselves a Decade Since Seattle," *Groundswell* 1 (2010); Team Colors Collective, *Wind(s) from Below: Radical Community Organizing to Make a Revolution Possible*.

47 Nietzsche, "On the Uses and Disadvantages of History for Life."

48 Ed Hedemann, ed. *War Resisters League Organizer's Manual*, rev. ed. (New York: War Resisters League, 1986).

49 La Botz, *Troublemaker's Handbook*, 9.

50 Eric Mann, *Playbook for Progressives: 16 Qualities of the Successful Organizer* (Boston: Beacon Press, 2011).

51 Giles Deleuze and Felix Guattari, *A Thousand Plateaus: Capitalism and Schizophrenia*, trans. Brian Massumi (Minneapolis: University of Minnesota Press, 1987).

52 Federici, *Revolution at Point Zero*, 37.

53 James, Lee, and Chalieu, *Facing Reality*, 125.

54 Raoul Vaneigem, *The Revolution of Everyday Life*, trans. Donald Nicholson-Smith (Oakland: PM Press, 2012), 27.

55 Michel Foucault, preface to Giles Deleuze and Felix Guattari, *Anti-Oedipus: Capitalism and Schizophrenia*, trans. Brian Massumi (Minneapolis: University of Minnesota Press, 1983).

Chapter 8. Conclusion: To Make a Revolution Possible

1 Cleaver, *Reading* Capital *Politically*, 57.

2 Gilles Deleuze and Felix Guattari, *Nomadology: The War Machine*, trans. Brian Massumi (New York: Semiotext(e), 1986), 111; Gilles Deleuze and Felix Guattari, *A Thousand Plateaus: Capitalism and Schizophrenia*, trans. Brian Massumi (Minneapolis: University of Minnesota Press, 1987), 417.

3 Cornell, *Unruly Equality*, 286.

INDEX

THE INSTITUTE FOR ANARCHIST STUDIES (IAS)

Anarchism emerged out of the socialist movement as a distinct politics in the nineteenth century. It asserted that it is necessary and possible to overthrow coercive and exploitative social relationships, and replace them with egalitarian, self-managed, and cooperative social forms. Anarchism thus gave new depth to the long struggle for freedom.

The primary concern of the classical anarchists was opposition to the state and capitalism. This was complemented by a politics of voluntarily association, mutual aid, and decentralization. Since the turn of the twentieth century and especially the 1960s, the anarchist critique has widened into a more generalized condemnation of domination and hierarchy. This has made it possible to understand and challenge a variety of social relationships—such as patriarchy, racism, and the devastation of nature, to mention a few—while confronting political and economic hierarchies. Given this, the ideal of a free society expanded to include sexual liberation, cultural diversity, and ecological harmony, as well as directly democratic institutions.

Anarchism's great refusal of all forms of domination renders it historically flexible, politically comprehensive, and consistently critical—as evidenced by its resurgence in today's global anticapitalist movement. Still, anarchism has yet to acquire the rigor and complexity needed to comprehend and transform the present.

The Institute for Anarchist Studies, established in 1996 to support the development of anarchism, is a grant-giving organization for radical writers. To date, we have funded over a hundred projects by authors from countries around the world. Equally important, we publish the Anarchist Interventions book series in collaboration with AK Press and Justseeds Artists' Cooperative, the print and online journal *Perspectives on Anarchist Theory*, and our new series of books in collaboration with AK Press beginning with *Octavia's Brood*. We organize educational events such as Anarchist Theory Tracks, talks and panels at conferences and events, and we maintain a Mutual Aid speakers bureau. The IAS is part of a larger movement to radically transform society. We are internally democratic and work in solidarity with people around the globe who share our values.

IAS, PO Box 90454, Portland, OR 97290
www.anarchist-studies.org
Email: anarchiststudies@gmail.com

AK Press is small, in terms of staff and resources, but we also manage to be one of the world's most productive anarchist publishing houses. We publish close to twenty books every year, and distribute thousands of other titles published by like-minded independent presses and projects from around the globe. We're entirely worker-run and democratically managed. We operate without a corporate structure—no boss, no managers, no bullshit.

The Friends of AK program is a way you can directly contribute to the continued existence of AK Press, and ensure that we're able to keep publishing books like this one! Friends pay $25 a month directly into our publishing account ($30 for Canada, $35 for international), and receive a copy of every book AK Press publishes for the duration of their membership! Friends also receive a discount on anything they order from our website or buy at a table: 50% on AK titles, and 20% on everything else. We have a Friends of AK ebook program as well: $15 a month gets you an electronic copy of every book we publish for the duration of your membership. You can even sponsor a very discounted membership for someone in prison.

Email friendsofak@akpress.org for more info, or visit the Friends of AK Press website: https://www.akpress.org/friends.html

There are always great book projects in the works—so sign up now to become a Friend of AK Press, and let the presses roll!